PENGUIN AFRICAN LIBRARY
Edited by Ronald Segal

Libya

RUTH FIRST

Ruth First was born and educated in South Africa. She took
up research in sociology but abandoned this work at the time of
the strike of the African miners to become a journalist and
editor on newspapers and journals identified with the African
national struggle in South Africa. She was a prominent
member of the opposition under constant fire from the South
African Government. In 1956 she was arrested along with 156
others and was involved in the subsequent prolonged treason
trial. In 1963 she was again arrested and held in solitary
confinement for 117 days under the notorious 'ninety-day'
law. The following year she went into political exile and has
since lived in London, writing on South Africa and independent
Africa. Her previous books are *South West Africa* (Penguin
Books, 1963) *117 Days* and *The Barrel of a Gun*, a study
coups d'état in Africa,; also published in Penguins; she
has edited *No Easy Walk to Freedom* by Nelson Mandela,
and with Ronald Segal, *South West Africa: Travesty of Trust*.
She is also co-author of *The South African Connection*,
published by Penguins in 1973.

RUTH FIRST

Libya

The Elusive Revolution

Penguin Books

Penguin Books Ltd, Harmondsworth,
Middlesex, England
Penguin Books Inc., 7110 Ambassador Road,
Baltimore, Maryland 21207, U.S.A.
Penguin Books Australia Ltd, Ringwood,
Victoria, Australia
Penguin Books Canada Ltd,
41 Steelcase Road West, Markham, Ontario, Canada
Penguin Books [N.Z.] Ltd
182-190 Wairau Road, Auckland 10, New Zealand

First published 1974
Copyright © Ruth First, 1974

Made and printed in Great Britain by
Hazell Watson & Viney Ltd,
Aylesbury, Bucks
Set in Monotype Plantin

Contents

Preface

This book is based on four visits to Libya in the years since 1969 when the Revolutionary Command Council under Colonel Mu'ammar Gadafi came to power, and a country previously unknown and obscure thrust itself on world attention.

I have concentrated on the period since 1969, on revolution – or coup? – on oil and on arab unity, for these are the themes of the new régime. The pre-revolution chapters are brief and selective, for they are intended to emphasize those issues which bear most directly on the causes of the change in the country's political system, and the direction the country has taken since the toppling of the monarchy. There is some fairly considerable material on economics, because the politics of Libya get extensive if often superficial coverage, but the economics of this oil-rich rentier state are far less well understood.

Scholars may shudder at my rendering of Arabic names, but I have used a transliteration most easily recognizable to non-Arabic readers; it is inconsistent here and there, as when there are quotations from sources using a different form.

My indebtedness to sources and to informants will show in the footnotes and references. There are Libyans to whom I am deeply indebted, not necessarily because they agreed with me or I with them, but because they talked about their country and their problems in ways which helped me to understand them. Official Libya, though it gave me generous assistance, was apprehensive: 'What will you write?' they asked. 'We have had so many bad experiences.' Some may think the criticism in this book springs from malice and arrogance of the kind they have come to take for granted from 'foreigners'. I can only say that I tried to understand Libya in its own context, not Europe's, and that I tried to measure its achievements against the need for revolutionary

7

change in Africa and the Middle East, which is the cause Libya so vocally espouses.

Note

The Libyan pound was re-named the Libyan dinar in 1969. There was no change of value. Numerous devaluations of international currencies have enhanced the value of the Libyan dinar (£L).

Until November 1967 when the pound sterling was devalued, the Libyan pound was equivalent. Thereafter the Libyan pound was equivalent to £1·14. Parity was maintained against the dollar, with the Libyan pound equivalent to US $2·8 until the dollar was devalued in 1972. The Libyan pound/dinar equivalents have moved as follows:

	US dollar	pound sterling
1951	2·8	1·0
1967	2·8	1·14
1972	3·04	1·20
1974	3·36	1·40

Part I: A Perverse Revolution

1 A Perverse Revolution

At first sight – as at last – there is no revolution more contradictory and perverse than the Libyan. It enjoys the vast wealth of
the oil-producing states in the Middle East, yet is determined
not to be another Kuwait or Saudi Arabia. It claims a social
revolution that will bring Libya into the company of the great
twentieth-century revolutions for social liberation, yet it zealous-
ly pursues a revival of Islamic fundamentalism. It was a rebellion
of young army men against the monarchical head of a religious
order, yet the cast of its own political thinking is not secular but
religious. It is a régime under which power is vested in eleven
young soldiers, yet it boasts of having shepherded a popular
revolution more mass-based than even China's. It has promoted
a cultural revolution against bureaucracy and called on the
popular masses to rise to their historic role, yet it suffocates any
political action or thought not initiated by the state. It reviles
the ancien régime for the corruption of the privileged classes
that grew in the shadow of oil, and sees Libya today as a society
without classes or social distinction, in which any tendencies
towards inequality will be combated by a return to the true ethic
of Islam. Yet even in rejecting the concept of class and class
struggle as alien to Arab or Libyan socialism, it confronts the
monopoly bastions of the capitalist world, the oil cartels. It is
dedicated to pan-Arabism, yet has prompted the resentment,
even the enmity, of Arab states, from the conservative shaikhdoms to the radicals, which it has reviled for their disparate
approach to Arab unity. It buys Mirages from France for use in
the 'national battle' for the liberation of Palestine, yet its leader
Colonel Gadafi explains setbacks in this struggle and future
tactics by passages in the Koran. Undaunted by the failure of
previous attempts at unity between Arab states, it is seeking to

hector a combined state of Libya and Egypt to its feet, despite the seemingly insuperable problems of federating two countries of such diverse domestic cast and such contradictory diplomatic postures on the very issue supposed to weld their unity, the battle for Palestine.

Libya boasts a tiny population of under two million, so remote from the Middle East battle-lines as to offer only a marginal contribution; yet she pursues a recklessly activist policy from Malta to Ulster, from Uganda to Ethiopia and the Yemen. When Britain connived at the handing over to Iran of two small islands in the Persian Gulf, Libya promptly nationalized the local holdings of British Petroleum, Britain's principal oil interest there, as a reprisal. She has intervened in the internal politics of both Uganda and the Sudan, flying plane-loads of troops and arms into Uganda on the strength of General Amin's false representation of an invasion; and masterminding the forcing down of a plane carrying Sudanese revolutionaries, and a Libyan–Egyptian intervention in the Sudan to mount a counter-revolution. Some of her foreign policy initiatives have been on the strength of provocative miscalculations: the fulsome welcome to the army coupmakers in Morocco was broadcast round the world even as the coup against the King was failing. She has attacked enemies and allies with equal sense of righteousness, clearly disconcerting her closest partners as much as her antagonists. Thus, though combined with Egypt and Syria in a Federation, she has publicly pilloried their governments for betraying the *fedayin* cause. Ignoring the judgement of friends and the strengths of the enemy, Libya has courted a policy of confrontation with Israel which, taking into account the objective strengths and weaknesses of the two sides, is in danger of substituting rhetoric for purpose.

By any rational political analysis, the contradictions and misjudgements of the Libyan revolution should have brought its sallies grinding to a halt; yet its journeys into pan-Arabism and abroad on the African continent continue to show a surprising endurance. Gadafi's simplistic formula for a united Arab, African, Asian, and Latin American world, together with the reformed young in advanced capitalist society, is based predominantly on a return to religion and refuses to take into account the wide range of other factors relevant to the debate and to the search within these continents for a new ideology and economic system. Yet in an Arab and African world demoralized by the failure of Third World initiatives, discouraged by the attempts at non-alignment which brought their countries not extra leverage but increased isolation from the world's power centres, Gadafi's speeches are capable of prompting unexpected attention. True, his solutions are absurdly simple – unity, morality, faith, determination – but perhaps other leaderships have grown too corrupt, obtuse, and sophisticated? There were even students at Paris's rebellious university of Vincennes who hailed Gadafi as the only Third World leader with any real stomach for struggle.

His speeches run over with smooth fanaticism yet he is capable of speaking painful and unpalatable truths. Arab régimes are rotten; Arab states have betrayed the Palestinian cause. Arab unity is hollow. Arab summit meetings are a waste of time. If you want something to die, he has said, send it to be buried in Arab League files in the skyscraper in Cairo.

There is something riveting about the audacity of his indictment and the simplicity of his solutions. In Cairo intellectuals who read his interviews in *Le Monde* and his speeches in their own newspapers bury their heads in their hands at his naïveté. In the Maghreb cities, Arab but also permeated by French culture, Gadafi has been seen as a latter-day Asterix absorbed in his picaresque adventures, and cut off from history and the world. What is it about Libya and Gadafi in the seventies which explains their eccentricities – this blinding gap between Libyan interpretation and Arab and world reality? Most observers are filled with scepticism; yet among some there remains the hope that in his impetuous innocence he will stumble upon some way to break the impasse in the Arab world. Is it to be a case of pristine Bedouin morality, steeped in the fundamentalist morality of the seventh century, riding in from the desert to reform twentieth-century statecraft? Is this possible in our day and age?

For Libya's young army government is pronouncing prescriptions for the Arab world already considered unworkable and outworn. There is an eerie sense of contemporary problems given previous solutions; of newcomers rushing in where more experienced partisans have learned not to tread; of policies discovered for the first time in a region where they have already run their course. It is surely this which accounts for the most predominant characteristic of the young Libyan régime: its sense of compelling anachronism, its appearance of being strangely displaced from its time.

Much of the explanation for this phenomenon must be found in the bombardment of Libya and Libyans by the forces of outside history. After Liberia and Ethiopia, she was the third independent state of Africa. But it was an arrested independence, Western-conducted and controlled. Libya came into her Arab own only in 1969, when the Western-supported monarchy was unseated. And this makes Libya nominally one of the first, but virtually the last, independent state of Africa, not counting the unliberated south. By the time she felt the first full flush of modern nationalism in state form, Egypt had already known the sensation for the better part of half a century. Libya was the newest Arab state; she emerged as the critic of the oldest Arab states which had been created in the aftermath not of the Second but of the First World War. No wonder the experiences that she found so daring were regarded as dated in other parts of the Middle East. But Libya's development had been retarded by both her history and her geography, which had in turn deformed her political experience. In the first half of the twentieth century she experienced rule by the Ottoman empire; then came foreign invasion and conquest, after a prolonged but savagely defeated armed popular resistance. The colonialism which followed was founded on metropolitan peasant settlement in an exclusive enclave economy. This was ended by war between European powers, some of whose most ferocious battles were fought on Libyan soil. It was followed by both the British and the French varieties of military and colonial caretaker occupation. When independence came in 1951, it was in response not to the internal thrust of Libyan actions but because it suited the strategic purpose of the West.

Less than two decades separated resistance and independence, but they could not have been more disturbing in their discontinuity. At one moment in time men were in insurrection against authority; at the next they were haphazardly co-opted into it. For the better part of thirty years in parts of Libya, if not the entire country, there had been two perilous options: to persist in what Berque has called a state of armed refusal, or to compromise and through expediency risk corruption by the alien régime in power. The anti-colonial war had prompted very different reactions from Bedouin* tribesmen and townsmen; from tribes that had allowed themselves to be drawn into the political orbit of the colonial administration; others that had remained aloof but passive; and still others that had resisted bodily to the end; between Cyrenaica where guerrilla bands, however reduced in size and striking power, fought until 1932, and Tripolitania, where active resistance ended before the twenties. Between the last episodes of the resistance and the end of Italian colonization, there was a span of not much more than ten years, but the stand that men had taken, of intransigence or compromise, suddenly became irrelevant. In Algeria, those who had fought the French army for eight years battled their way into control of the commanding heights of the revolutionary régime, and military and political gains were made one. In the parts of Libya where the resistance had been more prolonged if sporadic, it was also more dispersed and therefore localized; while the phase of primary tribal and religious resistance had not been followed by political opposition of the more modern type or the growth of a consistent nationalist ideology and movement which would in time inherit independence. In the rest of the Maghreb armed resistance was ended, but a tumultuous movement of strikes and demonstrations grew in its place; the masses began to take over political action from the tribes.[1] In Libya this did not happen in the same way. The country and a subdued population passed precipitately from colonization to independence, with sovereignty installed by the results of international and United Nations diplomacy. Thus even the coming of independence played its part in shattering what sense of historical and political continuity Libyans had managed to retain, and even the most favourable

* Bedouin from *badw* in Arabic, meaning nomad.

turn of events played havoc with the moral and ethical issues which preoccupy men in times of social and political disturbance.

By 1951 Libya had political sovereignty but little else beside. She was perhaps the poorest country in the world. The battles of the Second World War had devastated what infrastructure had been built and disrupted the economic life of even the Bedouin communities. Italian colonization did not seek to mould an élite, so that there had been virtually no education system capable of preparing men for government and administrative service. Obscure and illiterate men were plucked from their communities to occupy office. For a decade Libya was kept barely alive by American and British aid. The country lived on charity and felt the humiliation of poverty. Suddenly in 1959 oil was discovered; by 1961 crude was being produced and exported; and oil revenues began to course through the economy on a staggering scale from 1963 onwards. Once feeble and unnoticed, this was a country now not only financially self-reliant but wealthy enough to influence others. Independence had been unexpected, without prior indication let alone preparation for its coming. Oil was even more precipitate. It came despite the efforts of Libyans and yet transformed their lives. Humble men could suddenly become not only ministers but millionaires. (Most Libyans can cite you the case of the clerk under the British military administration who became both; or the baker from the Fezzan oasis who today lives in a Swiss château with his personal masseur.)

The accidents of history and geography which bestowed first an unexpected independence but even more importantly oil wealth, and the resulting collision of several periods of history – that of a bare subsistence society with a vengeful colonizing metropolis and then with the giant oil multi-nationals – have had a bewildering impact on Libyan social life and consciousness. Wealth so effortlessly acquired, solutions which so haphazardly present themselves, have helped to spread an illusion that converges only too easily with the use of Islam by Libya's regime. Opportunity has come in bursts from some external causation; faith, trust, and morality will surely produce solutions, for rationality and planning have indeed had little to do with

Libya's economic bonanzas. If *baraka* (blessing) is the reason, then this is beyond the effort of man. A by-product of blinding faith is a trust in recklessness; for if the twists in Libyan opportunity have been so unpredictable, and results have been so unaffected by effort, why not hazard more daring claims still and trust once again to belief? It is the sort of all-embracing faith which prompts the Libyan reply to the oil companies: 'We have lived 5,000 years without oil money; we can do it again.' It is as much philosophy as bargaining counter. It is this same haphazard experience of an imposed history that makes the timelessness of the Koran seem still more appropriate. To a Bedouin society thrust into the oil technology age, there seems little strange about applying the precepts of seventh-century Arabia to modern issues. Economic change has been imposed on the society from outside. Where most skilled manpower and virtually all expertise is imported, local society can absorb the benefits of the oil economy without having to change greatly in itself.

Having been plucked out of their history, Libyans are finding it a painful experience to return to it. Even when, in pre-European-conquest times, political association was achieved between its three spreading provinces, geography and parochial politics and economies made effectively close association difficult. Tripolitania's move towards unity with Cyrenaica had died out in the twenties; the independence Constitution of the fifties conferred national sovereignty but more effective power on the parts than on the centre; it was only the exigencies of the oil economy which achieved a constitutionally unified state. The army revolution of 1969 claimed to restore Libyans to their true identity and destiny; to make the final meaningful break with the colonial and pro-Western past. But Gadafi, like all fervent Arab nationalists, conceives of the Arab world as a single homogeneous whole and of the Arab people as a single nation bound by the common ties of language, religion, and history: even though the Arab world has not constituted a single political entity since Islam's expansion into an empire during the seventh and eighth centuries. It is a strain of nationalist fervour that ignores the diversity and differentiation in the Arab world; for Islam is expected to supply the indissoluble core of identity and communal heritage. Gadafi thus rejects a micro-nationalism, whether of the Libyan or any other strain. Libyans have been told that they are genuinely Libyan for the first time in their history. At the same time a people always overwhelmed by outsiders with superior skills is told that it is Arab above all. It is a bewildering experience to have simultaneously to absorb an immediate and a wider identity. The union with Egypt could not pose this question in a more direct and urgent form.

Yet it is precisely this return to the Arab world that is the pulse of the Libyan army revolution. For as the occupation of Suez and Farouk's enforced submission to Britain was the humiliation that gave Egypt to Nasser, so the occupation of Sinai by Israel after the Six Day War was the catalyst of the Libyan young officers' coup. The foreign policy of the monarchy had positioned Libya not towards Egypt and the Middle East but towards the West. The struggle to break free was thus the struggle to break into the Middle East and to become part of Arab aspirations. This is one reason why Libya, remote from the battlefields of the Middle East, insists on trying to settle the terms of the battle. Her late realization of her own identity is, for her, inseparable from the displacement of the Palestinians.

For an Arab world plunged into despair after the 1967 defeat, the Libyan coup – and the Sudanese, led by Nimeiry six months earlier – were signs of a possible revival in Arab fortunes. It was *Al Ahram*'s Heykal, sent to Libya to conduct the first on-the-spot investigation for Nasser, who pronounced the Libyan coup-makers as a young generation of a distinct quality. They were the post-setback generation, the new hope of the Arab world. Perhaps Egypt's revolution of 1952, which had so changed the face of the Middle East, would have a new beginning in Libya's Nasserite generation? For there was no question but that these were fervent young Nasserites, determined that the army would not only make the revolution but continue to lead it for its own good, and that it was the army-backed State which would initiate whatever political organization and ideology were judged suitable.

This is not only an essential theory for an army-led régime; it happens to coincide with the Libyan reality. For one of the consequences of Libya's disturbed contemporary experience is that indigenous political groupings, when they were able to form after the colonial conquest, were tiny, short-lived, and uncertain. Political party organization was banned by the monarchy in the first year of independence. The middle class, which informs the dominant politics of the more characteristic Middle East state, failed to gain any real political footing in Libya. This was largely because when money arrived, with the pumping of oil, to produce a small group of middlemen contractors, transporters, and property speculators, they thrived on patronage from un-bounded resources, and politics as a means to economic acquisi-tion was unnecessary. In the early sixties, small Arab Nationalist, Baathist, and Marxist groups appeared; but they never really took indigenous root; and, because they were imports, they pro-duced not any application of their policies to Libyan conditions, but the factional disputes which riddled their parent bodies in the Middle East and played such havoc with early attempts at pan-Arab strategies. Gadafi's standing indictment of the civilians of his generation and earlier ones was that they had been in-effective in opposition under the monarchy. They had failed to make the revolution. From this grew a sharp distaste for all voluntarist initiative and action. All 'factional' politics and all ideology other than the one produced by the state, whether Moslem Brother, Baathist, Marxist, or unlabelled, were declared illegal. Nasserite Egypt had arrived at the same point from a somewhat different national experience.

To Libya's strict adherence to these tenets of the Nasserite model, one must add Gadafi's own peculiar contribution of Islam as religion but also as politics. While few, if any, other than Beshir Hawady, among his army Revolutionary Command Council share his fanatical religious zeal, the cast and the content of their socialist persuasion is religious, not secular. Setbacks to the Arab cause are attributable, essentially, to human frailty and corruptibility, to the failure of true belief and a departure from the moral precepts of Islam. It makes for a dedicated but once again a fatalistic view of the world, for it reduces social and political action to the level of spiritual commitment, and the pursuit of policy to a moral cru·ade.

There is no denying the special cast given the Libyan revolution by the idiosyncratic character of Mu'ammar Gadafi. Much is impossible to understand without understanding him. The stories about his brushes with other Arab leaders, his intemperate outbursts, are legion. Some have even tried to explain the wild inconsistencies of his policies by the theory that he is an agent for a régime other than his own; I have even heard the notion that he is the most efficient *agent provocateur* that Israel or the United States could recruit. The objective consequence of some of his acts could very well spread despondency and defeat on his own side and satisfaction on the enemy's. But this is to reflect not on the man and his motivation, but on the play of forces in the world in an epoch when every weakness, division, error, and obfuscation among dependent peoples produces corresponding strengths for imperialism.

The obsession with the leader, even when it is the inimitable Gadafi, is precisely what should be avoided, for the sake of any real perspective. For to explain Libya by the temperament, eccentricity, even instability, of Gadafi is to make no meaningful explanation in terms of history and Libyan society. There is a rich and fertile source to be tapped in the study of personality. But while this might help in explaining Gadafi, what explains the Libyan response to him? For all the innovations of policy he has introduced, there is a long continuity between Libya before 1969 and after. Religion has always been an important part of the search for identity and expression. After all, Italy colonized for Christendom as well as for Sicilian settlers, and the resistance wars were fought in the interests of the true faith as part of national emancipation. Embryonic nationalist political expression has always been dominated and subdued by a political–religious state structure. If Gadafi's activism takes away the breath of Libyans accustomed to being despised or ignored, they are elated by his sheer bravado. He leaves circles of principally urban opinion as unconvinced in Benghazi and Tripoli as in Cairo and Damascus, but these circles are smaller in Libya than anywhere else; and his pronouncements undoubtedly fall on a receptive interior, and find an answering chord in the large constituency of the newly urbanized still struggling to integrate in a modern economy and a wider world.

The popular interpretation of Gadafi is a leader flushed with insatiable ambition to govern not only Libya but far beyond it; to establish himself as the new Nasser. It seems important to distinguish between a personal ambition to rule and Gadafi's conviction that he is more loyal to Nasser's mission than any other Arab leader of his time. He is gripped by a vision of the need to develop his country, transform the society, rediscover the true Islam, regenerate the Arab world, and unite it, and fire his generation with the same compulsions. How better to do this than by the continual example of the leader? Gadafi has himself shown insight into the personalization of Libyan – or Egyptian, or Arab – politics round the figure of the leader. The September 1969 revolution, he has said, represents principles, values, and ideals. It was trying to make the people sing the praise of facts, not persons, but such talk was considered strange in the Arab homeland. 'Nasser tried hard to make the masses from the Gulf to the Ocean, masses who had no faith in their abilities at the time, believe in themselves and shoulder their responsibilities. But the harder he tried to make them believe in themselves, the more they clung to his person.' Gadafi's resignation gestures, repeated at moments of frustration arising from the failure of the Libyan people to respond to the challenge, are attempts to break out of this style of personalized politics. Yet in the end Gadafi, like Nasser, perhaps despite himself but inevitably because of his methods and outlook, will encourage a popular belief in his infallibility. Will he, too, leave demoralization in his wake?

Not that he has not learned and changed. He continues the same bold forays into Arab policy. But the naïveté of the early attempts has been tempered by setbacks. Once at the first sound of a crisis, he climbed into his plane and flew from capital to capital urging immediate top-level summitry. These days he is disillusioned with summits. Once he composed a plan for the battle to regain Palestine; totalling the Arab armouries as though the arithmetic would provide the strategy. More recently, when the *fedayin* were under fire in Lebanon, he announced his offer of aid but told the Palestinian organizations that they themselves had to decide how best to deploy it. Recent speeches have shown a sophistication quite absent from earlier attempts, but also an underlying thread of desperation at the enormity of the problems. 'Like you,' he told a Libyan popular conference, 'I became independent on 1 September after 400 to 500 years of foreign rule ... You go to Algeria, Egypt, Feisal, Kuwait, and Jordan. I have met all these people. By God thoughts are confused. I no longer know the truth in the Arab world. Why? Because everyone gives you his own opinion ... By God I am confused. I cannot tell any more who is right.'

Yet the admission was not the start of some strengthening insight, but only a temporary lapse, for his characteristic style of government has continued uninterrupted: the same cloistered proceedings of the Revolutionary Command Council; the precipitate edict without reference to precedent and without consultation; the word of the speech becoming the letter of the law virtually overnight. (The 'cultural revolution' against the passive and bureaucratic and the agents of 'foreign' ideologies was announced on 16 April 1973; within days there were extensive round-ups of Libyans whose mistaken ideas were to be cured by a spell behind bars.) It is government by demagogy. Libyans agonized by the wilfulness of some decisions have cursed the mass media which give the spoken or written word instant universality and authority.

And yet Gadafi has infinite patience – and appetite – for prolonged public sessions when he invites the public, however select, to confront him. Though these public sessions are highly attractive, even exciting, as a form of popular or Bedouin democracy, they can be no substitution for institutionalized forms of participatory government. These forms will continue to elude a régime led by a closed army group with an ideology of army-guided government. For, however many committees are instigated from the top, there remains inertia and passivity at the bottom.

It is during these popular sessions, generally televised for successive days, that Brother Colonel Gadafi can be seen at his most magnetic, tireless, and obdurate. From him comes an inexhaustible flow; didactic, at times incoherent; peppered with snatches of half-formed opinions, cryptic self-spun philosophy, inaccurate or partial information; admonitions; confidences; some sound common sense, and as much prejudice. Few of his speeches do not contain the germ of at least one sound idea – but often only the germ of the idea, and little of its real development. For Gadafi's view of the world is uncomplicated by any real knowledge of it.

One of the problems in understanding contemporary Libya is to reconcile the significant and the seemingly absurd which flow from the use of fundamentalist religion to make a social revolution. On women: 'You (in the West) force women to work in factories. This is oppression of women. In Islam we do not sacrifice women for material gain. You have initiated the abortion of pregnant women, you have dispersed the family and broken up society. We have no problems whatsoever. You simply have to apply the Koran for ideal social living.' On the cultural revolution in People's China and Libya: 'In China the cultural revolution was led by the Red Army; in Libya it is the masses that lead. China is searching for an identity, for new principles to be inculcated in the minds of the people; we are consolidating something already in our minds. We need to go back to our origins.' On Sartre and existentialism: 'Sartre is a lost man. We have the answers to all the questions he puts. Why study these issues of existence since they are in the Koran? Only he who has no holy book can ask such questions.'[2] But the use of religion as resistance is nothing new. On the one hand foreign conquest has met with naked revolt. This is Jacques Berque's Islam as Revolution.[3] On the other hand, as superior invading forces prevailed, there has been the use of Islam as Refuge, a retreat but one which derived nonetheless from the same basic attitude of refusal. This refusal 'took refuge in a side of life that formed its

23

surest repository, namely religion'. Islam in North Africa withdrew into the 'fatal retreat of the *zawiya* of popular mysticism and xenophobic piety'. In the Maghreb maraboutism and saintly brotherhoods retained their vitality until the thirties: 'For believers [they] raised a rampart against the advance of enlightenment, still identified with that of the foreigner.'[4] Believing that all the guidance a man needs in running a state is to be found exclusively in the Koran, Gadafi has an essentially religious view of foreign exploitation. His distaste for urban life – because cities, if not creations of the West, are imitations of its culture – is synonymous with his view of corruption. His indictment of the values imposed by the money market – magazine pictures of women, the disturbing influences on young men who study in Europe and the United States – are characteristic of the xenophobic piety of those who needed to use Islam as resistance against foreign conquest. How closely the great majority of his people can approximate to the life-style and goals of their leader zealot is at issue, for his view of true religion as martyrdom for the cause could well be disturbingly alien to the petit-bourgeois yearnings of young Libyans flourishing under an oil economy.

Libya is a difficult country to know, let alone analyse. Central to the process of social change and the ideological ferment of Arab cities since the end of the Second World War has been the rise of an urban proletariat and the transformation of the status of women. In Libya the position of women is changing in only barely perceptible fashion. Except for the girls in school classrooms and the sprinkling at the university, the society is totally segregated. Half the society is accessible only in the home and then only to other women or the closest of masculine kin. The family is closed, private, and conservative. In the streets and public life, women are either not physically present or shrink anonymously behind the voluminous *baracan* which exposes only enough of one eye for the wearer to see where to walk.

If internal conservatism has stopped the emancipation of women, outside forces in the shape of oil have had profound and yet limited effects on the economy and on social formation. The oil industry does not bring the kind of industrialization that releases an urban working class of any size, for it runs on a tiny labour force that is in part imported. So the towns are swollen, but the urban population consists of a few first-generation workers, pedlars, and small shopkeepers, innumerable government employees, and a thin layer of the new rich. It is a society of social gaps, an unformed society even by the standards of underdeveloped economies, or one forming only very slowly.

Male society, which is interchangeable with civic life, is blocked out not into large easily recognizable and well-organized groupings – formal political parties have hardly ever existed – but into innumerable coteries, sometimes as peer groups of school or army class-mates, family or village or work associates, football clubs or circles of friends whose association may endure beyond friendship into some more durable relationship. Not here the seething political parties and working-class movement of the cities of the Maghreb and the Middle East. And in the country-side low population density and the absence of a viable agricultural economy combine to create a similar void in social and political organization.

Jacques Berque has remarked on the backwardness of sociological analysis in the Arab world, on the absence of analysis, the irregularity of reactions towards social phenomena, the scarcity of objective documentation.[5] Liberation from the past is making this, if anything, more and not less difficult in Libya. Historians, for instance, have been discouraged from studying the sources of support and weakness of the Sanusi régime and period, for all remnants of the old régime must be obliterated in the interests of the new. Where politics does not block enquiry, convention and Gadafi's insistence on unswerving adherence to the letter of the Koran invariably do.

There is insistence on the unchanging dogma of Islam. This, among other aspects, recognizes no distinction between the spiritual and the secular, for Islam in history did not differentiate between religion and state. There is thus the insistence that Moslem religious precepts form an integral part of the law of the state, regardless of the nature of the state. There is the role of orthodoxy in supporting established authority and setting up communal unity as the highest objective of social action.[6] There is the use of Islamic education less to instruct the child than to adapt him to the absolute, for 'the Koran is learnt by heart with a superb disregard of intelligibility'.[7]

All this makes Libya's an inarticulate and even a nervous revolution. Except for Gadafi, none of the coupmakers has said anything illuminating about its origins and meaning: their speeches are poor paraphrases of Gadafi's. An intellectual whom I tried to engage in a general discussion about pre-coup Libya and the causes behind the change advised: 'When you see Gadafi you can ask him about the causes of the revolution.' Civil servants – in a system that is a mix of Italian Bourbonic, Egyptian bureaucracy, and the army-induced system of closed hierarchical decision-making – are characteristically cautious; but doubly so under a régime in which no one except the Revolutionary Command Council feels secure enough to interpret policy on minor as much as on major issues. Those who were politically committed under the previous régime and were even persecuted for their opposition are reluctant to speak out. This régime has declared all 'party' politics to be treacherous to the purposes of the army-led State and during 1973 it rounded up and imprisoned persons suspected of political views, lest civilians try to steal or distort the revolution.

Yet, within Libya, many alarmed at the record of other military régimes recognize in the Free Officers the group that alone found the means to displace the monarchy: that transformed Libya from a rubber stamp of Anglo-American policy into a state with an international identity and voice; and that squeezed the oil companies in a masterful series of negotiations which brought benefits not only to Libya but to all Middle East oil producers. For whatever the rational reservations, there have been changes in foreign policy, in oil policy, and in domestic policy. The issue is why the changes have gone so far and no further; to what extent their limits are imposed by the army régime and Gadafi's singular style; and how much is generic to the Libyan condition. For one must try to guard against a vision of Libya bounded by the end of a European, or expatriate, or diplomatic nose. Much speculation about the Arab world is dominated by European preoccupations and the interpretations of European diplomacy.

The attempt should be to treat Libya as an intelligible whole. For whether or not Libya's example is relevant to other countries and systems, it has nonetheless to be understood and appreciated for having grown in its own climate.

Part II: The Limits of Independence

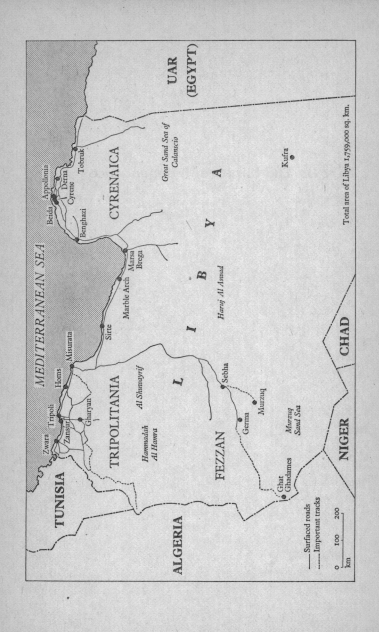

MEDITERRANEAN SEA

TUNISIA

ALGERIA

Zwara
Tripoli
Homs
Misurata
Zanzur
Gharyan
Sirte

TRIPOLITANIA

Hammadah
Al Hamra

Al Shuwayrif

L   I   B   Y   A

FEZZAN

Ghat
Ghadames

Germa
Murzuq

Murzuq
Sand Sea

Sebha

Haruj Al Aswad

NIGER

CHAD

Marble Arch

Marsa
Brega

Benghazi

Beida
Appollonia
Cyrene
Derna
Tobruk

CYRENAICA

Great Sand Sea of
Calanscio

Kufra

UAR
(EGYPT)

Total area of Libya 1,759,000 sq. km.

—— Surfaced roads
········ Important tracks

0   100   200
km

2 Hostage to History and Geography

The Ancient Greeks gave the name Libye to all North Africa west of Egypt, but for many centuries the terms Tripoli or Barbary (after the corsairs who practised piracy in the Mediterranean) were used instead. It was in 1934, after the completion of the Italian conquest of Cyrenaica and Tripolitania, that the two provinces were united under Italian over-rule as the colony of Libia. The independent State that was established in 1951 kept that name as the one associated with the region from ancient times.

The political divisions of the former provinces of Cyrenaica, Tripolitania, and Fezzan corresponded with the country's natural physical barriers and differences. Geography had made the ancient affiliations of the two coastal regions dissimilar – Cyrenaica's early history was influenced by Greece and Egypt, whereas Tripolitania fell under Rome and was close to Tunisia. The Arab invasions had unifying effects on the population, as did the Turkish occupation in the sixteenth century. But the three provinces were never closely unified, and successive foreign powers, whether they controlled all of modern Libya or only parts of it, generally continued to follow the natural divisions of the country in the shape of their administrations. Libya in more recent times has been not so much an artificial political entity as one which physical conditions mitigated against. The basis for the modern state was laid by international diplomacy after the end of the Second World War, but it was to be the demands of the oil economy which created a unified state.

In 1968 Libya's population was estimated at about 1·8 million.*
Approximately seven eighths of that population is clustered near

* Preliminary returns of the 1973 Census give the Libyan population as 2,257,037. (Men: 1,200,246; women: 1,056,791.)

the coast in the vicinity of Tripoli and Benghazi. The overall population density of the country is about 2·7 persons per square mile; in all Africa only Mauritania has a density as low as this. Only 2 per cent of the vast land area is arable. The 1964 census showed that of every 100 persons enumerated, 79 were settled, 9 were semi-nomadic, and 12 were nomadic. The settled population includes urban dwellers and agriculturists of fixed residence, though the latter may move during the planting and harvesting seasons. The semi-nomads move to the areas to which their tribes migrate during winter and summer in search of pastures for their livestock. The province with the highest population of semi-nomads was the Jebel Akhdar in the highlands and plateau areas of northern Cyrenaica. There is some settled farming along the coast, round the desert oases, and in the Tripolitanian hills, but shifting cultivation is the pattern in the semi-desert and the Cyrenaica Jebel. There is no substantial peasantry, which is one of the characteristics which most distinguishes Libya from the Arab societies of Syria, Iraq, Egypt, and the Maghreb.

Libya is and always has been hostage to a hostile geography. Twice the size of her neighbour Egypt, she stretches from the Mediterranean to deep into the sand seas of the Sahara; sharing a frontier with Sudan, and, across the Tibesti mountains, with Chad and Niger. A great burning desert void lies between the narrow coastal strip with its cities by the sea and the peoples of the interior clustered round the remote oases. The Greek geographer Strabo compared Libya to a leopard skin whose spots represented the settlements scattered in the desert. But if geography has held Libya's various parts in suspension from one another, it has also presented formidable obstacles to the successive invasions of twenty-five centuries; for while these have over-run the coastal strip, they penetrated little of the desert interior. From the Phoenicians, the Greeks in 600 B.C., and the Romans, through the Sicilian Normans and the Knights of St John in A.D. 1530, to the Ottoman empire twenty-one years later, and then Italy in 1911, each invasion has linked Libya to the foot-notes of yet another chapter in Mediterranean or Near East history. But who were the original Libyans?

Herodotus, writing about 445 B.C., recorded that a ten-day journey from western Egypt to the oasis of Augila reached the Garamantes, 'an exceedingly great nation who sow the earth they have laid on the salt'. Ancient geographers and historians made them out to be half legendary, endowed with fierce physical stamina, who clashed with the power of Rome as it thrust into the interior. Sifting field-work evidence from legend, archaeologists find that the earliest Garamantian site thus far discovered is Neolithic in culture and belongs to the first millennium B.C.[1] The Garamantes were Hamitic peoples. One investigator has argued their kinship to the Tuaregs; others that they were a Mediterranean Berber type. The Garamante kingdom was still in existence when the first Arab invaders reached and conquered Fezzan in the seventh century.[2] It seems certain that their capital was the city of Garama, today the site of Old Germa in the Wadi al Ajal in the Fezzan, ideally placed for the control of the Saharan trade routes if these flourished in antiquity as in medieval times.

When Rome was building its empire, the North African coastal fringes were joined to it, and in their offensive against the desert tribes, Roman generals even marched their legions against the Garamantes as far as Ghadames, 250 miles from the coast, and then to Germa, 350 miles south-east. The economy of Roman Tripolitania was agricultural, enriched by Saharan trade. Under the early empire the land was farmed by Berber peasants and smallholders. Later, larger state-owned or landowner properties forced the small farmer off the land, and the big estates were worked by the landless Berber.[3] There developed an urban élite which included Romanized Afro-Phoenicians; the name Tripolis, the Three Cities, was first used at the end of the second century. The tribes of the Sirtica desert raided but never conquered the towns of Tripolitania on the western coastline or Cyrenaica, the Greek city settlement on the eastern. It was the Vandals from Europe who ousted the Roman governing class but then abandoned the territory to the desert and its peoples. The Berber tribes reverted to nomad pastoralism. On the pre-desert slopes of southern Tunisia and Tripolitania there appeared in the fifth and sixth centuries A.D. the great Berber tribal confederation of the Zenata, camel-mounted pastoralists who augmented their resources by pillage.[4]

Mounted Arab forces first crossed into Cyrenaica in 642: with no resistance till they reached Tripolitania at the far end of the country. Fezzan was penetrated by 663. The Berbers, both the nomads of the interior and the farmers of the coastlands, were alternately cooperative and rebellious. In the mountains and the desert, where they guarded their independence for centuries, Islam was accepted, but Arabic and Arabs were not; and after the first Arab conquest, North Africa, including Libya, remained overwhelmingly Berber. The first Arab invasion was no more than a kind of preliminary colonizing effort that left small groups of newcomers in the country who were assimilated with the indigenous population. But in the eleventh century the tribes of Bani Hilal and Bani Sulaim,* which had crossed from the Arab peninsula into the Nile valley and then into North Africa, came with their flocks and their families, and over time they assimilated the Berbers and their social groupings. The Bani Hilal mostly moved westward into Tripolitania and Tunisia, while the Bani Sulaim settled primarily in Cyrenaica, to subjugate as clients the tribes of the earlier invasion. Scholars now doubt the view accepted since Ibn Khaldun that the Bani Hilal pastoralists were responsible for the destruction of agricultural prosperity in the Maghreb. It is now argued that the political and economic decline of the Maghreb preceded and facilitated the Hilalian invasions.[5]

In the Fezzan, Arab penetration was slowest, and for a while trade remained the monopoly of the Berber tribes and their camel caravans. Medieval Fezzan was an independent state on the great Saharan trade trail, with cities boasting markets,

* On Arab tribes, see Maxime Rodinson, *Mohammed* (Penguin, 1973): 'A tribe was made up of clans which, rightly or wrongly, acknowledged some kind of kinship. Each tribe had its eponymous ancestor. The ideologists and politicians of the desert worked out genealogies in which the ties of kinship attributed to these ancestors reflected the various relations between the groups that bore their names.' The basic groups of social and economic life were clans or sub-tribes, their numbers dictated by the necessities of life in the desert. Tribes were thus defined by kinship, and consisted of family groups which intermarried and cooperated in economic activity.

mosques, and baths; doctors of law; poets; and holy men. The desert was criss-crossed with caravans carrying not only local but also international traffic. The states of Kanem and Bornu were linked to North Africa by the trade route from Lake Chad to the Libyan coast.[6] Tripoli, standing at the narrowest crossing of the Sahara, was thus the gateway to the interior of Africa. The great trans-Saharan trade system was to be destroyed only in the last decades of the nineteenth century, when French and British imperial penetration of the Senegal and Niger–Benué river basins diverted commerce from the Sahara to the Atlantic. By then, too, the Mediterranean had become an economic backwater; for Western Europe's maritime states, exploiting the sea route to the Indies, had by-passed the North African outlets of the ancient African caravan routes.

Samir Amin has described[7] how Africa was predisposed by geography and history to a continental development, organized round the major inland river arteries, but was condemned by the entry of mercantilist trade to be 'developed' only along its narrow coastal zone. The domestic trade between herdsmen and crop farmers, the outflow of exports and the spread of imports had constituted a dense and integrated trading network dominated by African traders. For the colonial trading houses to capture this trade, they had to control its flow and re-direct it towards the coast; thus the colonial system destroyed African domestic trade and reduced the African traders to subordinate agents, or eliminated them altogether. For many of the societies of tropical Africa, the trans-Sahara trade had become the basis of their organization, and for centuries the Mediterranean societies and those of tropical Africa had been united; so that the vicissitudes of one had rapid repercussions on the others. The shifting of trade routes, especially the change of centre from the Mediterranean to the Atlantic, led to the decline of several formerly flourishing and autonomous African states. In particular it was to leave Libya, through which many of the trade arteries had coursed, high and dry.

From the mid-sixteenth century Libya was a province of the Ottoman empire, ruled by a Turkish Bey supported by Turkish officials and a body of Janissaries, or the Turkish mercenary military caste. But Ottoman rule in North Africa was never very firmly established, and effective authority passed after some time from the Sultan's representatives to military commanders and pirate captains. In 1711, after almost two centuries of rule from Constantinople, power was seized by the Karamanli, a leading family of Cologhli founded from an admixture of Janissary, Arab, and Berber. The Karamanli dynasty ruled for 125 years; and during this time it extended control to parts of both Cyrenaica and Fezzan, thus anticipating by over a century the shape of the Libyan state which the European powers were subsequently to claim as their creation. For as long as central African trade continued along the oasis routes to the ports of Cyrenaica and Tripolitania, there were well-established connections running from the Bedouin tribes of east and west, through the oasis dwellers, to the tribes of the deep interior, where the nomads of Libya controlled the routes and to a large extent supplied the transport for the caravans. Tripoli in the nineteenth century was the home of bankers and wholesalers and the headquarters for most of the trading firms operating in the interior. Ghadames, according to Barth, was the residence of wealthy merchants who embarked all their capital on commercial enterprises; and in all the southern termini like Timbuctoo and Kano there were resident agents of the Ghadames firms. Most of the men of the town were traders themselves and known all over the Sudan. Western travellers commented on the business acumen of the Ghadames people: 'They calculate with profound nicety the expense of carriage to distant countries, duties, customs, risk, trouble, the percentage that their goods will bear, and even do business by means of bills and unwritten agreements or promises.'[8]

In 1835, after the fall of Algiers to the French and Mohammed Ali's achievement of near-independence for Egypt, Turkey re-occupied Tripoli to prevent any further loss of territory that was nominally part of the Ottoman empire. As long as Libyans paid their taxes, Turkish rule was indifferent and remote. By then Turkey was the sick man of Europe, and her rule was inefficient and corrupt. The Turkish revolution of 1908 gave Tripolitania and Cyrenaica representation in the parliamentary régime then installed. And among the Tripolitanian representatives who went from Libya to Istanbul was Suleiman Baruni, who was to play an important part in the resistance of the next decade.[9] Something of the ferment of discussion current in the movement of Young Turks, concerning problems of religion and nationality, of freedom and loyalty and constitutionalism, reached the small groups of Turkish-influenced intellectuals in Libyan towns. But if small urban constituencies were being co-opted into the Turkish constitutional reform, in Cyrenaica the tribes were in effect ruled by the Sanusi on behalf of the Turks. It was, according to Evans-Pritchard, effectively a Turco-Sanusi condominium.[10]

It was the spread of the Sanusi order which had given a great fillip to Islam in the Sahara and also to trade. While commercially the Fezzan–Bornu route had been the most important till the mid 1850s, in the latter half of the century the Cyrenaica–Kufra–Waddai trade route on the other side of Libya began to overtake it. The prosperity of this caravan trade was largely the result of Sanusi enterprise and protection, and the order's wealth, as well as its temporal power, grew from its exploitation of the meagre resources of this region of the eastern Sahara.

The founder of the Sanusi order, Mohamed ibn Ali al-Sanusi, called the Grand Sanusi, was born in Oran in Algeria in the late 1780s of a family claiming descent from the Prophet's daughter, Fatima. Sayyid Mohamed studied at Fez where he came into contact with several of the fraternities of Morocco; then he set out, accompanied by disciples, through the Sahara and Tunisia, Tripolitania, and Cyrenaica to preach greater Islamic unity and a return to the religion of the Prophet, purged of the dross and irrelevance accumulated over centuries of decadence. In about 1843 he established his first *zawiya* in Cyrenaica in the Jebel Akhdar. The choice of Cyrenaica was not accidental:

Of all North African countries, Cyrenaica was a political vacuum, and the Grand Sanusi, who knew the area well, did not just tumble in it. Algeria was gradually being occupied by the French. Tunisia was undergoing a difficult period in her history . . . Egypt had already been ruled out ... In addition Cyrenaica provided an outlet to Central Africa, an area which the Grand Sanusi must have thought of as a possible field of expansion.[11]

It was the grandson of the Grand Sanusi, Sayyid Amir Mohamed Idris, who became head of the order in 1916 and was later to become King of Libya.

The Sanusi are Sunni or orthodox Moslems,*

which means that in faith and morals they accept the teachings of the Koran and the Sunna, a collection of traditions about the life and habits of the Prophet, whose example in all matters should be followed by believers. Most Orthodox Muslims recognise further doctrinal sources – like the *ijma*, general agreement among those of the faithful capable of holding an opinion on such matters, and *qiyas*, determinations of what should be believed or done by analogy with the teachings and life of the Prophet. The founder of the Sanusi order, like the founders of Wahhabism in Saudi Arabia, also a revivalist order with emphasis on the return to pristine Islam, rejected both.[12]

The Sanusi is therefore a highly orthodox order of Islam. Evans-Pritchard writes:

... the rigorous orthodoxy of the Order, and especially its insistence on conformity to the original teachings of the Prophet, meant that the faith and morals which the Prophet preached to the Bedouin of his day, and which they accepted, were equally suited to the Bedouin of Cyrenaica, who in all essentials were leading, and still lead, a life like to that of the Bedouin in Arabia in the seventh century.[13]

The Sanusi are also an order of Sufis. 'Orthodox Islam,' writes Evans-Pritchard,

tends to be a cold and formalistic religion. The gulf between God and man, spanned by the bridge of the Imans among the Shi'ites, is too wide for simple people, and its rules and regulations deprive it of warmth and colour. The need for personal contact and tenderness finds expression in the cult of Saints, in Sufi mysticism.[14]

Sufism, it has been said, 'appealed to the popular imagination because it supplied men with spiritual satisfaction and vitality as against the rigidity of the law and its teaching'.[15]

* Islam is divided principally between the Sunni and the Shi'a. The basis for the division was a dynastic quarrel in the early days of Islam, but it has since become one of rite and belief. See the *Cambridge History of Islam*.

In North Africa Islam had been to the end of the fourteenth century a religion of the towns and cities. Later this began to change. Islam became primarily rural.

The *zawiya* (monastery) replaced the mosque ... as a centre of learning ... Sufism gathered popularity ... and more and more the Shaikh became a saint and his *baraka* (blessing) rather more than his learning gave him an exalted position. The Sufi himself changed. He was no longer of the same calibre and integrity as the early mystics. The net result was that Islam grew narrower in outlook and lost sight of tolerance. Then the spirit of *tawakkul* (fatalism) spread among the Moslems ... The erudition and knowledge came to a standstill. Sufism gathered popularity but it lost its great tradition.[16]

Libya alone in North Africa was untouched by later reformist movements and teachings, like those of Mohamed Abdu, which proclaimed a return to the sources of the faith, yet contained a response to the challenge which faced Islam in the contemporary world, and whose approach opened the way to the development of a secular nationalism. The Sanusi movement was a revivalist movement pure and simple, aiming to restore what the Grand Sanusi conceived to be the original society of the Prophet.

The Sanusi order won over the nomad and semi-nomad Bedouin tribes of Cyrenaica, Tripolitania, and Egypt, and the oasis folk. It did not make much impression on the peasants and townsmen in northern Tripolitania and the Nile valley. 'The Order,' wrote Evans-Pritchard, 'poured its vitality southwards along the trade routes to the interior of Africa, into the Fezzan and the various regions (then) called the French Sahara and French Equatorial Africa.'[17] The headquarters of the Order and the seat of its Islamic university were at Jahgub, an oasis which bisected one of the trade routes from the coast to the Sahara. Alongside the prophets, the learned men and the cultivators of the oasis *zawiyas*, flourished the traders who controlled the slave traffic at its peak. Many of the brethren of the *zawiyas* acted as guides, transport providers, and caravan escorts from the depots and resthouses for slave and other caravans along the route. Indeed, many of them were themselves merchants and slave traders, 'charging fees in money and in kind for the honour and protection they bring to the caravans with which they may be travelling; in fact the holier the person, the more he charges'.[18] The Sanusi profited both by directly engaging in trade and transport and through customs dues collected at the centres through which the caravans passed.[19]

In small-scale societies as these in Africa, where dominant classes were able to extract only limited surpluses due to the difficult ecological conditions and the low development of the productive forces, long-distance trade of the kind dominated by the Sanusi played a decisive role in transferring some of the surplus of one society to another, and in providing the basis of the wealth and power of the ruling groups.[20] The Sanusi headed a religious–political organization; but at the same time their leading families constituted a ruling class, from their control over resources of land and water and over trade.[21] It was the Sanusi organization that clashed with France's colonial armies as they advanced northwards from the then French-held Congo to Lake Chad; and as the twentieth century opened, the Sanusi, in alliance with African states and tribes, were fighting a *jihad* against the advancing French forces. Sanusi envoys recruited volunteers as far north as Benghazi to fight with the Tuareg round Lake Chad.[22] And by 1902, the French advance had been temporarily blocked at Kanem. It was in this mobilization against French colonialism's threat to their trading monopoly that the Sanusi tested their network of alliances and its military capacity. By then practically all the oases, the nomadic population between Egypt and the Sudan and Tuareg territory, were Sanusi. Some of the more prosperous town merchants who had dealings with the Bedouin tribes and sent caravans into the Sahara found it advisable to be received into the Order, and for this reason there was in all the towns of Libya a body of the richer citizens who belonged to it.[23]

But essentially the strength of the Sanusi Order was that it coordinated its lodges to the tribal structure of Cyrenaica, which was particularly favourable to the growth of a politico-religious movement. It was a region cut off by deserts from neighbouring countries; it had a homogeneous population and a tribal system which embraced common traditions; above all the Bedouin tribes needed some authority lying outside their segmentary

tribal system which could compose inter-tribal and inter-
sectional disputes and bind the tribes together.[24] When necessary the Sanusi used the Turkish administration to buttress their
position in their dealings with the tribes, and at other times
combined with the tribes to resist encroachments on its preroga-
tives by the Turkish administration. British intelligence reports
were convinced that a Sanusi revolt against the Turkish occupation was brewing in the years immediately before the Italian
invasion. But by then, the struggle against the advancing French
colonial armies was running aground; and since there was a
danger that two European powers would encircle Sanusi control
from the coast and the interior, the Sanusi turned to an alliance
with Turkey and the indispensable military help this would
bring.[25]

By the time of the Italian occupation almost all Libyans were
Arabic-speaking Moslems of Arab–Berber descent; for with the
merger of the Arab and Berber streams over the centuries, the
country came to have a more or less unified population. But
there were enclaves of groups less uniform and closer to their
original affinities. In Tripolitania, small communities of Berber
still live as settled farmers along the northern fringes of the Jebel
Nafusa, at Jefren and at Gharyan, and on the coast at Zwara.[26]
The majority of these follow the Kharedjite sect of Islam, more
egalitarian than the orthodox Sunni and chosen in its time to
signify resentment of their Arab conquerors. In the coastal
towns of merchants, pedlars, and functionaries, the Turkish
strain was strong. In southern Libya a tiny community of Tebu
are suspected to be the last survivors of the early Garamantes.
Perhaps 7,000 of the North African population of Tuareg live in
south-west Libya, mostly round the Ghat area. Once important
middlemen for the caravan trade, they were economically ruined
by its collapse. In 1917 there was a Tuareg revolt, aided by the
Sanusi as part of their anti-French campaign, which ambushed
and virtually wiped out a platoon of French camel corps. When
the revolt spread, there were even Allied fears for the safety of
Northern Nigeria.

In the Fezzan, Arab, Berber, Tebu, and Hausa and Bornu

peoples are inextricably mingled, former black slaves having become lower-class sharecroppers or semi-serfs working for an imposed ruling group of Arab, Berber, or Tuareg landowners. In the desert oases, whether in the Fezzan group or round Kufra to the east, communities are more sedentary than nomad; cultivating irrigated gardens on the fringes or round the palm groves. The soil is worked by the hoe, and returns for labour are small. An analysis of three Libyan oases (Ghat, Ghadames, and Murzuq) showed that the distribution of water resources was monopolized by a restricted set of family groups. In Ghat, for instance, this dominant group constituted only fifteen families among over 200 registered proprietors. Customary land usage was likewise controlled by large families who similarly dominated social and political life.[27]

There were, thus, vertical divisions running through oasis society; but there were also horizontal divisions among the tribes of the Fezzan, and among the Bedouin of Cyrenaica, a region of part herdsmen, part cultivators. The actual as well as the legendary lines of descent from the original Arab invasions had become the structural basis of a tribal system that strongly influenced the economic and political processes of twentieth-century Cyrenaica. The tribes divide between the Sa'adi and the Marabtin. The Sa'adi are the nine tribes which hold the country by right of conquest;[28] the Marabtin are the modern descendants of Arabs of the first invasion, with some Berber admixture, who were subjugated by the new invaders and compelled to pay tribute. Thus a Sa'adi tribesman has rights to the country's resources which a client cannot claim. The Marabtin, who cannot claim nobility by descent, are vassal tribes and use the earth and water by grace of the free tribes. The core of the distinction was thus property rights, for the client tribes had to be granted access to land and water by their patrons, and this privilege had to be periodically renewed. Shortage of land was not a problem, but clients had to supplicate for use of water points each year. Water, or access to it, was the prime resource.[29] The clients were thus compelled to produce a surplus; and over-production still left them debarred from political power. Yet because the economy was marginal, with near-drought conditions over many years, the differences between patron and client tribes began to fall away; and the Sanusi, who claimed adherents among both did much to lessen the differential between client and free.[30] By the beginning of the century the Marabtin, though still traditionally vassals of the Sa'adi, were partially absorbed into the free tribes and no longer necessarily paid taxes for the land on which they moved. Yet while in the ordinary run of life it was often difficult to distinguish between patron and client groups, as late as the independence election of 1950, when the patron group had vast land resources under its control, all the candidates for the semi-desert areas were noblemen.[31] It was especially under the Italian administration that the division between client and free tribes was seen as an opening through which to drive a wedge between the Bedouin population, and some of the Marabtin took advantage of the opportunity afforded.

The bulk of the traditional urban dwellers were either descendants of merchants or marabouts from other parts of North Africa or Turkish officials of the Ottoman administration. In later years – especially after the Second World War and the discovery of oil – large numbers of Bedouin tribal adherents also moved to the towns. And though many of these continued to give primary allegiance to their tribal units within the interior, the strong bonds of rigid tribal discipline and common land ownership were missing. Thus urban representatives of the post-independence parliament were members of prominent town tribe families, and electoral contests were determined not only by rallying urban support but also by mustering Bedouin tribal links with the interior.

Yet essentially within Cyrenaica, the Sanusi remained a rural and a Bedouin Order and directed its affairs from the desert. This ran to the heart of how the Bedouin resistance against the Italian occupation was sustained for so long, and why the conqueror could not easily win. For, Evans-Pritchard writes,[32] while tribes and town affected one another politically, essentially town and country kept apart, with the towns dependent on the country and not the country on the towns. For in Cyrenaica there was no client peasantry bound by debt, no need of protection and trade monopoly to the towns. The Bedouin did not settle on the land where they could be easy prey to the usurer, overseer, and town collector. There was nothing in the Bedouin way of life which gave an opening to the usurer. Moreover the towns had no monopoly of trade, for if necessary the Bedouin could go without urban supplies or obtain them overland from Egypt as they did during the war with Italy. Consequently there were no rich landowning families living in the towns at the expense of the countryside; no aghas, beys, or pashas. And what small educated middle class existed outside the small official circle, lacked both wealth and influence. In general it may be said in Cyrenaica that the towns were not parasites on the country but had their functions as trading centres and suppliers. The markets were free, not tied to town societies. Nor could the Bedouin be coerced by force of law. The tribes were largely inaccessible and they were stronger than the towns, even with the administration behind them. The Bedouin were not afraid of the Turkish administration and they did not use the courts. The Turkish administration centred in the towns had to operate through the leading tribal shaikhs, and through the Sanusi lodges. After the invasion the Italian administration was to find the whole system operating against rather than through it.

3 Resistance but Conquest

Italy, it was said, occupied Libya so as to breathe more freely in a Mediterranean stifling with the possessions and naval bases of France and Britain.[1] The colonization lasted thirty-two years, from 1911 to 1943, and together with that of Algeria, where the occupation was far more prolonged and the struggle even more cataclysmic – and of Palestine where the occupation was anomalous but bitter – this was the most severe occupation experienced by an Arab country in modern times. The object of the colonization was to incorporate Libya as Italy's fourth shore: it was to be colonization by peasant settlement, and the advent to power of Mussolini's Fascist order opened Libya to mass emigration financed and organized by the State.

Though Italy's acquisition of a North African colony has been characterized as part of the pre-First-World-War European diplomatic game, the Bank of Rome had begun its economic penetration in the last decades of the previous century. The colony was initially to be acquired by purchase. Between 1907 and 1908 the Bank of Rome's deposits in Tripoli more than doubled, and they continued to rise. This helps explain why, when in 1913 there were secret negotiations between Italy and the Sanusi, a representative of the Bank of Rome was present throughout.[2]

Libyans were divided in their reception of the invaders. In Tripoli town, where a brief insurrection provoked harsh reprisals against civilians, the new colonists found a defeatist élite and submissive traditional heads. Such opposition as expressed itself was furtive; as in the efforts at persuading rich Tripolitanians to send their wealth to Egypt.[3] Some important families, notably the Muntassers, were pro-Italian from the start and throughout the occupation; and it was largely with the help of collaborator chiefs that Italy occupied much of Tripolitania during 1912. But in the interior, both east and west, resistance rose. Turkish commanders and their troops had retreated into the hinterland, where they were joined by commanders sent from Constantinople to help direct the war effort. But above all the tribes had ridden in to fight alongside the Turkish irregulars. Italy had expected Libyans to welcome her as relief from the clutches of a dying Ottoman empire; instead she faced combined Turkish–Libyan resistance. A year after the invasion there was military stalemate. The Italian forces were in command of the coastal enclaves and of the sea, but thousands of tribesmen were under arms.

In 1912 Italy and Turkey suddenly negotiated a peace. Libyans were stupefied. It was an ambiguous settlement, essentially enabling Turkey to disengage. It ostensibly granted independence to Tripolitania and Cyrenaica and yet recognized Italian sovereignty. Overnight the war changed its character. It ceased to be one in which a foreign power was trying to seize a colony from a tired empire; and became an anti-colonial war by an indigenous people, battling to retain their lands and their independent way of life.

Once Turkey had deserted them, leaders from all parts of Tripolitania met at Azzizia to discuss their strategy.[4] Two positions were defined, and they were to recur and re-form in varying combinations throughout the struggle. On the one hand, a peace party was ready for conciliation and submission; on the other, a camp of irreconcilables pressed for armed resistance. The meeting was no sooner over than, led by Suleiman Baruni who had represented Tripolitania in the Turkish parliament and who had returned to Libya to fight the invasion, there began to rally a great cluster of tribes to demand an independent Berber province, administered by an elected assembly with headquarters at Jefren in the Jebel Nafusa, and with an outlet to the sea.

By August 1914, when the European war broke out, the first phase of the war in Libya was over. Italy still held only the towns of the coast; and in the interior, she had suffered the worst defeat since the Battle of Adowa against the Ethiopians. The struggle for the autonomy of the Jebel had been defeated, but

Baruni had slipped through the frontier into Tunisia and had
got away to Constantinople, from where he was shortly to return
to try once more to rally resistance. In Tripolitania Italian
troops had been routed when Ramadan Esh Shitewi es Aweihli,
chief of Misurata, went into battle ostensibly on the Italian side
but ordered his troops to turn and fire on them. In Cyrenaica
and the Fezzan, despite heavy losses, the tribes had begun the
guerrilla warfare so suited to their terrain and their traditions of
turbulent independence. When parts of Cyrenaica were overrun,
resistance flared in the Fezzan, led by Sanusi forces supported
by Tuareg and Tebu from even the furthest corners of the
desert. At one stage the Italians were forced to retreat into
southern Algeria for French protection. It was apparent that as
long as the bedouin were at large and unsubdued, there was bound
to be resistance, and that the Sanusi Order was able to organize
the united resistance that Tripolitania alone was unable to
summon.

Italy entered the European war in 1915 on Britain's side, and
with Turkey on Germany's, Turkish commanders re-entered
Libya with some advisers and arms. It was under Turkish and
German pressure that the Sanusi, under the leadership of Sayyid
Ahmed al-Sharif, still trying to protect the Order's trade system,
and desperately in need of Turkish arms, launched an abortive
assault on British posts in western Egypt. His leadership did not
survive this episode. After his defeat at Mersa Matruh by
British forces, he handed over control to Sayyid Mohamed Idris
(later King Idris I), who promptly entered into negotiations with
Britain. British intelligence sources had early noted the 'difference of opinion in the Sanusi family on the war and other
matters'.[5] If Italy had misjudged the Libyan reaction to its
invasion, so did Britain; though she subsequently exercised
pressure through both the Khedive in Egypt and the Amir of
Arabia to advise the Sanusi to bring the hostilities to an end.[6]
(The War Office in Cairo insisted that the proclamation under
the Sanusi seal to fight had been fabricated by a Turkish
official.)[7] By the time that a truce was signed in 1916, Britain
was convinced that the Sanusi head 'had been made to understand thoroughly that he was to be recognized only as the

religious leader of his sect and not as chief of a political entity, and second, that he must make peace with both powers (Britain and Italy) or with neither'.[8] Under the truce, the Sanusi were to recognize *de facto* Italian order in the towns, while the Italian administration recognized the *de facto* rule of the Order in the country.

By the early twenties Italy was on the verge of social revolution at home and in no condition to pursue an aggressive war in Libya, although this was precisely the time when she might have taken advantage of the country's internal divisions. Tripolitania, sharing in the optimism that swept the Arab world immediately after the war, had taken advantage of a liberal régime in Rome to assert its independence in the declaration of an Arab Republic, al-Jumhuriya al-Trabulsiya. Following the treaty with Italy managed by Britain, Cyrenaica also boasted a parliament, under what had become virtually a system of weak indirect rule by Italy. Cyrenaica's rejection of the Italian presence – except as traders on the coast – was as unequivocal as that of the Tripolitanian Republic. Italy found herself paying regular subsidies to the army, police force, and the Sanusi tribal shaikhs and notables; while even Sanusi officials, scribes, chiefs of irregular bands, informers, and political counsellors were on the payroll. Idris was recognized as Amir, and had his own flag, along with a handsome monthly subsidy. In return the tribes were supposed to disband and disarm. Idris visited Rome to negotiate a sizable indemnity for the *zawiyas* destroyed in the war and even promised to remove those shaikhs who had embittered relations between the government and the people.[9]

Also in Rome a delegation from the Tripolitanian Republic lobbied left-wing deputies to reiterate their total rejection of Italian sovereignty of any kind. One of its members subsequently attended the Moslem Revolutionary Congress in Moscow. From spasmodic tribal rebellion to a dangerous pan-Islamic plot? British and other Western intelligence circles were duly alarmed.[10] But if some events in Tripolitania carried dangerous overtones of the feared Abd al Krim rebellion against the Spanish, which had overflowed into Morocco; if any rebellion or any profession of independence, let alone Arab nationalism, sounded ominously like Bolshevik revolution, within the Libyan resistance there were also complex conflicting and enfeebling tendencies. This was inevitable within social movements and leaderships of such varying social bases and consciousness. Some sought to retain a foothold in urban trading communities under Italian commercial control by turning collaborator. Some saw the defeat of Italy as the return of Libya to the Turkish fold. Some were inspired by a messianic religious order when messianic resistance against Italian conquest had a close affinity to nationalism. Some fought to protect or re-assert regional and local interests and leadership claims. Some were inspired by republicanism and visions of national autonomy. The Tripolitanian Republic placed Arab nationalism on the agenda. In the end it was not these advanced ideas of anti-colonialism which were able to build a viable and united resistance, but the Bedouin stateless society, which managed to develop the rudiments of a state in the face of external attack, and which converted its physical means of primary resistance into a prolonged popular and guerrilla war against the colonizing enemy.

In Tripolitania, on the other hand, with Italy still in only paper control, discordant claims and internecine strife were prevalent. The Italian administration helped to play off Berber against Arab, and to exploit Berber conflicts in the traditional north–south feuds for the control of the Jebel. The uneasy alliance of forces that had founded the Tripolitanian Republic broke apart. In Misurata, one-time partners in the Republic, the Orfella and the forces of Ramadan Esh Shitewi es Aweihli, clashed, and the latter was killed. Earlier, in 1916, an attempt by the Sanusi to unite the country under their flag had failed because of the long-standing conflict between the Bedouin and interior groupings of Tripolitania, to which most of the Sanusi supporters belonged, and the urban and coastal forces. The two sides had met in battle and the Sanusi had withdrawn, to set the limit of Sanusi influence in the interior.

Even before the Fascist march on Rome, Italy was disillusioned with her attempt at rule by compromise in Libya, and her generals prepared to change their tactics and commence the reconquest of Tripolitania. It was as renewed offensives were imminent that Tripolitania, which had been unable to produce leader or political force capable of uniting the disparate strains in the region, turned to the Sanusi as a possible source of unity. In April 1922 Idris was offered recognition as the Amir of all Libya. His dilemma was acute: to accept would snap already strained relations with Italy; to refuse meant offending Tripolitania. He was already compromised among his followers for his treaties with Italy. Idris played for time and then left the country for Egypt, 'where he had long made financial preparations for this eventuality out of the Italian subsidies'.[11] Idris did not return to Cyrenaica until almost the end of the Second World War in 1943. Though many of the Shaikhs and Brothers of the Sanusi Order played a leading part in the prolonged resistance that followed, the Sanusi family as such 'played an inconspicuous and inglorious part in the resistance'.[12] Idris was a quietist. He was 'temperamentally prone to vacillation and evasion', with an 'aversion for directness in thought or action'.[13] This and his long exiled isolation from the struggle of his people notwithstanding, Britain continued – as she had from 1914, when Idris had first made contact with British political authorities in Cairo on his way from Mecca – to favour and promote his pretensions to leadership of the Bedouin in Cyrenaica.

By 1923, with Idris in exile, with the Fascist take-over of Italy complete, with the hope of a solid anti-Italian front of Cyrenaica and Tripolitania foundering, and with Italian forces re-occupying all the coast from Tunisia to the Gulf of Sirte, the second Sanusi–Italian war of 1923–32 had started. The classic account – by a Westerner – of this guerrilla war is by Evans-Pritchard,[14] the eminent British anthropologist who had served as Political Officer to the British Military Administration of Cyrenaica. He describes it as a war of the Bedouin, asserting that the townsmen played little active part in the resistance, even where they sympathized with it. Some of the tribes remained passive and some collaborated, for they had a history of intercourse with the towns and the Turkish administration, and when the Italians took over from Turkey that intercourse was resumed. But the nomadic warlike and powerful looked not to the coast but southwards to the desert:

Beyond striking-distance by horse-patrols, these hardy wanderers of the steppe, whose history was nothing more than a long record of tribal wars, had paid scant attention to the Turks, had refused in the first Italian war to make terms, had disdainfully turned their backs on the intruders during the ensuing years of peace, and were now to offer a stubborn resistance to renewed aggression.

The interior, and not the towns, offered the terrain and other conditions for guerrilla war. But the stress on countryside rather than generalized resistance is probably overdone. For many who fought in the Jebel were from the towns; and in the end martyrs and collaborators were of fairly similar proportion among Bedouin and townsmen.

Italian tactics were to exploit old feuds, to run furrows of blood (*solci di sangue*) between tribe and tribe and one section and another, and to seek out collaborationists to be used against the patriots, or the *rebelli*. But even among those guilty of the worst complicity, the Bedouin who joined the Italian forces as irregulars, police, labourers, and camelmen, there was assistance to the patriots when the opportunity presented itself. Battalions drawn from the submissive elements of the population constituted a sort of supply depot of men, arms, and ammunition for the Sanusi formations. Omar Mukhtar, the indomitable and best-known soldier–patriot of the resistance, was said to have agents in every Italian post. Some supposedly submissive populations allowed their horses to graze far from their camps so that the patriots could borrow them for operational purposes. 'So useful was a submitted population to the patriots that the tribal shaikhs sometimes arranged among themselves who should submit and who take the field.' Even the tribal shaikhs on government subsidy paid a tithe to Omar Mukhtar. There were said to be two governments of Cyrenaica, Italian and Sanusi, and they were the government of the day and the government of the night. Each Bedouin tribe maintained its own guerrilla band; and though by the end of the war the guerrillas did not total more than 600 to 700, since only a certain number of men could maintain themselves on the country and move through it with speed and secrecy, the resistance flourished on the support of the population. 'All Cyrenaica was hard hostile rock beneath the shallowest covering of local collaboration.' The Italians found themselves fighting not an army but a people.

There were, according to Evans-Pritchard, roughly three military phases in the war. In the first the Italians attempted to subdue the Bedouin through the use of regular army units. In the second they made greater use of aeroplanes and small motorized units. In the final stage they employed the strategy of massive concentration camps and the pacification methods of modern counter-insurgency campaigns.

In the later phase of the resistance, when Graziani was determined to wrest the initiative from the guerrillas, he re-organized his forces in the *guerra senza quartiere* into small mobile patrols, to keep the whole of the forest country under surveillance and to attack the enemy wherever they met him giving him no rest. To prevent the guerrillas from obtaining supplies and reinforcements from the civilian population, he disarmed the tribesmen, confiscating from them thousands of rifles and millions of rounds of ammunition, and made possession of arms a capital offence. He instituted the *tribunale volante*, a military court flown from point to point: to try, and execute, all who had dealings of any kind with the guerrillas. He reduced the Libyan units by more than two thirds with the intention of eventually disbanding them altogether. In the meanwhile he distributed among the 750 Libyans retained in service rifles of a different calibre from the rifles in patriot hands to prevent leakage of ammunition. At the same time he closed the Sanusiya lodges, confiscated their estates, and exiled their shaikhs.

For years a considerable part of the guerrilla supplies had come from Egypt, paid for by Bedouin produce, by money raised by customs charges, and by funds collected throughout the Arab and Moslem world. The guerrillas steadily found themselves cut off from local sources of supply and forced more and more to rely on Egypt for the bare necessities of life and of war. When the patrolling of the frontier by armoured cars and planes, with instructions to destroy any caravans they spotted, did not prevent supplies from coming in or refugees from going out, Graziani ran a line of barbed wire entanglements from the sea to the sand dunes in the south, a distance of over 300 kilometres.[15] Thus was the country scourged into submission.[16]

By the close of the struggle the Bedouin population of Cyrenaica was reduced by a half to two thirds through death and emigration; while the Sanusi Order was disrupted, and its lands confiscated and, when suitable, handed out to Italian colonists. Italian administrative policy was directed at compelling the Bedouin to settle – but away from the fertile plateau. By 1935 these lands had been reserved for metropolitan colonization. The aim was to abolish the traditional Bedouin way of life altogether and to make the Bedouin themselves peasant-tenants of the State, and wage labourers. This required the destruction of their tribal and kinship institutions – tribal shaikhs were displaced by direct military rule – and an end to patriarchal agriculture. It was hoped to avoid the growth of a metropolitan proletariat, by making the Bedouin a cheap reserve of labour for general unskilled work and/or seasonal labour on the farms of the colonists. For political reasons the Italian administration also created Arab colonization centres similar to those built for Italian immigrants. Like the Italian, the Arab colonist was first to be salaried labour, then partner with the State, then mortgagee and finally owner. The administration found difficulty in creating Arab colonists, however, for the Bedouin showed no inclination to work as serfs.[17] In the administration Arabs were employed in only minor posts, so that almost no élite was formed. By 1940 there were only fourteen Arabs employed in the civil service other than in menial jobs. And these Arab bureaucrats were mostly townsmen from Derna and Benghazi; some of them were members of respectable families from the Turkish days, but most had a record of close and active collaboration with the Italian system as spies, guides, interpreters, and overseers of concentration camps. Towards the end of Italian rule these were being replaced by a new class of officials brought up in the towns under Italian rule and educated in Italian–Arab schools. Evans-Pritchard describes them as markedly preoccupied with their own affairs, uninterested in the benefit of the people as a whole, and hostile to the Bedouin. They were easily susceptible to disaffection nonetheless, and very ready to cooperate with the

British when the war brought them into Cyrenaica.[18] With the onset of independence, these same officials were absorbed into that government administration.

Italian land acquisition had totalled less than 10,000 hectares by the end of 1923, but it rose to twenty times that area in the next five years.[19] By 1940 Italian colonizing efforts were making possible the intensive use of irrigated land by Italian colonists. There were orchards in the coastal plain and northern hill lands in the west, and crops were being grown from Zwara to Misurata. In Cyrenaica settlement estates were still in the early stages of reclamation when the Second World War broke out; but again the land was producing more than it had done probably since Roman cultivation times[20] – for Italian settlers.

Mussolini had declared in 1934: 'Civilization, in fact, is what Italy is creating on the Fourth Shore of our sea (Libya–R.F.); Western civilization in general and Fascist civilization in particular.' But it was less for Fascist ideals than in expectation of a worthwhile return on their investments, a commentator writes,[21] that Italian capitalists, led by the colony's most energetic governor, started large-scale agricultural development in Tripolitania. The governor, Guiseppi Volpi, himself acquired a big estate near Misurata, and encouraged others to follow his example. Land was sold, mortgaged, or rented in large concessions by the State and was worked, under Italian supervision and with Italian capital, by hired Libyan labour and by some Italian peasant families. The colonial government acquired land either by confiscating it from 'rebels', or, following a decree of 1922, by taking over uncultivated land for 'public use'. The government invoked Turkish and Moslem land-tenure laws which, broadly speaking, recognized as its owner anyone who settled on and cultivated previously untilled and ownerless ground.[22] But the big concession system was not part of official Fascist colonial policy. Mussolini wanted Italy's landless peasants and unemployed to settle in Libya with their families and establish their own farms; 'he did not approve of scarce Italian capital being used to pay Libyans to work rich men's estates.'[23] In later years the concessionaires were obliged to employ and settle Italian families on the land under long-term contracts. When 'demographic colonization' really got going in the thirties, state-aided peasant colonists were recruited in thousands at a time. Methods used in the Pontine Marshes and other Fascist land-settlement and reclamation schemes in Italy were applied. This involved generous state aid to make colonial farming a success. 'Demographic colonization' was costly, and the state was estimated to have spent over £4 million (pre-war) on the 1938 migration alone, even before the colonists arrived on Libyan soil. Had the war not broken out there would have been 100,000 settlers in the country by 1942, and the settlement of half a million was planned by the early sixties.

Fascist Libya, it has been said,[24] was not an African colony, but a colony of Europeans in Africa, where 'immigrants were encouraged and helped by the state to acquire and farm land, and where rule by the mother country was first and foremost in the interests of these settlers'. Colonialism in Libya was practised according to the theories of Fascism. Libyans were enrolled in the army and fought in the Abyssinian campaign; they gave the Fascist salute, wore black shirts, and cheered Mussolini. Libyan youth had its own Fascist organization. But above all Libyans provided a core of manual labourers. In 1939 Libyans were given their first opportunity to apply for Special Italian Citizenship (*Cittadinanza italiana speciale*). 'The small Libyan intellectual class,' Wright observes:

was either in exile or voiceless and all opposition had been too recently and ruthlessly stamped out for embryo independence movements to cause trouble. The traditional structure of tribal authority was deliberately weakened by the appointment of one 'leader' to as few as twelve tribesmen. In Fezzan the Italians abolished the Jemaa, or councils of family heads, which were genuine popular assemblies, and instead exercised authority through suitable Mudirs. Fascism taught Libyans, as well as Italians, to do as they were told.[25]

By 1938 the colony had a population of just over 880,000 of which 10 per cent (89,000) were Italians and about 86 per cent (763,000) Libyan Moslems.

Freya Stark paid a visit to Bengazi just before the war. She described colonial Italians strolling in family phalanxes at leisure after the working hours of the day . . . in the squares . . . and here I gradually began to be puzzled. Something was missing and I noticed that it was the raucous Arab voice of the Levant. The crowds moved in a silence that sounded European to anyone familiar with the East . . . I discovered a boot-black . . . when he had done polishing my shoes I thanked him in Arabic; he looked at me, startled and fled without being paid. I began to feel a quagmire beneath this gay little town, a deadening substratum of fear. 'There must be Arabs somewhere,' I thought and spent what remained of the daylight trying to find them; and did eventually, in a little ghetto of squalid streets far back from the sea. A throttled horror made me wish never to visit Benghazi again.[26]

Only months after Italy entered the Second World War, she used her Libyan bases to push deep into Egypt. The prize was Cairo and control of the Suez Canal.

Britain and France raced one another for possession of Libya's parts. Free French forces under General Leclerc staged a forced march over forgotten caravan routes and surprised the Italian post at Murzuq. Then General Leclerc began to advance his forces northwards. British officers, sent to him at Fort Lamy, carried a letter signed by General Alexander asserting the desirability of a British military administration. But General Leclerc had received instructions from General de Gaulle that the British officers posted to him should be returned to Cairo, and that any territory occupied by the Fighting Free French was to be administered under General Leclerc's authority.[27]

Since General Leclerc was an independent commander and was not under the immediate orders of either General Alexander or General Montgomery, it was not possible on legal grounds to dispute the attitude adopted by General de Gaulle and it only remained for us to press the War Office to endeavour to come to some amicable arrangement with the Free French authorities in London.[28]

Throughout the war, uncertainty remained about who was to be responsible for the administration of the conquered territory; North Africa was still under discussion within the British and American High Command.[29] In 1944 a query to Britain's Foreign Office from the Treasury about the future of Libya brought the response: 'All we can possibly say is that we simply do not know.'[30] Its forecast was that none of the Libyan areas would return to *direct* Italian rule, although there was a possibility of the Italians being admitted to a share at least in the rule of Tripolitania. Major Evans-Pritchard, then of the British Military Administration of Cyrenaica, wrote a memorandum at the beginning of 1944 maintaining that Cyrenaica was closely bound to Egypt and suggesting that it be placed under Egyptian sovereignty as a semi-autonomous state. His memorandum was forwarded to Anthony Eden by the British Ambassador in Cairo. It prompted a Chiefs of Staff memorandum shortly afterwards which urged that Cyrenaica become an autonomous principality under Egyptian suzerainty but with international supervision and adequate safeguards which would include 'naval and air base facilities in the Benghazi area'. Tripolitania, it was suggested, should be restored to Italy, subject to Britain's retaining an airfield at Castel Benito as a staging point. As for the French in the Fezzan, 'any reasonable frontier adjustment should be agreed to'.[31]

During the early British military occupation of Cyrenaica, there had been consternation among the Sanusi at the continuance of the Italian administrative structure, and it was at this time that Idris made representations to the British government for a commitment that it would not countenance the return of Cyrenaica to Italy.[32] Not long afterwards, the British administration received a petition from a 'clique of Tripolitanian refugees' who had always been opposed to the Sanusi and had refused to take part in the formation of Britain's Libyan–Arab force, based on the Sanusi army and which subsequently developed into Libya's army. The Tripolitanians had requested permission to recruit their own force; this was refused on the grounds that Britain could not have two rival Libyan forces operating. One of the petitioners was a younger brother of Ramadan Esh Shitewi es Aweilih. The petitioners proposed the formation of a committee of leading Tripolitanians to maintain relations with the British administration; the suggestion had a cold reception.[33] The wartime reserve of Tripolitanians about taking part in British military operations – expressed in 1940 at a meeting of émigrés in Cairo – arose from their insistence on a firm prior commitment from Britain for the future independence of their country. They objected, further, to the application by Idris of the term 'Sanusi' to all who desired to cooperate. They were prepared to come forward but without acknowledging Sanusi leadership, for they objected to Sanusi leadership over Tripolitania.[34] But Britain had decided which forces within Libya to support, and all others were irrelevant.

4   Independence through Cold-War Diplomacy

War has been called the midwife not only of revolutions, but of nations. While the World War of 1914–18 was a turning-point in the formation of the older-established Arab states, and it was the Second World War of 1939–45 which transformed the political face of Asia, it was the Cold War which gave Libya formal independence. This is not to say that the state of Libya must be seen entirely as a diplomatic creation of the West.[1] The political association of Tripolitania, Cyrenaica, and the Fezzan antedated the Italian conquest by hundreds of years, as in the establishment of an Ottoman administration for the region; and, above all, common cause, if not unified structures, had grown against the Italian invader. But once the Italian occupation had been replaced by British and French, it was committees of the United Nations which brought about the formation of a Libyan government and played overseer to the transfer of power from the administrations of the occupying powers.

With Italy defeated in war and Britain and France in occupation of Libya, the colonial powers with which the United Nations had to deal, whatever their interests in the region, had not been the country's original colonial masters; this made the task of formalizing Libya's independence far easier. The story of that accession to independence is nonetheless bewildering. It winds through the tortuous diplomacy of the major powers as they adjusted to the power balances of the post-war world, for the creation of the independent state of Libya was directly determined by their shifting interests and changing perceptions. Unlike Europe's experience of the growth of nation-states, Libya was created a state from without, and only then did she begin to try to assemble a nation from the parts which over centuries had been separated from one another by successive foreign occupations as well as her hostile geography.

In the post-war North African region, Libya's independence was something of an anomaly. It was 1955 and 1956, and in the case of Algeria 1962, before the Maghreb countries attained sovereign government. The independence they struggled for, a prostrate and ruined Libya suddenly had thrust upon her by a diplomatic pact of the Big Powers and the small. It was a measure of the confidence of the powers which traditionally controlled the Mediterranean that nothing present or promised in Libyan post-independence politics was likely to disturb the balance in the region.

Perhaps it was an inevitable culmination of a past in which a succession of alien powers had arbitrarily disposed of Libya that the fiercest controversies over the form of her independence took place not inside the country but in the corridors and cabinet rooms of the big powers. There the focus was not on the needs and problems of Libya but on the state interests of the power-brokers in an area that had been a central battleground of the war and was a strategic prize in any future conflict. But while initially the competitive purposes of the powers worked against the chances of a united Libya, for they pulled her several parts to their own centres of strategic gravity, ultimately the agreement between the governments of the West that at all costs the Soviet Union had to be kept out of the Mediterranean served to subdue their contesting claims and permitted an at least nominally independent Libya to break out of the diplomatic impasse. In its protracted passage through interminable international proceedings, the Libyan issue showed all the signs of being an instrument of outside purposes. Among the powers there were eccentric switches of policy and inexplicable changes of pace. In 1948 a four-power commission visited the country and unanimously agreed that Libya was neither economically self-supporting, nor politically ready for independence. A year later a United Nations resolution decided her independence.

After the war, as much as during it, the Italian colonies of Somaliland, Eritrea, Ethiopia, and Libya were strategic outposts for the control of north-east Africa and the eastern basin of the

Mediterranean. But though the other three controlled the land bridge between the Mediterranean and the Persian Gulf, it is Libya's coastline that runs for 1,200 miles opposite the belly of Europe, from Sicily to Cyprus. During the critical war years of 1941 and 1942, the Axis had demonstrated that possession of the Tripoli–Benghazi–Sicily triangle, together with control of the Aegean islands, could effectively nullify sea-power in the eastern Mediterranean. After the war it was the requirements of strategic air warfare – lands spacious and desolate enough for the long-range land-based bomber – which placed a premium on Libya's shores and vast spaces, which were ideal for reconnoitring and controlling sea routes, and for asserting and protecting further-flung operations.

At the Potsdam conference, the Big Four had agreed that under the peace treaty, Italy would renounce all right and title to these territories, and their disposal would be the joint decision of the United States, Britain, France, and the Soviet Union. Between them Britain and France now held *de facto* control, and they were anxious to keep it. After her reverses in Egypt and Palestine, Britain's Middle East defence system was in danger of collapse, and she needed a compensatory balance in the Mediterranean, as close as possible to the Suez Canal. Her military administration in Cyrenaica could not have been better placed. In the big-power negotiations which ensued, Britain's purpose was a British-sponsored Sanusi amirate over Cyrenaica; which made her the principal protagonist for a divided Libya. France was anxious to hold on to the Fezzan, already securely garrisoned by her troops; for her colonial empire in North Africa was in jeopardy, and the Fezzan not only linked French possessions in the Maghreb with those in Central Africa but was also a buffer territory protecting the exposed flank of her empire in Algeria. France thus laid claim to Fezzan and all Libya south of the Tropic of Cancer; while arguing for the return of Tripolitania to Italy, since this would placate the defeated power in Europe and would at the same time provide another controlled area adjoining the French-run Maghreb.

But if Britain and France were the powers on the ground in Libya, determined to remain there in one form or another, the balance of power in the Mediterranean, as in the Middle East, the Pacific, and the Far East, was coming essentially to be controlled by the United States.[2] The war had transformed the world's industrial power structure. Three quarters of the world's invested capital and two thirds of industrial capacity were concentrated inside the United States. United States troops were stationed on every continent and in scores of countries, among them Libya. By the end of the war the United States had spent 100 million dollars on developing Wheelus airfield, on the outskirts of Tripoli. It was the first American air base in Africa. Yet as late as 1947, though the United States had given notice of her intention to maintain the Wheelus base, there seemed to be no serious disposition on her part to expand it. The Middle East was considered, as it had been for more than a century, an area in which Britain's interests and responsibilities were paramount. In the immediate post-war years America saw herself acting as a mediator between Britain and the Soviet Union in the Mediterranean. Her policy was one of 'limited diplomacy' in the Middle East; and until 1951, when Greece and Turkey were enrolled in NATO and the United States became a direct contestant in the Mediterranean, she seemed to be fumbling for a policy on Libya. The State Department's Office of European Affairs was obsessed with the role of the Soviet Union in the Mediterranean and was in favour of the return of Libya to Italy. But the Office of Near Eastern and African Affairs saw the newly devised system of international trusteeship as a way of taking the territory 'out of European politics'; for, it was argued, the war had already amply demonstrated the security interests of the United States in North and West Africa, not to mention the oil areas of the 'not so distant Middle East'.[3]

Accordingly, the United States proposed a ten-year period of collective trusteeship under United Nations auspices, after which Libya would become independent. This, argued Secretary of State Byrnes, would ensure that Libya would not be developed for the military advantage of any one power; though the United States indicated that she was interested, with Britain's agreement, in a permanent air base.[4] The Soviet Union argued that as

Britain was already in military occupation of Tripolitania and Cyrenaica, and France of the Fezzan, the country should be divided into four instead of three parts; with each to be administered by one of the Big Four, and with herself in Tripolitania. Thus, wrote an appreciative American government commentator, were Britain and France 'rescued from the thankless task' of leading the opposition to the United States proposal for trusteeship; now all three of the Western powers could unite against the fourth party to the talks, and against any 'intrusion of the Soviet camel's nose into the Libyan tent'.[5]

The issue was thus deadlocked between the Big Four, and as time went by it became steadily more intractable. Relations between the powers deteriorated sharply over issues like German reparations, the Balkans, and Iran. On Libya, three of the Big Four changed their positions. Washington and Whitehall differed over details; but on the whole there was a convergence of American, British, French, and Italian policies, and a sharpening cleavage between these and the Soviet Union's. The United States tried not to veer too far from Britain's position, but at the same time she needed to find a suitable compromise with France and Italy so as not to rupture the *entente* that was shaping round the Marshall Plan.

Italian claims that the blatant imperialism of the recent past had vanished with Mussolini began to find sympathetic ears among those who calculated that Italy could be useful in the balancing of Mediterranean power. The powers that had forced Italy to surrender all claim to her colonies were the same ones now lending support to her claims for their restoration. There had also been second thoughts in Washington about the principle of international trusteeship. For if the principle was good enough for Libya, might it not be extended to the handling of all enemy colonies? The United States was not prepared to have any trusteeship principle applied to the Pacific Islands. It seemed best to drop this proposal and search for some compromise between the British and French positions. Britain, however, also changed her policy at this point, finding it difficult to discount the pressures of the Arab League and the Sanusi, who harped constantly on Eden's House of Commons pledge of 1942, that under no circumstances would the Sanusi of Cyrenaica fall at the end of the war under Italian domination.[6]

Ernest Bevin, then Britain's Foreign Secretary, decided to seize the initiative with a proposal for independence of Libya. The United States agreed on independence within a specified time, but after a period of trusteeship under Italy. Foreign Minister Molotov, for the Soviet Union, argued that Britain's independence proposal was predicated on British domination of the country through its ties with Cyrenaica and was thus unacceptable. Instead he proposed a plan for four individual trusteeships, each under one of the Big Four. It was almost identical to the American proposal of six months earlier, and would have left Cyrenaica to Britain and the Fezzan to France. But it was by now too late. Under the pretext of a programme designed ostensibly to contain expansion by Communist powers, but in fact to contain social revolution wherever it might break out, the United States was launched into the Cold War; this power now precipitately abandoned its original trusteeship position. Next the Soviet Union changed the plan for Big Four trusteeships and supported the return of Libya to Italy, under trusteeship supervision; for in Italy the 1948 election offered the prospect of a strong swing to the Left. The proposal was calculated to thwart British control over Cyrenaica and to lose her Benghazi and Tobruk, the two important coastal positions in British strategy in the eastern Mediterranean.

The powers were still deadlocked. When the Four-Power Commission of Foreign Ministers sent fact-finding missions to Libya itself, to ascertain the views of the local population, the facts adduced by the contesting powers differed almost as widely as their policies. The British–French–United States version laid emphasis on the difference and separateness of the three zones. (A French annotation to this report read conveniently: 'In the Fezzan the inhabitants appear to be content with the present administration and to have given little thought to a change of régime.') The Soviet text stressed not diversity but the essential unity of Libya:

Local differences accentuated in the post-war period, owing to the artificial political division of this integral territory, recede into the background before its natural and social unity ... The post-war differentiating factors connected mainly with foreign interests are an obstacle to the normal economic and social development of Libya and are largely counter-balanced by the integrating factors connected with the national interests of the Libyans themselves.

The upshot of both texts was nonetheless that the territory was too dependent on foreign aid to be ready for immediate independence.

The Peace Treaty had provided that if the Big Four could not agree on Libya, the issue was to be taken to the General Assembly of the United Nations. A rather different set of rules applied there. A unanimous decision was no longer necessary, and no power exercised a veto. There was more room for compromise, though also more opportunity for an almost unlimited range and number of proposals (as was shown by the rush of disparate solutions). Libyan parties and organizations could be heard. Debates were conducted in public.

This did not keep Britain and Italy from a final fling of secret diplomacy in the shape of the Bevin–Sforza agreement. The two foreign secretaries, Ernest Bevin and Count Carlo Sforza, arranged between themselves a package deal which gave Britain trusteeship over Cyrenaica; Italy, trusteeship over Tripolitania, and France, trusteeship over the Fezzan. It was now four years after the end of the war, and Britain was more anxious than ever to consolidate her position in the Mediterranean and the Near East, while Italy was still hoping to regain at least part of her lost empire. The agreement was a blatant infringement of the terms of the Peace Treaty, which both Britain and Italy had signed. It was supported by the United States and by the Latin American countries which had been mobilized by Italian diplomacy. It was repudiated by the Soviet Union, and by the Arab and Asian states. It provoked heated protests in Libya. But it seemed that Britain might succeed in steamrollering the plan through the General Assembly. When a count was taken, it was found that a single vote might tip the balance either way. A Libyan canvasser in the lobbies, who worked at the time as an official of the Arab League, found the decisive vote in the shape of the Haitian delegate, M. Émile Saint Lot. M. Saint Lot did not return to Haiti. In Tripoli, however, there is a street named after him.

With the defeat of the Bevin–Sforza deal, a solution seemed more elusive than ever. But suddenly and unexpectedly independence for Libya was in the air. Two weeks after the defeat of the Bevin–Sforza plan, Britain announced that she had granted partial self-government to Cyrenaica and that in time this was to be followed by independence. Britain was to retain control of foreign relations and defence; and all airfields and military installations would continue to be occupied by British troops. But the Sanusi government would handle internal affairs. Britain was to build on a presence she already had, and the implication was that France could proceed to do the same.

Britain made the decision unilaterally, behind the back of the United Nations but after due consultation with the United States and France (and South Africa, Canada, and New Zealand, her dominions). The Italian government had been informed before the public announcement,[7] and Italy promptly dropped her own claims.

Why the switch in Anglo-American policy? It was apparently in the summer of 1949 that the United States and Britain had set to work and had succeeded in convincing Italy that the solution would be to grant all of Libya independence as soon as possible.[8] The reasons that these two powers decided to push for independence are not as yet explicitly stated in any public official document.[9] But it had dawned on them that, first, they would not achieve the required measure of international agreement for British control over Libya, whether in whole or in part, unless this was linked with the promise of independence; and, secondly, that any trusteeship agreement, whether collective or single-nation, would involve the surrender of their bases. Villard, who had chaired the State Department's sub-committee on the future of the Italian colonies and who was to be his country's first ambassador to independent Libya, subsequently set out the case with some frankness:

It may be worth noting that if Libya had passed under any form of United Nations trusteeship, it would have been impossible for the Territory to play a part in the defence arrangements of the free world. Under the U.N. trusteeship system the administrator of a trust territory cannot establish military bases; only in the case of a strategic trusteeship as in the former Japanese islands of the Pacific are fortifications allowed; and a 'strategic trusteeship' is subject to veto in the Security Council.

But, he added:

As an independent entity Libya could freely enter into treaties or arrangements with the Western powers looking towards the defence of the Mediterranean and North Africa. This is exactly what the Soviet Union feared and what Libya did. The strategic sector of African seacoast which had proved so important in the mechanized war of the desert was coming into its own as a place of equal importance in the air age.[10]

It was only at a late stage in the long drawn-out diplomatic deadlock over Libya that Western policy makers came to this recognition. But once the Cold War had begun to grow hot – the Korean War broke out in 1950 – United States military planners resolved that the bases in Libya were not only useful but indispensable. Suitably handled, the grant of independence would make Libya safe for American and British bases and would keep the Soviet Union out of the Mediterranean. (It also, to Britain's satisfaction, got France out of the Fezzan, after many decades of Anglo-French rivalry in Central Africa.) Italy was mollified by being given the trusteeship of Somalia in return for the withdrawal of all claims over Libya. And in the Arab world the bestowal of independence upon Libya helped Anglo-American exertions to woo the Arab League and Arab states in the Cold War and, especially after the defeat of Arab forces in Palestine in 1948, to conciliate Arab opinion.

Thus it was recognized, admittedly late in the day, that far from independence being an obstacle, it could prove indispensable to the full utilization of Libya's strategic position, as long as there was the certainty that Libya could be depended upon to join the strategic alliance of the Western powers. This was where

Britain's carefully laid designs for Cyrenaica fitted. The United Nations resolution for Libyan independence was adopted in November 1949 and provided that independence for Libya was to become effective by the beginning of 1952 at the latest.[11] Ten weeks before the resolution went through the General Assembly, Britain anticipated it by granting internal autonomy to Cyrenaica. His Majesty's Government, Britain's delegate told the United Nations:

could not continue to refuse the people of Cyrenaica its indisputable right to the greatest possible measure of self-government consistent with the international obligations of the United Kingdom Government . . . The Government has therefore given the Emir of Cyrenaica absolute powers in the internal affairs of that territory . . . Faced with a demand from representatives of the people of Cyrenaica for independence . . . the Government . . . had decided . . . it could do no less than grant Cyrenaica that full measure of self-government . . .[12]

Britain's domination of the Arab world had been characterized by its reliance on existing political structures built into a relationship of patronage with the imperial power, and this functioned most smoothly in the areas where traditionalism held strongest sway. The Sanusi monarchy was an ideal basis for the application of this pattern to Libya. Britain would introduce legal and constitutional changes to transform a patriarchal amirate into a constitutional monarchy leaning heavily on British tutelage; simultaneously Britain's control over the Sanusi-run part of Libya would determine the pattern of control in the rest of the country. By the time that the independence resolution was passed and the United Nations was beginning to assemble the machinery for the preparation of independence, the former British military administration had already gone over to the services of the Cyrenaican government. The former Chief Administrator had become British Resident controlling foreign affairs and defence. A draft of Cyrenaican laws to replace the Italian legal code was in the press. Plans were afoot to build a Cyrenaican army on the model of Jordan's Arab Legion. And a treaty was being prepared to give Cyrenaica nominal independence with continuing British control of defence facilities. When United Nations teams arrived in the country, negotiations for the signing of a defence treaty were already completed. Britain had begun to pre-empt the decisions that the new state had yet to take.

The United Nations Commissioner in Libya, Adrian Pelt,[13] the former UN Assistant Secretary-General from the Netherlands, saw his mission as a race against time; for if the timetable for independence was not adhered to, the future of Libya would once again have become a pawn in the game played by the powers, and there might have been a reversion to the Bevin–Sforza agreement or something similar, which would have defeated any prospect of a unified state. So he stuck rigorously to the letter of the UN Resolution and its time-limit, and succeeded in steering Libya to independence within the prescribed period even if he could not steer past the obstacles erected by the occupying powers and the political forces they patronized.

The emphasis of the UN Resolution was on the creation of an independent and unified state. France dragged her feet to the end by suggesting, even when the resolution had been adopted, that the three separate governments of the three zones should be granted independence in the near future but not at any fixed time. She was still fearful of the chain reaction in North Africa to the establishment of a new independent state, and there was a smell of oil in the Saharan air, if French and other geologists were right.[14] M. Couve de Murville's statement, Pelt commented, sounded like a forecast of the policies which the United Kingdom and France were to follow in Libya in 1950 and the first part of 1951, when the powers in occupation devised plans not aimed at unity but at autonomy for their separate spheres of influence.[15] In this respect, Pelt added, 'the already semi-independent status conferred on Cyrenaica created a disquieting precedent that was in utter conflict with the General Assembly resolution'.

On the eve of his departure for Libya, the UN Commissioner received a confidential memorandum from the British Foreign Office setting out a plan not for any steps towards a unified state but for Tripolitanian regional self-government and autonomy on the Cyrenaican model. One of the effects on Tripolitania was to divide older traditional leaders, whose political ambitions had been stifled under the Italian occupation and who were strongly tempted by the opportunities they saw in the British plan, from the younger nationalist generation, which understood that local government according to Britain's specifications would jeopardize the goal of Libyan unity.

Once the UN Resolution was adopted, France introduced into the Fezzan administrative measures similar to those enacted by Britain in Cyrenaica and proposed for Tripolitania. She installed a transitional régime with powers confined to internal policy which were vested in the Fezzan's traditional head Saif Ahmed Seif al-Nasr, a prominent member of the Sanusi Order whose property had been confiscated under the Italian administration, and who had returned from Chad with the Free French forces. Seif al-Nasr, it was announced, had been elected *chef du territoire* by an assembly of representatives. But in fact this area of scattered oasis villages remained under the control of the French military administration which, like the British, used the period of transition to make suitable dispositions for the shape of independence.

Pelt has described the identity of purpose between British and French policy and yet the difference between the way these two colonial administrations went about it:

In Tripolitania the British authorities used indirect tactics, carefully supporting certain political parties and opposing others, in an endeavour to promote controlled emancipation ... In the economic and social fields British policy had been considerably more constructive, particularly in the educational factor, though its implementation was hampered by the 'care and maintenance' mentality born of the knowledge that British rule in the territory was not intended to endure ... In Cyrenaica, where the United Kingdom had more immediate and more lasting interests both its constitutional and economic and social policies had been taken considerably further ... In the Fezzan by contrast the French administration, while ostensibly trying to match British policy in Cyrenaica, went about matters in its own way; in practice it held up constitutional development by repressive measures, the intensity of which varied from oasis to oasis and village to village. At the same time it introduced economic measures which considerably improved living conditions in the territory.[16]

French policy thus showed a dual aspect: 'conservative in the political field but progressive in the economic and social sectors'.

Trying to convince the British Foreign Office that the premature establishment of an independent Cyrenaica would endanger the creation of a united Libya and that any bilateral British–Cyrenaican agreement would run counter to the UN decision, the UN Commissioner sought a prolonged audience with the Sanusi Amir. And during this discussion it emerged that the Amir was already fully engaged in long-term treaty negotiations with Britain which would allow British forces to remain on Cyrenaican soil in return for badly needed financial aid. Idris did not feel free to show his copy of the draft treaty to the UN Commissioner but he suggested that the latter ask Britain for a copy. The British Resident replied that it was a confidential document which could not be divulged without authority from the Foreign Office. By the time a copy of the draft treaty was handed to the Commissioner, 'every Tom, Dick and Harry in Benghazi knew that a treaty was being negotiated between the Amir and the United Kingdom and that its signing was expected in the near future'.[17]

Pelt bent his energies to persuading Britain that no agreement committing the as yet unborn state to a military pact should be signed until a provisional Libyan government had been constituted. It was evidently not so much the principle of the military treaty but the inexpediency of its timing that would be damaging to the UN mission. In the course of a long session at the Foreign Office 'gradually it became clear that an understanding might be reached subject to Cabinet approval'.[18] This 'understanding deferred the *quid pro quo* pact between Britain and Cyrenaica till after the declaration of independence'. But it also recorded the opinion not only of the British government but also of the UN Commissioner that a 'federal structure for the future Libyan state seemed to be in conformity with its physical conditions and political tendencies, and that the Amir appeared to be indicated as the probable head of such a state'.[19] Britain thus agreed to defer her plans for the Treaty; but in return the UN Commissioner had virtually agreed to underwrite them. Most of Britain's plans for Libya were falling well into place.

It was by now no secret that immediately after the declaration of independence, the agreements whose conclusion the UN

Commissioner's intervention had postponed would be signed by the new Libyan government with Britain, and also with France, to regularize the presence of foreign troops on Libyan soil. Libyan beggars could not be choosers, Pelt commented, but he was anxious that the United Nations should not be implicated in the financial–military bargain for fear of Arab nationalist reaction and its consequences in the United Nations. He therefore advised Libya's provisional government on the financial terms of the treaties. But he covered himself in his report to the General Assembly by arguing that the government he had advised had ceased to exist as soon as foreign relations and defence powers accrued to it; that any agreement concerning foreign troops and military installations on Libyan soil was the responsibility of the new sovereign independent government; and that his function had in fact ceased momentarily before it had come into being.[20] Not that Pelt found much room to manoeuvre. Britain was underwriting the budget deficit under a set of temporary arrangements which were to make way for the formal treaty. And at the time Pelt tried to prevent the conclusion of the treaty, the treasury was empty and there were no monies to finance the first budget. Britain argued that only a formal agreement would justify further outlays by the British taxpayer. Pelt attempted to negotiate an interim loan, but his approach to Egypt's Wafd government failed; as Idris, well briefed by Britain, had warned that it would. It was a blatant case of a treaty in exchange for support.[21]

Though Britain had already decided the issue, the shape of the coming government was the subject of protracted argument among Libyans. The National Congress Party of Tripolitania, representing a large part of the coastal population, advocated a unitary form of state and proportional territorial representation in the National Assembly. Cyrenaica, supported by Fezzan, and by parts of the Tripolitanian interior, insisted, as a precondition of her participation, on a federal state and parity representation which would outweigh Tripolitania. Essentially because a federation was the only form of Libyan state that Idris – backed by Britain and the United States – was prepared to rule, this was the inevitable outcome. For by then it had come to be accepted by all sides – by some for religious and traditional reasons, but by others for reasons of political expediency in the interests of a single state – that the recognition of the Amir as monarch was the imperative, in fact the only, basis of any unified state. The throne was offered him in December 1951. All effective decisions were taken before the first Libyan National Assembly met to draw up the Constitution. On the UN Committee of twenty-one which paved the way, Egypt and Pakistan backed the unitary aspirations of Tripolitanian nationalists. But in the end Cyrenaica got its way. The National Assembly was not elected but selected, with the Mufti of Tripolitania composing the list of members from those in the province likely to agree with Cyrenaica and the Fezzan on the federal principle. The Tripolitanian Congress Party had originally advocated the selection principle; now it found itself, through this tactical error, largely excluded from significant decision, while the National Assembly reinforced itself by rejecting any referendum on the constitution that it had prepared. The UN Commissioner felt that the appointment rather than the election of the National Assembly left 'grave doubts in my mind as to whether it will have the necessary moral and political authority to elaborate a final and definite Constitution for Libya'.[22] In the months before independence there were angry demonstrations in Tripoli by crowds calling for a united Libya. Over 800 people were arrested on one occasion. But federation was the only form of state Idris would accept and in transferring power to Idris in Cyrenaica, Britain had decreed that if there was to be an independent Libyan state, it would be under the Sanusi crown. Nationalist groupings and independent individuals were completely outmanoeuvred. They found themselves powerless to reject the terms of the Constitution. Time was the ransom: if time ran out for the United Nations mandate, the future of Libya would once again become a bargaining point between the powers.

Towards the end of the transition period, when the Cyrenaican and Fezzan conditions had prevailed on all the principal issues, Britain and France, once reluctant about imminent independence, and the United States, were suddenly eager to achieve it. The UN Commissioner had to warn that this would cause speculation on 'hidden motives' and 'Machiavellian designs', one of which was the 'premature urging of independence upon a still inadequate Libyan government in order to enable the three more highly organized territorial governments to continue to function quasi-independently under an illusory federation'.[23] The UN Commissioner commented that it would be an exaggeration to pretend that all Libyans were happy on Independence Day. The protagonists of a unitary state found the new state insufficiently centralized; too dominated by the country's traditional forces; and providing excessive autonomy for the three provinces, so that foreign or local influence could undermine the authority of the central government. There was also grave doubt that a country as poor as Libya could support the financial burden of a federal structure.[24]

Britain and France had taken considerable care in shaping the political character of the new state and in ensuring the hegemony of patriarchal and tribal structures over such urban nationalist forces as had emerged. If Libya had to be insulated from the currents of Arab nationalism, imperial rule and patriarchal government had much in common. The original colonial power having been displaced by the war, the transition to independence appeared to have been amicably enough negotiated. The price, however, was a state heavily committed to the West. This was to be the fundamental cause of the coup d'état which overturned the monarchy eighteen years later.

5 Palace Power

Libya found herself a federated state under a Sanusi monarch. Though resistance against Italian conquest had generated the rudiments of a state among the Bedouin, the war had in turn worked its destruction. By the end of the war the Sanusi Order had been destroyed as an organization, political, economic, and religious; and it persisted only as a sentiment 'with the Head of the Order in exile in Egypt retaining the allegiance of the Bedouin who saw in his freedom the hope of their own'.[1] Whereas during the Italian period Britain was prepared to recognize Idris only as head of a religious order, during the war-time mobilization he was recognized as Amir, put on stipend and authorized to recruit troops. For the needs of war propaganda, Sanusi, Cyrenaica, and Libya had been used as interchangeable concepts. Ultimately Tripolitania was forced to recognize that if she did not accept the Sanusi crown, Cyrenaica would go her own way, and hope for a unified state would be lost.

Yet even Cyrenaica, the stronghold of the Sanusi, was by no means monolithic. There were tribes and important urban centres that were opposed to Idris' installation as their monarch and Britain's instrument of control. The city of Derna in particular, the east's intellectual and political centre, was opposed to the shaping of the new state on religious lines. The Omar Mukhtar Society, formed by Libyan exiles in Egypt, came home to become the centre in Benghazi for young nationalists who were critics of the British military administration and its sponsorship of Cyrenaica separatism, and who demanded union with Tripolitania. It pressed for democratic structures and was even mildly republican. Like the Tripolitanians, the Society eventually accepted the Sanusi monarchy in the interests of a unified state;

though by independence it had been suppressed, and its leaders were in prison for a civil disobedience campaign against the pre-independence Cyrenaican administration.

Idris's amirate was supported by Sanusi sentiment but also by the symbiosis nurtured over years between himself and Britain. The bolstering of traditional monarchies, even the creation of client rulers, was a well-tested device in the Middle East for offsetting nationalism, pan-Arabism, the pressure of the masses, and a host of related evils. Client monarchies with an impeccable record of loyalty to the British were relied upon in Iraq under Feisal, in Transjordan under his brother Abdullah, and in the Trucial States along the Arab Gulf. The House of Sanusi was comfortingly reminiscent of the Hashemite kingdom in its muster of the forces of religion behind those of a tribal principality, with Bedouin tribesmen readily available for recruitment into an internal security force. The first British Ambassador who arrived at the moment of independence came fresh from service in Jordan and was representative of the Foreign Office generation that had nurtured the Amirates as the mainstay of British influence in the Middle East during the 'safe' years. The policy of shoring up dynastic and tribal authority was in full swing from the outset, to the consternation not only of Libyans but also of the younger generation of Arabists in the Foreign Office which had begun to perceive new social forces stirring in the Middle East and North Africa. It was not that the supervision was unwelcome; the King could conceive of nothing else, and if some of his ministers sought some other source of patronage, they envisaged the United States. The first American Ambassador chaperoned his men in the first Cabinet; they included the Minister of War 'whose undisguised ambition is to be sent to the United States', and the Finance Minister.[2] The economic aid dispensations under the Wheelus base agreement involved the United States in as many policy decisions as any Libyan ministry. In their day, the oil companies helped steer decisions. The story is told of the oil company executive who closed his interview with the Minister of Petroleum by saying 'I'm on my way to see the King; is there anything you want me to tell him?' By 1967 United States private investment in Libya stood at

$456 million, the second highest United States investment stake on the continent after that in South Africa.

The constitution of the new state[3] had been drawn before the state was yet in existence, on expert advice and allegedly from several celebrated models. It claimed affinity with the American constitution; but if it was an American-type federal instrument, it was one grafted on to a traditional tribal society. It provided for a federal representative government of two chambers, together with a hereditary monarchy. Laws could be initiated by the elected House of Representatives, or by the nominated Senate, or by the King. The King himself had the power to veto legislation and to dissolve the elected parliament at his sole discretion. It was the King's absolute privilege to appoint the provincial governors or *wali*; they were answerable to neither an executive nor a legislative body. Seen from outside, Libya was one nation; experienced within, the provinces could act almost autonomously, for the federal government was dependent on the provincial governments for the implementation of its legislation. The Parliament offered only the semblance of democratic government. In theory the Cabinet was responsible to Parliament; but in practice it was an instrument of the King.

It was a Palace system of power.[4] The strength of the Palace system derived from two principal sources: the claim to religious legitimacy on which the Arab monarchies were founded and the religious orders they led (thus the Alawite monarchy in Morocco and the Hashemite Kingdom of Jordan as descendants of the Prophet's family, and the Wahhibiyya and Sanusi movements of Saudi Arabia and Libya); and a tribal, regional, and even class constituency (as in Egypt where the strength of the monarchy derived from the landowning pasha class) whose fortune was indissolubly linked with the monarchical régime.

In Cyrenaica the authority of the King as Sanusi head had derived from the coincidence of the Sanusi lodges or *zawiyah* with the main points in the distribution of power in Bedouin society and economy; the shaikhs, and especially those whose authority spanned several groups, were the links between the head of the system and the corporate property-owning tribal clans, where land was owned by the tribe as a whole, in the sense that the tribe had the exclusive right to graze and use the water resources within a traditionally defined area. The political authority of the monarchy was exercised through tribal notables who made up the Diwan or royal household. The Diwan was reinforced by the Sanusi hierarchy which controlled virtually a parallel administration through its *zawiyas* and religious schools, its system of patron–client tribal relationships, and the traditional functions of the tribal shaikhs on government stipend. The inner conclave of the King and its parallel system of authority was unwritten in the constitution, but it was this court government of trusted advisers and confidants among the tribal nobility, together with a judicious selection of townsmen picked for their loyalty to the monarchy and their complicity with this system of patronage, that ran the political system. Premiers were selected for their regional origins and loyalties, and Cabinet appointments followed a rough and ready principle of tribal balance. There were ministries over which the King customarily reserved his sole right of choice, and these were the senior portfolios of Finance, Petroleum, Defence, and Interior, to which were appointed the notables of the tribes that constituted the foundations of Sanusi power in the Jebel Akhdar: principally the Barassa, but also the Ebedat, the al Hassa, the al Derisa, and al Awagir. Appointments of Tripolitanians were made in consultation with prominent families, some of whom had maintained a foothold in government from the Karamanlis through to the Turkish period and to the Italian.[5] Here it was not the web of social and religious groupings that was the basis of the political system but the use of government office and appointments to the administration.

The King controlled the Cabinet through his control of the Prime Minister. Cabinets were shuffled and ministers shifted frequently; this promoted ministerial instability but effectively prevented individuals from consolidating their influence. The King governed often by default rather than initiative. His technique of dealing with disputes was increasingly one of withdrawal – his retirement to Tobruk effectively removed him from the centre of government intrigue – but this entrenched authority not in the Cabinet but in the Royal Diwan. Here the pillar of the régime were notables of the Barassa tribe and their family connections which linked together, for instance, Premier Hussein Maziq, Mahmoud Qwalatein, Commander of the Cyrenaica Defence Force (CYDEF), the King's praetorian guard in the east, and – through marriage – the Shalhi family, grandsons of the King's former retainer, who had inherited his influence in the Royal Diwan but had also become the byword for the régime's corruption.

By the end of the first year of independence, Libya had become a non-party state. A constitution intended to accommodate the monarchy had worked the other way, so that the monarchy and its traditional support had constrained the constitution. February 1952 was the first and the last occasion when elections were fought between political parties. By then the argument over the shape of independence had resolved itself into a contest for political power between two principal tendencies. The one was Cyrenaican traditional society, joined in the west by the Istiqlal party under the leadership of Salim al-Muntasser. This party represented the interests of well-established Tripolitanian business families, which had contemplated rebuilding links with Italian interests after the war but which thereafter formed associations with the British military administration and, through it, with the Sanusi. The other political tendency had formed round Bashir Bey Sa'dawi during the protests against the Bevin–Sforza Plan, when several political groupings had merged to form the National Congress Party. Rejecting the leadership of traditional society and its British associations, this tendency leaned instead to the Middle East and the Arab League.

The National Congress Party had been confident that it would sweep the board in Tripolitania and thus win an overall majority in the country which would clear the way to a revision of the constitution and an abandonment of the federal system. The party won all the seats in Tripoli City, but in the rest of the country, including Tripolitania's countryside, pro-government candidates scored a sweeping victory. The Congress Party concluded that government officials had tampered with the poll and rigged the counting; the results were no sooner announced than the party's supporters invaded government buildings, cut telephone wires, and interrupted transport and communications. The government ordered widespread arrests, banned the Congress Party, and expelled Sa'dawi to Egypt. The political system had crumbled even as it was still being erected.

Like the measures taken before independence against the Omar Mukhtar Society, the outlawing of the National Congress Party had serious consequences for the subsequent shape, or shapelessness, of Libyan politics. Neither of these two groupings had anything like a popular base or a coherent programme except on immediate issues; they were compacts of politically like-minded individuals and élitist intellectuals rather than mass-based campaigning movements. But they were advances on tribal and patriarchal politics, with their factional and personality intrigues. Had they survived, they might have inaugurated a style of politics that Libya had never known. After this, the party system never reappeared. When nationalist and radical groupings developed they had to function in semi-clandestine fashion.

The monarchy had rid itself of a troublesome opposition in the part of the country where it had always been insecure; but it had also rid the country of any productive political life. Libya, unlike its Maghreb neighbours, had achieved independence not because of but despite the absence of any strong nationalist movement; under independence this movement, always internally divided along regional as well as policy lines, far from reorganizing and gaining in impetus, shrivelled and died altogether. Individual opposition members abandoned politics or crossed the floor to join their one-time antagonists. Politics became the assertion of family, factional, tribal, and parochial interests and the Cabinet remained the instrument of the Palace. In subsequent elections most of the candidates were government nominees. Voting criteria were tribal and family ties and the personal influence of the candidate. Since political parties and programmes were suppressed, and government was immune to public pressure from within its own ranks or those of an opposition, governments fell essentially through conflict between them and the Palace system.[6] A recurring source of crisis lay in the respective powers of King and Cabinet over the provinces.

Several prime ministers resigned as a result of the interference by the Palace, direct or indirect. In seventeen years of the monarchy, there were eleven governments in all, and over 200 ministers. When the days of penury were over and the government became the major distributor of the spoils from the oil economy, the groups that had always been the dominant political constituents of the system became in turn its economic beneficiaries. Ministries seemed to change hands even faster, for men feathered their nests quickly while the chance was there.

It was oil – struck in 1955, and coursing richly through the economy by the sixties – that worked changes on the nature of government. For the British-supported monarchical structures were inadequate to the new economy, and the entry of United States capital introduced the United States policy preoccupations with North Africa. In 1963, scarcely two years after the first oil shipment, a royal decree abolished the federal system; it had proved impossible to cope with the exigencies of oil exploitation and manage the funds it generated without a centralized state.[7] From this time Libya also took a more Arab stance on foreign affairs as a counter to the influence of Nasser's Egypt and Algeria. The press was liberalized. But attempts to curtail the influence of tribal shaikhs in government provoked them: one instance was the CYDEF security force onslaught on the 1964 student demonstrations which brought down the government of the day and installed one that better represented the old Palace order.

The oil decade opened with a grand financial scandal that set the tone for the *enrichissez-vous* activities of the ruling group. It prompted a letter from the King to government heads which quoted the Koran on the evil of taking bribes and practising nepotism and squandering the country's wealth in secret and in public. Central figure in the Fezzan road scandal[8] was Sayyid Abd-Allah 'Abid, a senior member of the Sanusi family, who had formed a politics-for-business triumvirate with a former premier, Ben Halim, and the King's adviser, Shalhi. Favouritism had landed the contract, and government profligacy funded it. The affair was a prototype for the style of corruption that was setting in. Whereas tribes had formerly used their patrons at court to augment their prestige and influence, now the tribal notable became a political and a financial manipulator, for a larger share of government resource allocation and jobs and appointments to the favoured tribe and area. Old feuds and the regional competition between Tripolitania and Cyrenaica are said to have cost millions in rivalry over allocations.

Tribal links remained strong but the beginnings of class differentiation began to cut across tribal links as a class of new rich grew under the oil economy. Palace power politics were the prerogative of a few score; now wealth came to be concentrated in much the same hands. When foreign firms needed go-betweens for contract negotiations, ministers and members of Parliament had ready access to government departments and tender boards. There were such tales as the truck driver translated into the director of a transport firm from one day to the next; but the outstanding instances of the emerging bourgeoisie were among the men at the heart of government and close to the monarchy who manipulated high offices for business. Omar Shalhi was the most notorious example. Almost no capital went into industry. The Libyan private sector established itself in real estate and property speculation; in transport, catering, and other services auxiliary to the oil industry; in import and export and foreign trade.

After 1967 and the shaken summer of the Six Day War, an attempt was made to modernize government once again and to accommodate the rising élite of technicians and professionals. In engineer Ben Halim's Cabinet some years earlier, he had been the sole technocrat among traditionalists. Under Abdul Hamid Bakkush, a battery of young educated men gave government a new aspect; Bakkush himself, a former legal adviser to an oil company, was a protégé of the Muntassers, and a technocrat used by the traditional families. Into his Cabinet he took several of his contemporaries who were proving their ability in planning and administrative capacities. Under Bakkush, French interests also established themselves; not least a French oil company. It was also Bakkush who finalized the missiles contract with the British Aircraft Corporation, and began the building of an enlarged army. The old traditional oligarchy was being joined by an embryonic local bourgeoisie: still scattered and without cohesion; restricted to non-productive commercial and speculative economic activity, and with the prospect of commanding only a tiny share of an economy dominated by foreign monopoly capital; but beginning to play the dominant role once held by tribal notables.

Ideological politics, as distinct from the politics of the tribe and the Palace, began slowly and tentatively as the nationalist stirrings of the Arab world began to impinge upon Libya. Egypt had always been a dominant influence. Not only the Sanusi head but many thousands of Libyans had lived there in exile. When the British military administrators reorganized the education system in the forties, they based it upon the Egyptian. Libyan schools continued for many years to be staffed by more Egyptian than Libyan teachers. The law was administered and interpreted by Egyptian judges. When independence began to produce the first generations of university students, the majority attended Egyptian universities, and Libyan students became involved in Egyptian and Middle East politics. Libya's first army officers were trained in the Baghdad academy, but also in Cairo. Egyptian intelligence recruited its usual quota of agents and used them over the years to pursue not only Egypt's intelligence purposes in Libya but also her political purposes, with the usual blurring of the two roles. Until there were Libyan Arabic newspapers, the reading public relied on imports from Cairo and Beirut; and if Gadafi's consciousness of the world outside Libya was formed by Cairo Radio, he was representative of the generations for whom the transistor radio was Libya's most continuous link with the rest of the Arab world.

Libyan political groupings were influenced by the two tendencies of Nasserism and Baathism. Nasser was the charismatic cult figure of the Arab world, leader of a triumphant army-led revolution and a state of 'inter-class' politics, and spearhead of an aggressive diplomacy against the West. The Baathists accepted secularism, saw economic development as the essential condition for social change, and relied on a political party, but, like the Nasserites, they used the army to take power, and though they had a certain view of social classes, were aggressively anti-Marxist. The two enjoyed a honeymoon period in the late fifties and then celebrated a marriage with the proclamation of the United Arab Republic of Nasserite Egypt and Baathist Syria. But the attempt failed three years later when Syria seceded; and with the break-up of the union, Libyan ideological politics inherited the divisions between them. During 1961 and 1962 the Baathists were at their peak strength, among them officers graduated from the Baghdad Academy; and an important trial took place on charges of forming cells of the Baath Party. The court ordered the dissolution of Baathist cells, the confiscation of funds and the deportation of the non-Libyans among those accused. After the break-up of the Union with Syria there was a strong anti-Baathist reaction in Libya exploited by Cairo Radio. The Baathist groups went into decline, and Nasserism became the ascendant tendency. After the Nasser-Kassem clash, Nasserites and Baathists grouped together against a Marxist tendency, but the Nasserite-Baathist dispute of the mid-1960s separated the strands once again. New alliances formed loosely of Marxists and Baathists on the one hand and Nasserites on the other, but all the groups were weak and shaky, and strained by Middle East political vacillations.

Mass politics, though on a limited scale, were initiated within the student movement when students demonstrated in defiance of the police in 1964, schools went on strike, and the authorities had to close the university. Libyan students in Britain and West Germany staged sympathy occupations of their embassies; and government mediators agreed to demands for the reopening of the university, the release of the arrested students, and recognition of a students' union. The first conference of the Libyan Students' Union was held in 1966, and it opted for the Leftist tendency within the Arab Nationalist Movement; pledging support of the Vietnam revolution; demanding a more radical approach to the Palestine problem; criticizing the government's oil policy; and demanding the liquidation of the bases. During the Six Day War the students carried their fury off the campus and into the towns. The student movement forged links with the trade union movement. At the height of the crisis, petroleum and dock workers struck and refused to permit the pumping of oil and the loading of tankers.

Apart from these militant political strikes, trade union organization was spasmodic and permeated both by the patronage system of the régime and that of American-style labour boss methods that had percolated through contact with CIO–AFL leadership and the ICFTU. Salem Shiteh became president of the first general labour union, but he was inspired by United States notions of a federation of unions from the Maghreb to Egypt, as counter to the Arab Labour Federation; and though he controlled ten company-style trade unions, the most important of all, that of petroleum, dock, and tobacco workers, broke away and formed a second federation, with more radical orientation. This last was under the leadership, among others, of Rajab Neihum, who had tried to organize workers under the Italian occupation; and of Suleiman Maghrabi, a US-trained lawyer, who organized the 1967 oil workers' strike and was to become the first prime minister after the Gadafi coup. By the middle sixties Shiteh had become a member of parliament: it subsequently emerged in court evidence that his election campaign had been funded by the Minister of the Interior. By then his unions were suitably docile; and militant worker action, like the radical political groupings, rose and declined with the general fortunes of Middle East Arab politics.

The government resorted to a mass trial in 1967 to bring even these activities to a stop. Though the Arab Nationalist Movement had virtually ceased to exist in Libya after internal convulsions between the nationalist tendency on the right and the Marxist tendency on the left, the police had infiltrated a splinter group and professed to have discovered a conspiracy. The trial was used to remove the militant leadership of the unions, to discredit the student movement as politically inspired and to defeat its struggle for the recognition of a student union.

The régime worked at disarming its critics in several ways. It made public concessions to Arab nationalism which muted internal opposition and saved Libya the embarrassment of being attacked on Cairo Radio. When there was a furore against the bases, the government started negotiations for their withdrawal which lasted till the fuss had died down. The patriarchal régime sought to avoid confrontation and to ignore criticism rather than contend with it. Acts of opposition tended to be isolated from public response by being casually handled by the régime. Prison sentences were not excessively severe. The traditional leader tended to treat critics as errant rather than rebellious, and more than once the pressure for arrests and prosecutions came not from him but from the professionals and lawyers in government.

The critics of the régime were isolated from the mass of the people, and a certain tolerance towards the outspoken sons of the petit-bourgeoisie did no harm. Critics were disarmed by concessions to pan-Arabism, and once oil began to flow the régime had ample resources to make material as well as rhetorical concessions. Employment and housing opportunities multiplied; students were indulged and civil servants pampered. Prosperity helped to fund assent. At the same time Libyan attempts at ideological and political mobilization had been so dependent upon inspiration from outside that when this faltered it had profoundly demoralizing effects on Libyans.

6 A Base for Imperialism

Anglo-American policy saw Libya as less a country or a state than a strategic position for a series of military bases. One day before independence was proclaimed the British Ambassador arrived to present his credentials and, formally and this time publicly, to open negotiations for a long-term treaty of alliance between Britain and Libya. Its broad outline had by now been agreed with the United States and with France.[1] The treaty was finally sealed in 1953, for in between it had been considered expedient for Libya to apply for Arab League membership. When this gesture to Arab solidarity was sealed, Libya gave Britain alternative bases to those she evacuated in the Suez Canal zone. The Twenty-Year Treaty consisted of two separate agreements, signed on the same day, which granted Britain 'facilities within the territory of Libya for military purposes' and in exchange undertook to pay annual subsidies to the Libyan budget. The treaty's 'military purposes' included exclusive and uninterrupted use for military purposes of specified land and buildings and the right of British aircraft to fly over, and in an emergency, to land and take off from any of Libya's territory. Britain's Tenth Armoured Division was based in Libya, and there was a large air base at Al Adem, fifteen miles south of Tobruk, and a detachment of RAF personnel at Idris airport near Tripoli which provided staging posts on the strategic air corridors to East Africa, the Indian Ocean, and the Far East.

Wheelus base, eight miles out of Tripoli, had been captured by British forces from the Italian air force. The US air force began operations there in 1944, and abandoned its use in 1947; but at the time of the Korean crisis, the field was reactivated, and the base integrated into the United States Strategic Air Command. The negotiations formalizing the United States presence in Libya were prolonged 'but there was never any doubt in the mind of either party that a mutually satisfactory arrangement would eventually be placed on the books'.[2] When American foreign policy failed to enfold the whole of the Middle East into its embrace, King Idris went personally as the emissary of the Baghdad Pact to Turkey and Lebanon. Wheelus was duly inspected by John Foster Dulles. 'For its part,' said the American Ambassador, 'Libya has acquired a powerful new protector in addition to its British ally. As a stakeholder in Libya's future, the United States, it stands to reason, will have a natural interest in the defence of that none too strongly unified country.'[3]

France was eager to conclude an agreement like those with Britain and the United States, but Algeria was the stumbling block. Until 1954 France had the right to keep three companies in the Fezzan in return for a subsidy to the province's budgetary deficit; but Libya's Parliament then insisted that the garrisons be withdrawn, and France was granted limited air and surface transit rights only, at Sebha, Ghat, and Ghadames. Franco–Libyan relations were not improved by border incidents, which led to the setting up of a Franco-Libyan commission to investigate frontier claims.[4]

Whereas the Wheelus base had functioned originally as an air transport centre, with the signing of the treaty it became a primary training base for NATO forces. It could be used by strategic nuclear bombers and provided direct access to southern Russia across Turkey; and in 1956 the headquarters of the US Seventeenth Air Force was transferred from Morocco to Wheelus. But its major function was to provide target practice for tactical fighter pilots rotating from stations in Britain, West Germany, and France. Wheelus was also the headquarters of the Mediterranean Communications region and was used for certain combined operations in Africa; one of these was the 1960 airborne United Nations intervention in the Congo.[5] The American subsidy for the base, under the seventeen-year agreement, was at least double that paid by Britain. In 1958 the Libyan government pressed for substantial increases in US aid and complained about the uncertain annual dispensations. The amount was increased and channelled through the Libyan

Ministry of Finance. In the late fifties the United States undertook a military aid programme to train and equip an army unit
in the handling of modern transport, and to help the infant air
force get off the ground. By 1964 about a quarter of the officer
personnel in the Libyan army had been trained in the United
States.

Like the Saudi ruling house, King Idris distrusted a regular
army. Each time an army overthrew or threatened to overthrow
a Middle East monarchy, the surviving dynasties took a close
look at their own forces and tightened procedures for screening
officer loyalty. Libya, like Saudi Arabia and Jordan, saw
tribally-based levies as the mainstay of internal security and an
essential counter-balance to any army attempt to seize power. By
the end of the war in 1945 the Libyan–Arab Force, recruited
from Sanusi forces in exile, consisted of five infantry battalions.
The British military administration demobilized three and transformed the remaining two into a para-military force. CYDEF
began as a force commanded by British officers. The Tripolitanian Defence Force (TRIDEF) equivalent was built to similar
strength, and a smaller gendarmerie force was built in the
Fezzan.

After independence the story got about, at least into the
British press, that Glubb Pasha was about to relinquish his
Jordan command to train a crack Arab Legion for Libya. But
the army was eventually placed under a Libyan-born commander-
in-chief who had served in the Turkish army, and then an army
chief of staff from royalist Iraq. Army training was undertaken
by a British military mission, but also by the Iraqi military
academy in Baghdad, before the Kassem revolution there in
1958. As part of a five-year agreement signed in London in 1958,
Britain agreed to provide free of cost the small arms and equipment for the expansion of the army to 5,000 men by 1963, and
to train advisers for all units.[6] In 1957 a military academy was
opened in Benghazi, and the first officers graduated in 1960.
This self-reliance in officer training was unusual for so small a
country and army, but it was another of the King's safeguards
against the infection of his army from contact with coup-making
or coup-thinking officers from other countries.

By 1965, after eight years of organizing and recruiting a regular force, the army did not exceed 6,500 men organized in infantry battalions together with two small artillery battalions, an armoured car squadron, and a company of engineers. The para-military security force mustered almost twice as many men.[7] The garrisons of the regular army were about equally divided between the two capitals, separated on land by more than 700 miles without a railway connection. The formula for controlling the armed forces remained one of keeping the regular army and the tribal security forces divided and posting the latter in or near the urban centres. From 1965 to 1969 the United States sold increasing amounts of military equipment to Libya. Such aid was given, by official report, not only to enable the Libyans to refuse Soviet offers of military assistance, but also because of the 'vulnerability of Libya's internal situation as demonstrated during the 1956 Suez expedition'.[8]

That Suez invasion had precisely the opposite effect to that intended in Libya as well as in Egypt. Far from being toppled, Nasser had achieved the status of an Arab national hero, even in countries like Libya where nationalism had stirred late. Each time tension rose in the Middle East, the crisis was reflected in Libya by a commotion over the military bases. During the 1956 Suez crisis, Libya had formally rejected a British approach for facilities in Libya; and this had a direct bearing on the Defence White Paper the year after, which reduced the number of British troops in the country; though after the Iraqi revolution of 1958 Libya asked for the return of troops previously withdrawn.[9] But the high point in the agitation over the bases occurred in 1964, and again in 1967 during the Six Day War.

During 1963 there had been rumblings in the Libyan Parliament about Libya's departure from the prevalent African policy of non-alignment. The politicians who raised the question were persuaded to remain away when the answer was due, thus technically saving the government the embarrassment of a reply. The question thus remained unofficially unanswered. As 1964 opened Nasser convened a conference of Arab states in Cairo to plan action against Israel's diversion of the River Jordan. King Idris broadcast his support of the meeting but he did not attend. When school and university students demonstrated in Benghazi in favour of the conference, they were dispersed by the Cyrenaica Defence Force; two students were killed and several injured in the clashes. Tripoli staged a mock funeral as a protest. The Prime Minister resigned. He had asked the King for the resignation of the CYDEF commander, who was the brother-in-law of the King's adviser Omar Shalhi; but the King preferred to do without his Prime Minister at a time when several alleged plots against the régime had been uncovered. The CYDEF commander was less dispensable than the Prime Minister. The following month Egypt asked Libya for assurances that the bases would not be used against Arab states in the event of a war against Israel. The Prime Minister, under pressure from Parliament, informed Britain and the United States that the Libyan government would not be prepared to renew or extend the base agreements. The King announced his abdication. After staged demonstrations for days outside his Palace in Tobruk, he was prevailed upon to change his mind.[10] The Cabinet was reshuffled. Britain and the United States took their cue and offered to run down their military strength over a period of time. The *Daily Telegraph* was more than usually alarmist: 'Britain to Quit Libya in a Fortnight'.[11] Six months later the talks about the bases were still in progress, though it was announced that both powers had accepted evacuation in principle. The same month King Idris personally led the Libyan delegation to the Arab Summit Conference at Alexandria, and Libya joined the Arab Joint Defence Council. In the following year Britain carefully timed an announcement of the withdrawal of men from the garrisons in Tripoli, Benghazi, and Tobruk, to coincide with the assembling of the new Parliament. The United States official record of the episode reads: 'The United States Government affirmed its adherence to the principle of withdrawal which enabled formulas to be found which permitted the King Idris and the Libyan government to allow us to continue our use of Wheelus Airfield Base.'[12] The bases were to go, but they remained.

During the Six Day War the United States discovered 'another restive Arab nation'.[13] Libya seemed to explode in an emotional frenzy of Arab nationalism. The Libyan government threatened to expel the Americans from Wheelus. Together with Saudi Arabia, Kuwait, and other Gulf states, Libya shut off oil production, though briefly. The Oasis consortium office was seized by workers and held for five hours. The United States information library in Benghazi was sacked. The demands for the removal of the bases were renewed. In Washington officials put out the statement that the base would be wound up before the scheduled date of 1971. The Pentagon was said to be seeking another location for gunnery training; but, like London, Washington was hoping that the Libyan request would be withdrawn 'in a calmer moment'.[14] Once again a prime minister resigned, and his successor instituted a fresh set of talks about the future of the bases. The government that came to office in the autumn of 1967 was a new breed for Libya. The Palace and traditional elements were still there but beside them sat young technicians and 'modernists', who, while they did not represent any popular masses, were beginning to perceive Libya and the Arab world in a new light. When in 1968 Libya embarked on a spectacular defence programme, it was under pressure inside of Libya from these new elements, not least the army officers and their civil service support, and outside from changing Western defence and strategic perspectives.

NATO purposes remained constant, and the geography ostensibly unchanging. But geography is affected by the state of technology and weaponry – not least the increased range of aircraft – and new modes of warfare were beginning to diminish the importance of staging bases. By the mid 1960s Wheelus was still useful, but it was no longer indispensable. The instruments for the defence of American interests had moved largely outside Arab borders to adjacent areas where the Sixth Fleet was stationed, and to American defence installations in other parts of the world. The United States was also asking itself political questions: 'Was the British air base in Libya, or the naval base at Aden, so essential to the defence of the free world that the United States could risk a rupture of its Arab relations to defend them?'[15]

Yet Libya remained important. Apart from her strategic position in the Mediterranean, there was her role in countering radical Arab nationalism in the Maghreb and the Middle East. And there was oil. By 1968 Libya was already the largest supplier of oil to Britain, and to Italy, and the third largest to France. Libyan oil flows could not have been more timely for Britain. Britain's oil imports from the Persian Gulf area made sound strategic sense as long as Britain could maintain an influence over the political situation in the Gulf by a permanent military presence there, which could be rapidly reinforced by a naval presence from the Mediterranean. The Six Day War closed the Canal and rapid access from the Mediterranean. In January 1968 Britain's Labour government announced the withdrawal of British armed forces from both the Gulf and the Far East by the end of 1971. The development of new and substantial sources of oil west of Suez under the control of a friendly government became an urgent strategic need. Libya met Britain's requirements exactly.[16] But Libya's oil resources also meant that she could pay for her 'own' defence, and thus foot the bill for the West. There was a significant pattern to Britain's withdrawals from her spheres of interest. The handsome arms deal with Saudi Arabia was negotiated as Britain was withdrawing from Aden; it left Saudi Arabia, which unlike Britain could well afford it, with the burden of protecting British interests in the region. The treaty with Kuwait under which Britain had undertaken the military protection of that country expired in 1968, when Britain concluded a deal with Kuwait for the sale of Vickers tanks. Britain announced her withdrawal east of Suez when she had begun to meet the demand for equipment from the Persian Gulf states, many of which were establishing armies for the first time. By the time Britain was ready to withdraw or shrink her military presence in Libya, the British Aircraft Corporation weapons system was being readied to take over.

In 1966 Britain had created a Defence Sales Organization in the Ministry of Defence which soon more than earned its keep in foreign exchange. Britain's lagging arms exports had been stung by a series of American sales coups. The United States Government arms sales office (The International Security Affairs

Division of the Department of Defence) had edged Britain out of an important Saudi Arabian aircraft deal, but was reputed to have a stand-off agreement with Britain on the supply of arms to Libya: that if British forces stayed in Aden for two years longer, then the United States would allow Britain to sell certain planes to Libya. Whatever arrangement existed was broken by the Whitehall announcement in May 1968 that it had won an order to install a complete missile air defence system in Libya. The package was not made public in all its detail but was believed to have been worth at least £145 million in its initial stages, rising to £500 million over the next five years. Britain was to supply Rapier and Thunderbird ground-to-air missiles and attendant radar installations. BAC also won a large contract to instruct the Libyan army in the operation of the missiles system; and the next stage was expected to be the purchase of British military aircraft. Yet another deal involved Chieftain tanks and a new tank with a 120 mm. gun 'which had proved hard to sell abroad despite its high reputation with the British Army of Occupation of the Rhine'.[17] The Libyan commitment was to develop and reorganize its armed forces on modern lines.

Even the £102 million package for Saudi Arabia was outstripped by the Libyan deal. It was the largest missile system order ever won by a British firm and the most valuable export deal of any kind. It was also an example of the new hard-sell partnership evolved between Whitehall and the aircraft industry. But, said a critic, 'no one in Britain had ever asked why Libya needs these weapons, who its enemies are, or from what quarter the country is being threatened. Nor was Britain really interested in selling Libya weapons until it became rich through oil revenues. Then all of a sudden the country needed extremely sophisticated weapons.'[18] Who was the likely enemy? *Flight International*[19] had a try:

Libya's new oil wealth resulted in her eastern neighbour Egypt making expansionist noises in Libya's direction, and Nasserite sympathisers in Libya, encouraged by Cairo, were taking maximum advantage of the sociological strain which has resulted from the sudden wealth and western know-how coming to a poor and federal desert Kingdom.

The fact was that the Libyan defence deal had less to do with war than with business. Journalists trying to unravel the story of super-arms salesmen described the 'hard sell' behind the Libyan deal:

How is an arms deal made ? ... Several factors worked together to push the Libyan Government ... First was the discovery of oil six years ago which both gave the country revenues ... with which to buy arms, and something more than millions of acres of desert and a tiny population ... to defend from predatory aggression ... At the same time the neighbouring governments of Algeria and the United Arab Republic began to display considerable political hostility towards Libya for the friendly attitude its government under King Idris was continuing to show towards Britain and the U.S. ...

But what sort of defence should Libya provide for herself? Large ground forces were clearly out of the question, and in any case a ruler anxious to stay in power in a new country does not act in his own interest if he creates a real military élite. At this point the announcement of Saudi Arabia's fighter and missile deal with Britain provided a catalyst. Here was an entirely defensive force capable of deterring an invader but hardly able to be turned against the country's own government ... The final touch was given by the Six Day War. This showed that there was little point in going for a defence system that was susceptible to a surprise raid because of its immobility. Libya's requirements could therefore be met by a highly mobile combination of radar, communications, missiles and aircraft that would be capable of detecting and intercepting an attack of the kind Israel launched against the Arab world last June ... And as it happened most of the elements of such a package were becoming available in Britain.

As for Britain's interests:

There could be no objection. First there was the ever-pressing problem of exports; any windfall here was, as always, welcome. And second, from a strategic-commercial point of view, Libya stands as the only source of mid-eastern oil that would remain unaffected by the long-term closure of the Suez Canal.[20]

Inside Libya the King's resistance to a large and powerful army was being countered by the rise of a small but vociferous group of younger technical and professional men, both in and out of uniform, who saw in the absence of an impressive army one more proof that Libya was cut off from the mainstream of Arab nationalism. The King was not receptive to the arguments of this group but he lent a ready ear to the proposals of his British defence advisers. They produced the ideal solution to his anxiety: an army based on a sophisticated missile system could defend Libya and the West, but could not be turned into a coup-making instrument. But the defence package served to feed other conflicts in the army: between sections of the Defence Ministry divided by connections with both British and United States defence commitments in Libya; and inside the officer corps, where senior officer opposition took the form of objections to aspects of the army retraining support contract, and middle-level and junior officers were preoccupied with the currents of political as well as army opposition to the régime.

By 1969 there was a growing belief that the enfeebled King was losing his judgement and that his authority was evaporating. The Shalhi family was amassing ever greater power. Omar Shalhi achieved nomination as the King's special adviser; and this, together with the control of the army by his brother Colonel Abdul Aziz Shalhi following the retirement of the former chief-of-staff, convinced many that the balance of power was moving rapidly into the hands of the Shalhi group, which might well decide it was strong enough to rule without the King or the Crown Prince.

In August clandestine leaflets appeared. For the first time they attacked the King by name, as well as the Shalhi brothers, and the arms deals that Libya was concluding with Britain. The King pressed for the discovery and rounding up of the culprits. He also threatened once again to abdicate. The army promised that the pamphleteers would be found.

Part III: An Army for Islam

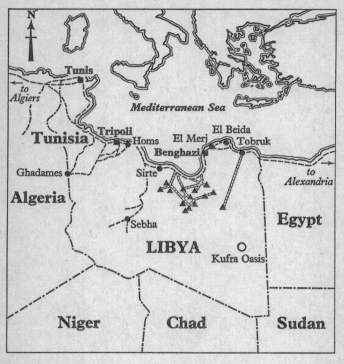

—————— Main Roads

▲ ▲▲ Oil Wells

════════════ Oil Pipelines

7 The Intervention of the Army

When the news of the Libyan coup d'état on 1 September 1969 reached Cairo, Nasser sent Mohammed Hussanein Heykal, editor of *Al Ahram*, and his close political confidant, to make the first on-the-spot investigation for Egypt. At Benghazi airport Heykal looked past the young army officers who met him and asked: 'Where is Abdul Aziz?' He was referring to Abdul Aziz Shalhi, the brother of Omar Shalhi, and commander-in-chief of the army.

Colonel Shalhi had in fact been arrested on coup day, upbraiding the soldiers sent to fetch him: 'Go away, you fools. It's not today, it's the fourth.' A Libyan coup had been expected; the problem was, whose? There were in fact at least two and probably three distinct take-over conspiracies under way inside the Libyan army. One of them was for a classic coup by colonels. Both Nasser and Shalhi had anticipated the wrong coup.

Abdul Aziz Shalhi had been backwards and forwards to Cairo during 1969. There he was reputed to have enjoyed rapid and easy access to Nasser and the top echelons of the Egyptian army; he was himself a product of the Cairo military academy. Whether independently or as a result of the same intelligence briefings, by 1969 both Egypt and the United States had come to the conclusion that while a scramble for power was inevitable when the King died, the monarchy's survival might be in doubt even while he lived. Intrigues in and around the Palace made the ruling group far from homogenous. Tripolitania was restive under what it regarded as rule from Cyrenaica. Western powers and oil interests were already persuaded that a more 'modern' administration, less subject to tribal pressures and less stigmatized by corruption, would pre-empt opposition to the monarchy polarizing into radicalism, as had happened during the 1964 and 1967 demonstrations. In the Middle East the two classic sources of opposition had traditionally been the students and the army. A strike from the army seemed only a matter of time.

By 1969 the army was about 10,000 strong, but it was a rather static force. It was top heavy with senior officers – seventy-four colonels for instance, by 1969 – and this imbalance was a source of grievance with junior and middle officers. It could not do field training without the express permission of the King. This was another safeguard against the army acting as coup-maker.

After Egypt's defeat in the Six Day War, together with the decline in prestige of all the Arab armies, there was strong pressure for the Libyan army to be enlarged and better equipped. Britain's General Mogg arrived to set up the Anglo-Libyan Board of Reorganization for the purpose. The plan that emerged, inspired by British military advisers, was for the reorganization of Libya's army into two brigades, one armoured and one infantry, based on the British Aircraft Corporation tanks and self-propelled guns. The Ministry of Defence and its advisers had devised a conscription system which was due to enrol its first recruits on 8 September. But until Libyan officers had been put through training courses, British officers were to be seconded to the Libyan army; and this, together with a new British-installed sophisticated logistics maintenance system, made it plain that the entire army expansion plan was totally dependent upon Britain and British officers. This was seen by young and middle-ranking officers as Britain's way of colonizing the Libyan army and it brought to a head the rumbles against the régime's subservience to Western defence interests. The contract for the anti-aircraft missiles and tanks was signed in April 1969, but negotiations over some of the sub-contracting began to stall as even senior officers began to express reservations about the project.

In Libya the 'revolution' stands or falls by Gadafi's official version. It provides for a continuous history of planning: with Gadafi, from schoolboy to president, its visionary, theoretician, and leader of a close-knit conspiratorial group. It makes the young officers the natural heirs and custodians of power, because they alone not only conceived but organized and carried through the revolution. The version is, however, silent on some of the key events. This is relevant not only to the physical seizure of power but also to the presence in the first Council of Ministers after the coup of two senior army officers of the rank of colonel. By the end of 1969 they had been arraigned for treason before a court martial. The following year there were further plots and trials involving army officers among others. Why was the revolution so early devouring its children? Part of the answer lies in the chronicle of the coup which the official version does not provide, because it strives to repeat the Nasserite model of a Free Officer revolution.

Revolution as a concept can have no definite time period because it undergoes natural growth and happens in its own time, Gadafi has said. 'When things on earth change against the norms of nature, there must be a revolution.'

Pressed for a more detailed and coherent account of the planning of the revolution, Gadafi has written:

It is impossible to give a specific date for the beginning of the Libyan revolution (*thawrah*) – no one can determine the beginning of any revolution.

This differs from a coup (*inqilab*) which is a casual event occurring at the pleasure of senior officers. These sometimes issue orders from positions of legal authority for the movement of troops and officers who bring about everything but their masters' orders. These may not be discussed and are followed without certainty or conviction.

A revolution is the opposite, even if the practical application of the idea partakes of the same appearance as a military coup. A revolution is a vital necessity which grows naturally in the consciousness of the society as a whole ... The necessity for complete and radical change ... produces ... a man of revolution, a man of comprehensive and complete change, a man who is as if born again in a new age.[1]

As for the practical organization of the revolution:

... the collection of men and the provision of weapons – a specific time for them can be determined.

The practical steps of the revolution, including the beginning of secret meetings, began in 1959, when my colleagues and I were students in secondary school.

The first command committee was formed while we were students in secondary schools in the town of Sebha to be exact. Our number began to increase and to branch out within the ranks of the youth. One can (thus) fix a date for planning and preparation of the revolution. We go back ten years to 1959.

What inspired them?

Our souls were in revolt against the backwardness enveloping our country and its land, whose best gifts and riches were being lost through plunder, and against the isolation imposed on our people in a vain attempt to hold it back from the path of the Arab people and from its greatest cause.

We met as a group of friends to plan a long hard path for ourselves. It would, however, lead to a goal we had promised ourselves to achieve.

Gadafi had been expelled from school for his part in organizing a demonstration against Syria's secession from the United Arab Republic. He found the doors of all the government schools of Fezzan closed to him. He moved from that province to Tripolitania and enrolled at Misurata's secondary school to sit examinations for the college preparatory certificate. By then, even earlier at school in Sebha, Gadafi maintains, the young men of his group had decided that the ideal way to revolution was through the Military Academy.

Why not political activity?

The opposition parties and groups were weak. They did not have the strength for confrontation and did not have definite ideas . . . As for the people, they proceeded in their opposition without organization. As for the ideological parties, there was a small group of the Arab Baath Party whose movement was suppressed by the authorities, and later a small group of Arab Nationalists appeared. Socialist revolutionary thought existed among a few individuals without organization.

In 1964 Gadafi entered the Military Academy. He instructed some of his friends to do the same:

MEHEISHY: I was surprised. I never thought of doing that. But Gadafi insisted. When we parted the decision was not really firm. Later Gadafi wrote me a letter: 'You are to submit your papers to the Academy', signed Gadafi.

GADAFI: I wish to remind Meheishy he once asked me if I was connected with any of the political parties. I said no. I have no connection whatever with any political group. I do not believe in their aims.

INTERVIEWER: You are against political influences?

MEHEISHY: We are but we supported Nasser's ideas ... Gadafi had some civilian contacts but once we joined the Academy (our organization) changed from civilian to military, from no power to power. We decided the military was the best means to achieve revolution.[2]

According to Gadafi's version, the central committee of the Free Unionist Officers was regularly convened from this time onwards. No meetings constituted a quorum unless all the members were present. Meetings were arranged to coincide with holidays and feast days. 'We tired ourselves most of all over the meetings ... the reason for our exhaustion was that they were held outside the cities and on holidays ... we travelled hundreds of miles accompanied by sleeplessness and heat or cold, according to the season ... Cars were expensive, while our salaries were small and our families poor. However, by praising God and with his help we were successful. We passed the many check points without registering, sometimes with a trick and sometimes through a personal acquaintance. We slept out of doors and met under trees, in the shelter of boulders, or in desert tents.'

The Central Committee, said Gadafi, 'imposed on itself a stern code of ethics which others could perhaps not endure'. The members were forbidden alcohol, gambling, and night clubs. They practised their daily prayers and studied diligently. The code was imposed on all members of the movement. But in order not to attract attention, the movement was not strict with any of its members who played cards.

Here and there in Gadafi's accounts are references to a popular committee, or a 'civilian command to heighten popular consciousness'. While some members of the original Sebha group joined the army, others had 'headed for universities and civilian activities'. The composition of this group is shadowy. After 1964 nothing more was heard of popular civilian committees. Those civilians whom the RCC subsequently appointed to government and the civil service were selected because they were personally known and trusted by the young officers, not because they had been part of any sustained organization.

Gadafi told me: 'The civilians who identified with us in those days were very slow. They met from time to time but very infrequently. They had no discipline, unlike those of us in the army. It was military discipline that helped us to continue working.'[3] In fact once the Gadafi group joined the Military Academy, the activities of the civilian group were frozen. Gadafi revealed this during the four-hour discussion on Libyan television in which six RCC members participated on the first anniversary of the coup.

INTERVIEWER: The civilian group knew nothing about the revolution?

GADAFI: Absolutely not. All we told them was 'keep going' but we never integrated them except in our thoughts.

ABUBAKR YUNIS, intervening: At that time the trend in the country was Nasserite–Nationalist, and there was strong support for the unity of Egypt with Syria. There were political activities. I joined in. But when I saw how disunited they were I submitted my resignation. I decided that civilians would not do anything for the country.

In May 1968 army promotion examinations in Tripoli brought a number of young officers together at the Garrison Command Camp. Gadafi pressed for an assessment of Free Officer support not only in the army but also among the cadets of the academy who would graduate that August. It was during this meeting, according to Gadafi, that it was decided to start thinking seriously in some months' time of setting a date for action.

He began to take soundings within the senior officer corps. Each member of the central committee was instructed to report on officers who were not Free Officers. 'Consequently we received piles of confidential reports on various commanders, and the picture became clear to us by comparing these reports with our personal impressions.' In January 1969 Gadafi wrote a memorandum to Abdul Salaam Jalloud and sent it from Benghazi to Tripoli through a corporal in the First Signals Corps. It contained a short message of four lines ordering all officers of the Free Officer Movement to ascertain whether they had sufficient strength to overcome and control all armed forces at a given signal. They were instructed to conduct a survey of men, armour, and ammunition, to ensure accuracy of the assessment. It was found that the movement had 'achieved superiority' and that in consequence the time was ripe for action.

I therefore wrote by hand in the Gar Younes Camp our first military order on behalf of the Central Committee. Copies were made and distributed to all Free Officer Movement formations. In order that I should devote my whole attention to the action in hand, I took forty-five days leave, my first leave since I joined the army. During this time I held many meetings with members of the Central Committee and other officers. Most of these meetings were held in the house of Abdul Salaam Jalloud at Zawyet El Dahmani in Tripoli, and the house of Mohammed el Mgarief in Benghazi. I checked personally the strength of each Free Officer Movement formation and held a separate meeting with every individual commander of each formation. As a result of my findings we decided to go into action on 12 March.

But on the night of 12 March, Um Khalthoum, the great Egyptian singer, was due to give a public recital to an audience that would include not only many of the régime's civilian luminaries but also senior army officers who would have had, as a matter of coup-making course, to be rounded up. 'We decided,' Gadafi said, 'it would be unethical to disturb the civilians.' The date was postponed to 24 March.

As this date approached, the Free Officers noticed that the army was being alerted. Armoured units from Homs and Tarhuna were concentrated in the central barracks at Bab al Azzizia. Several units were ordered to hand in their trucks, and these were moved from Tripoli and concentrated in a camp near Benghazi. Units had their ammunition recalled. Military intelligence officers kept night watches at barracks and on ammunition stores. Colonel Shalhi and some of his staff made night tours of the city of Benghazi. 'They were taking counter-action as though they knew about our plans,' Gadafi said. 'That was a bad time for us.' Some of the Free Officers telephoned Gadafi to come urgently to Tripoli. He arrived the same night. It was decided to continue with the plans for action on the Sunday night of 24

March, and some of the leading officers stationed at Sebha garrison took leave in readiness. But on 19 March the King flew from Tripoli to Tobruk, close to the protective arm of the British forces stationed there. The plan was once again called off and there ensued a lull of some months in the conspiracy.

On 2 September a batch of young officers was due to be posted to training courses in Britain. The Free Officers who had been living on their nerves for the better part of the year began to feel that they were virtually being watched; and that even if they were not, the postings would seriously drain their manpower resources. Zero hour was fixed for 1st September, one day before the officer postings abroad. The King was out of the country, resting at a Turkish spa.*

As it happened, it was propitious timing. The young officer plot was on the point of being uncovered inside the army. Furthermore, a great deal of evidence points to the fact that if the junior officers had not brought off their action, a more senior plot would have pre-empted it.

The Free Officer Movement was only one of the subterranean currents in the army. The circles and factions that made government an intrigue for career and business were present, too, in the army. As Gadafi has said in one of the more perceptive passages of his account: 'The régime was preoccupied with internal struggles. The senior officers revolved in the orbit of these struggles and were preoccupied by the competition for positions.' There was a group in support of the King. There was also the group of the General Staff under Colonel Shalhi. And there was the important group of middle-level officers, mostly of the rank of major, who were products of the Baghdad Academy, pan-Arab and nationalist oriented, some of them socialists. This group had considerable strength in the officer corps and a small leadership nucleus. It was specially well represented in military

* When he heard the news of the coup he moved from Turkey to a small port on the Greek coast with his retinue. As he arrived a dozen young Libyan naval and air force cadets on training schemes in Greece occupied the Libyan Embassy in Athens in the name of the revolution. Later the King moved his exile to Cairo where he was in October 1971 when a Libyan people's court trying cases of corruption sentenced him to death *in absentia*.

intelligence quarters. The Free Officers drew their support from the non-commissioned officers. The existence of their organization was said to be an open secret at certain levels in the army, though its chances of any effective action were heavily discounted. When news of a Free Officer plot reached Colonel Shalhi, military intelligence played it down – perhaps thus deliberately seeking to protect it – and though an inquiry was ordered, this was inconclusive.

The men who subsequently emerged as the leadership of the Free Officer Movement were – with two exceptions – the seventh (1963) batch of graduates of the Military Academy. The two exceptions, Meheishy and Mgarief, graduated a year later as part of the eighth batch. Such organization as was maintained in a group posted throughout the army was a result of Gadafi's indefatigable efforts – or imagination, for there is evidence that the group was far from as cohesively organized as he makes out.

Apart from the seventh and eighth batches, new recruits had been selected from each year's intake at the Academy, and the Free Officers were counting heavily on the batch of second lieutenants due to be graduated that August; for these would be posted to army units throughout the country, and by the night of 1 September there was a good chance they would be functioning as duty officers, already briefed by one of the Free Officers who was a platoon commander at the Academy, Mohamed Nejm.

According to Gadafi, it was at a very late stage in the preparations for the coup, between March and September 1969, that some of the senior officers were sounded out for their support: 'When we felt we were strong and in control of the army.'

We disclosed the matter to them but often found deep in them a profound despair and disbelief of what they were hearing. The reluctant among them sought to frighten us with (mention of) bases, tribes, and security forces, but we trusted in God's help . . .

I say with respect to contacts with and disclosures to the high ranks that the result was almost nil.

One of the exceptions was Lieutenant-Colonel Adam al-Hawwaz. He was 'among the excellent officers devoted to his military duty. All loved him and would have admitted him into the movement had it not been for the kidney illness with which he was afflicted . . . We put him aside with the others we had put aside until such time as we had risked all and succeeded.'

Colonel Adam al-Hawwaz was the officer responsible for the static communications company based at Benghazi. He was popular and admired in the army and had a reputation for integrity and democratic persuasions. He had also been one of the British Embassy's most valuable contact men in the army. On coup day he acted as RCC front man to the foreign embassies in Benghazi. There is no information on precisely how he came to play this role. But more unexpected still was the crucial part played by the second senior officer who helped pull off the Free Officer plot. This was Lieutenant-Colonel Musa Ahmed. He was a member of the Hassa tribe, which had a longstanding history of friction with the dominant Barassa tribe, itself the pillar of the Sanusi régime. Musa Ahmed was reputed to have close contacts with the American Embassy. The mystery of the September 1969 coup in Libya is how these two senior officers were drawn into the Free Officer operation. For it was Musa Ahmed who immobilized the headquarters of the Cyrenaica Defence Force – the first ring of defence round the King and his régime – and without this action the coup had absolutely no hope of success.

There is evidence that in the week before the coup, Gadafi approached some of the middle-ranking Baathist officers for their cooperation. It was refused:[4] these officers were laying plans for an action of their own. But while they drew back from the Free Officer plot, which seemed unlikely to succeed, their inner leadership group did not convey their decision to their supporters throughout the army. The result was when the Free Officer action started, numbers of middle-ranking officers not part of its planning nonetheless sided with it and helped its completion and stabilization in the vital post-coup period.

As coup date approached, there were thus several layers of active conspiracy in the officer corps; and over the army as a whole, an air of disillusionment with the régime. The Free Officer plot absorbed elements that by no means constituted a homogenous conspiracy. Several officers took part in the coup without knowing who was leading it. The mingling of these streams of conspiracy contributed to the coup's success, but were to promote the first crises of the new régime.

The headquarters of the CYDEF strike force, with its formidable armoury of heavy weapons including tanks, was at Gurnada camp east of Beida and a few miles from Appollonia. On the night of 31 August a group led by Lieutenant-Colonel Musa Ahmed (who had just been assigned to Benghazi army headquarters to handle the forthcoming conscription programme) met together at the bar of the Cyrene Motel, which is situated between the ruins of Cyrene and the crossroads that lead on the one hand to Beida and on the other to Gurnada. The group drank for a while and eventually left the motel at about 3 a.m., driving south to the crossroads. But there, instead of proceeding to Beida, it drove to Gurnada. That camp had for some unexplained reason been placed on alert that evening, with a company on stand-by. But the duty officer in charge of the guard company Captain Abdullah Shuayb, who belonged to the same tribe as Musa Ahmed and had a sense of personal loyalty to him, had been made party to the Colonel's plan. He called off the alert and ordered the return of weapons. Musa Ahmed's group, drawn principally from the signal corps of the army's Fifth Battalion at Derna, travelling in Landrovers and Volkswagens and armed with hand weapons, disarmed the guard at the gate, burst in and took the arsenal and then the camp by surprise. There was some brief shooting in which one man was killed and about fifteen were wounded. The CYDEF commander, Brigadier Sanusi Fezzani, the one man who might have rallied the CYDEF force to challenge the coup-makers, was asleep at his home when a group of soldiers came to arrest him. General Mukhtar Bu Shar was arrested while speeding towards the Gurnada camp; he had made the mistake of driving out to investigate instead of proceeding straight to his headquarters to rally his force.

Only when Gurnada was secure and the King's praetorian guard immobilized in its stronghold, did the plotters move on Beida, Benghazi, and Tripoli. There was a period of a few hours until the outcome of the Gurnada operation was clear; and then a call to Benghazi, where Gadafi, Kharuby, and Mgarief were standing by, brought the rest of the plan into action. The coup-makers had the use of the army's new military signals system installed a month earlier. By 6.30 a.m. Gadafi was at Benghazi's broadcasting station to announce the accession to power of a Revolutionary Command Council.

Like the capture of Baghdad by Kassem in 1958, Tripoli was taken by armoured car regiments on a night training exercise. TRIDEF's commanding officer summoned a British technician training the security force in the use of vigilant missiles and – as though an external attack threatened – ordered him to 'put the missiles up'. This would have taken at least twenty-four hours.

In Fezzan the takeover was the easiest of all, and the security force was not even disarmed. Its commander remained at his post for the first week, though firmly under the thumb of Lieutenant Rifi, who was in touch with the RCC groups in Tripoli and Benghazi. Tobruk was the last to fall. On day three after the coup, a group of CYDEF armoured cars arrived at the camp to appeal to the British force for intervention; but by then power had passed well out of the hands of the old régime, and the appeal had a cool reception.

It had been a copybook putsch. In a matter of hours a small group of audacious young men had overthrown government and seized control of the state, with a minimum deployment of forces and almost no bloodshed. For all the claims of a long and con-tinuous conspiratorial history, there were signs of hurried last-minute preparations: some members of the inner circle were alerted only the night of the operation. In Tripoli the coup-makers were acutely short of ammunition. Yet the seizure of power was almost effortless: above all in Cyrenaica, where the régime's first ring of defence had been built. In the very steps it had taken for its protection, the régime had created a source of weakness in building two competing armed forces in inevitable rivalry with one another. Furthermore, tribal loyalty had been proved ineffective in defending a modern state; and within the army Colonel Shalhi was too preoccupied with his own imminent plot to take others seriously.

According to one of the King's aides, the King dismissed the coup as a 'trifling affair' and vowed he would return to resume power: though not without Britain's help, apparently. On 1 September the British government received a message from the Libyan Ambassador in Ankara requesting British intervention 'to restore order and peace and to protect lives'. The following day the King sent a special emissary to London in the shape of Omar al-Shalhi. Shalhi was granted a twenty-minute interview with the Foreign Secretary Michael Stewart: 'at his own request' according to Whitehall. Foreign Office officials were silent about the substance of the meeting, but 'it was understood' that the Foreign Secretary had listened to a message from the King rather than advancing any proposals for the British government to meet the situation in Libya. In some quarters in the Arab world* it was claimed that there was a secret protocol in the Defence treaty between Libya and Britain. But if there was, it was not invoked.

In Libya for a while and abroad for much longer, there was widespread confusion about the provenance and parentage of the coup. The first guess of the diplomatic corps was that it was Baathist-inspired, and had links with Iraq. Iraq was the first country to recognize the new régime, followed hours later by Egypt. In London, as late as a week after the change, it was suggested, in a widely speculative article, that King Idris might himself have been party to the 'revolution', in order to ease the succession to a young modern middle-of-the-road 'socialist' and go-ahead politician, none other than a former Premier, Abdul Hamid Bakkush. Bakkush was in prison by the second day of the coup. To others the fact that the Crown Prince had broadcast his acceptance of the coup was a sign of his connection with it, and not simply his use by the coup-makers to claim legitimacy. The speculation was fast and loose; no one really seemed to know whose coup this was.

The first cable sent to the government of Egypt was signed in the name of one Colonel Saad ed-Din Bushweir Abu

* On 5 September 1969 four days after the coup, *Al Ahram* in Cairo published what it claimed was the full text of the Anglo–Libyan Treaty code-named Raford.

Schweirib. Early radio broadcasts after the takeover proclaimed him the chairman of the new Council of the Revolution. But on the fifth day of the coup it emerged that the Colonel, whoever he was, was not the chairman after all. The Middle East News Agency published an interview with the real chairman who, it said, intended to remain anonymous for the time being, as did the other members of the Revolutionary Council. This was the first time it was announced, again by this anonymous spokesman, that the coup had been carried out by an organization of Free Officers. Colonel Abu Schweirib was no longer in the army and had not even been in Libya when his name was announced. Who chose him as the straw man of the coup? Some thought that on the strength of his reputation as a fervent pro-Nasserite army officer, a group of officers running Tripoli's broadcasting station had guessed him into the leadership of the coup. For a few brief days he was cast in the role of Libya's Neguib, until its Nasser came forward and announced himself.

In Tripoli the foreign embassies were complaining that the coup had to them taken on an Arabian Nights atmosphere. The British Embassy had twice in three days been briefed by completely unknown men, captains in the Libyan army. None gave his name. Whitehall complained that Britain was unable to recognize a régime about which virtually nothing was known, and she could make no decision about arms deliveries. On the other hand, delay in British recognition would risk giving other countries a valuable start in acquiring influence with the new Libyan leaders.

It was eight full days before the new government announced the name of its new commander-in-chief of the army; and another four days before he was identified as head of government, too, in the shape of chairman of the Revolutionary Command Council. It was January 1970, four full months after the coup d'état, before the country was told the full membership of the Revolutionary Command Council.[5] When Gadafi was eventually announced as the leader, he refused to supply any biographical details, and he banned pictures of himself; only very gradually did these begin to creep into the papers. It was Nasser who warned the young men of the RCC that the revolution would be stolen from them if they did not identify themselves. This was in December 1969, and then the names and photographs of the RCC were published for the first time. Only two army officers appeared in the first Council of Ministers, and they were the colonels who were not members of the Free Officer Movement.

Egypt's initial response to the news of the Libyan coup and the subsequent blackout of news was one of great alarm. No one knew who the coup-makers were, and the fear was that it had been a move sponsored by the United States as part of a plan to encircle Egypt. (In the Sudan the right-wing Ansar had just attempted a rising against the Nimeiry régime.) Heykal returned from Libya brimming with enthusiasm. 'I can say,' he wrote in *Al Ahram*, 'that I have toured the Arab world, east and west . . . (but) what I saw in Libya affected me more deeply than anything else. This is a different type of youth . . . the post-setback generation of young people whose upbringing and schooling was dominated by the sufferings of the setback.' Egyptian anxieties were, however, not entirely placated till after Nasser's own visit to Libya and his meeting with Gadafi. It was Nasser's deliberate decision that Gadafi be built as the charismatic leader of a group that had until then presented itself as a collective; this was his way of tightening Egypt's grip on the Libyan régime and preventing other influences rushing in to fill what seemed suspiciously like an ideological vacuum.

Until the actual take-over of power, Egypt's intelligence services had maintained contacts with several of the groupings in the Libyan army. Egyptian dossiers on the Libyan opposition were reputed to be more complete than the records of the Libyan police. Yet if anything persuaded observers that, though inspired by Nasser's example, Gadafi had organized his coup autonomously from Cairo, it was his success. This was because the intermingling of political purpose with police methods so characteristic of Egypt's dealings in other Arab countries had invariably served to stifle political groupings. Nasserites were seen as potential Egyptian intelligence agents; Baathists, as critics of Nasserism, and thus enemy agents; and Cairo's insistence on tight control usually robbed a movement of any right to determine its own tactics. Gadafi was emphatic from the start that he had never consulted Nasser, though he had been tempted to do so before success was assured. Yet many in Libya doubted that these obscure young men could have brought off their coup without outside help.

Suspicion was aroused not so much by the ease with which the coup-makers seized power, but because they were allowed to endure. It was recognized that the passage of the Free Officer coup had been obscured and thus eased by the preparations for the Shalhi coup and, though this was less well known, by the coup-making proneness of the middle officers. It was also recognized that the United States might not only have accommodated but even encouraged a change from the monarchy. But if the Shalhis had been the substitute candidates, why was Gadafi acceptable instead? Until more is known about the CIA's role in Libya and the decision of Musa Ahmed and Hawwaz to join the Free Officers it will be difficult to say. One possibility that would need investigation is that, as in the case of the Free Officer revolution in Egypt in 1952, there was a last-minute insinuation of American influence into the network of conspirators. The Shalhis had always been more pro-British than pro-American; perhaps an alternative candidate was needed, preferably from the Nasserite generation, to prevent anti-West sentiment from getting out of hand. Alternatively Gadafi's appearance on the scene might have taken the United States as much by surprise as everyone else, but they played down their apprehension with the expectation of exerting influence over him.

In a coup d'état nothing succeeds like success, especially in an oil-rich country. There was a rush by foreign powers to get on good terms with the young officers, however anonymous. For their part, the RCC members were anxious not to alarm foreign interests in Libya. RCC members visited the embassies of countries which had oil companies operating in Libya three times in the three days immediately after the coup, to reassure them that they would honour agreements and protect the foreign communities. An RCC statement broadcast over the radio gave the assurance that existing oil concession agreements would be honoured: 'The pumping of oil at Libyan ports will continue as usual. Work will continue according to the rules and regulations previously in force.'

Immediate steps were taken to secure the army: officers above the rank of major were arrested, pensioned off, or posted abroad. The bank accounts of senior officers, as of leading civilians, were frozen. Army pay for the ranks was doubled. Those who took part in the coup operation were granted the Medal of Bravery. After appropriate purging the security forces were absorbed into the army proper. Overnight the Libyan army doubled in size. Yet it was still considered too small and it began to recruit from a generation that needed little convincing that the road to power lay through the Military Academy.[6]

There is a significant pattern in the social composition of the RCC group and the Free Officers around them which makes this a revolution of the oases and the interior against the established society of the large families and dominant tribes. These are the representatives of the generation and the social strata that sent its sons into the army because they did not qualify for university entrance – the Military Academy enrolled students without the general education certificate – and had no other outlets and opportunities.

Only two members of the RCC were members of majority tribes: Mgarief, a member of the Sa'adi tribe the al-Magharba, whose wife was a daughter of the one-time Minister of Communications and army chief of staff; and Abu Bakr Yunis, who belongs to an important tribe from the Augila oasis in Chad that had emigrated into Libya; he and Mgarief met at a boarding school in Derna. The others came, with one exception, from minor tribes and poor families. The exception was Meheishy, born in Misurata of a father who was a provincial administrator and from a Circassian Turkish family. An important group in the RCC – and very many among the Free Officers – were born at oases in the interior, where they were the country's second-class citizens, the children of nomads or lowly cultivators, in the last days of the Italian occupation. Gadafi was born in Sirte, in the desert that reaches to the coastline between Tripolitania and Cyrenaica, of a family which he claims still lives in a tent, and he spent his formative years in Sebha in the Fezzan.[7] Beshir Hawady comes of a poor family in Uaddan in the Fezzan; Jalloud, from a Fezzan oasis in Wadi Shati. Those born on the coast were mostly from the lower social strata, not the dominant tribes, or the traditional citizenry of the coast, or the new rich families.[8]

Despite the repeated assertion that the Free Officer plot was long-enduring and closely organized, there is no doubt it was not a group revolution but almost entirely the achievement of one man, Mu'ammar Gadafi. His vision might have been continuous from his schooldays, when he modelled himself on Nasser's career; but the Free Officer central committee was less an organization than a loyal malleable group around him, and it was he who hand-picked the RCC. After the coup, between sixty and eighty young officers constituted the core of RCC support in the army,[9] and a few were transferred into the administration – though on nothing like the Egyptian scale, perhaps because it was still so early.[10] Many of the army officers who performed crucial roles during the coup were not part of or loyal to the Free Officer group and they were gradually eliminated from the army. The coup had been military in conception, planning, organization, and execution, carried out without the participation or knowledge of any organized civilians or even sections among the intellectuals. Its success was more due to the sclerosis of the old system than to the vitality and broad support of its challenger. It released a wave of spontaneous popular enthusiasm but from the outset excluded the active participation of the mass of people in any autonomous organization of their own. The domination of the army was established from the outset in the hegemony of the RCC. While Gadafi frequently talked of his urge to abandon politics for the army, he accepted Nasser's famous dictum that the army must permanently patrol society. Unlike the typical African coup d'état, in countries south of the Sahara, which declares a moratorium on politics and leans on the administration alone, Libya's coup followed the model of the Middle East nationalist coup, which takes over established nationalist parties to legitimize army rule (as in Syria), or creates a political organization directed by the army-state to infuse society with the ideology of the young officers and so promote mass support.[11] The danger was that without a precise ideological formation or a consolidated power-base and without institutionalized support in the society, the army régime depended on the loyalty of the army officer corps and relied on the machinery of the police and security apparatus as the major means of political control. However far-reaching and ambitious any changes introduced by the RCC régime – above all in foreign policy, for the new government turned Libya's face forcibly from the West towards the Arab world – the continued domination by the army, and the refusal of the régime to permit any autonomous popular organization or initiative – were to make it less a revolution than a coup d'état.

The first counter-coup plot was exposed less than four months after the new régime took power. The trial of the two colonels, together with fifteen other army officers, was based largely on circumstantial evidence, its proceedings were rapid and sentences pre-emptory. What might have become a plot against the régime was snuffed out even before it had begun. It had been detected by the RCC's strong man in the eastern province, Mustapha Kharuby. Before the trial opened, Gadafi went on television to reveal the details of the plot. It had been motivated, he claimed, by personal grudges and the 'sensitivity' of senior officers against the Free Officers who were in power but lower in rank. There was a charge of foreign instigation and involvement, but this was never substantiated and proved false. In mid 1970 al-Hawwaz and Musa Ahmed were sentenced to life imprisonment, and the others to varying terms. Street demonstrations protesting at the lightness of the sentences prompted a re-trial two days later which sentenced four of the accused to death by firing squad; four others to life imprisonment; the remainder to long prison terms. (The death sentences were not carried out.)[12] The accused were all army officers, but a diverse group politically. Like the two colonels, the others had helped the coup to success; but unlike them, many had both radical views and influence in the army that discomfited the Free Officers.[13]

Six months later another plot was detected in which the key conspirators were Abdullah Abid Sanusi, Omar Shalhi (in exile in Switzerland), the Seif al-Nasr family together with a number of retired security force officers, and some contractors linked with the old régime. Arms had been smuggled into the Fezzan from Chad, and the plot called for the arrival of foreign mercenaries at Sebba airport and garrison. Twenty men stood trial; among them, four living abroad but tried *in absentia*, and sentenced to long prison terms.[14] The new régime has carried out no executions. Simultaneously with this plot, there was alleged to be another in Benghazi uncovered by Egyptian intelligence personnel working inside the Libyan army; this time the plotters were army officers but also dissident intellectuals. During 1973 a large number of military cadets on courses in the Cairo Military Academy were detained as they returned home. A régime that had come to power by conspiracy was reaping conspiracies in its turn.

8 Religion as Politics

The proclamation of the Libyan Republic on 1 September 1969 was passionate:

In the name of God, the Compassionate, the Merciful, O great Libyan people: To execute your free will, to realize your precious aspirations, truly to answer your repeated call demanding change and purification, urging work and initiative, and eager for revolution and assault, your armed forces have destroyed the reactionary, backward, and decadent régime whose putrid odour assailed one's nose and the vision of whose attributes made one's eyes tremble. With one blow from your heroic army, the idols collapsed and the graven images shattered. In one terrible moment of fate, the darkness of ages – from the rule of the Turks to the tyranny of the Italians and the era of reaction, bribery, intercession, favouritism, treason, and treachery – was dispersed. Thus, from now on, Libya is deemed a free, sovereign republic under the name of the Libyan Arab Republic – ascending with God's help to exalted heights, proceeding in the path of freedom, unity and social justice, guaranteeing the right of equality to its citizens, and opening before them the doors of honourable work – with none terrorized, none cheated, none oppressed, no master and no servant, but free brothers in the shadow of a society over which flutters, God willing, the banner of prosperity and equality. Extend your hands, open your hearts, forget your rancours, and stand together against the enemy of the Arab nation, the enemy of Islam, the enemy of humanity, who burned our holy places and shattered our honour. Thus will we build glory, revive our heritage, and revenge an honour wounded and a right usurped. O you who witnessed the holy war of Omar al-Mukhtar for Libya, Arabism, and Islam, O you who fought the good fight with Ahmad al-Sharif, O sons of the steppe, O sons of the desert, O sons of the ancient cities, O sons of the upright countryside, O sons of the villages – our beloved and beautiful villages – the hour of work has come. Forward.[1]

Between those in power and the populace at large the radio was the sole link, but behind the scenes the RCC, meeting in continuous session, was casting about for civilian intermediaries. A small circle of Benghazi students whom Gadafi knew and trusted was asked to recommend civilians for appointment to a new government, but the contacts were casual, almost haphazard. Five days after the take-over, a group of Benghazi intellectuals who had been in opposition to the monarchy addressed a nine-page memorandum to the RCC. It welcomed the revolution, for the Libyan people had been eager for change, but a real revolution had to more than merely arise from the aspirations of the masses; it had to give them the means to express their support through the organization of trade unions, women, students, and intellectuals. In other words, they said, a revolution had to be built not from the top but at the base. Any other politics would degenerate into intrigue. The Benghazi group received no reply but heard informally that the RCC had rejected its representations as coming from a political party. In November the memorandum was presented once again, together with a request for an appointment with Colonel Gadafi. The request was never granted.[2]

On the eighth day after the coup, a Council of Ministers was announced, of two army men holding the portfolios of Defence and the Interior, and seven civilians, under the premiership of Dr Mahmoud Suleiman Maghrabi, who had been serving a term of imprisonment for his leading part in the strike of dock workers during the Six Day War. Apart from Maghrabi, Salah Boweisir, and Anis Ahmad Shitawy, who became ministers of Foreign Affairs and Petroleum respectively, the other appointments were of relatively obscure personalities.[3]

From the outset the RCC functioned as a closed system of authority with supreme power.[4] Its members worked round the clock, generally in the Azzizia Barracks, where Gadafi took up residence and which the RCC made its working headquarters. If the twelve young men consulted at all, it was to seek confirmation of their acts among their friends the Free Officers. There was the minimum of contact between the RCC and the Council of Ministers; the former was busy reorganizing the army,[5] finding its Arab and foreign feet, and exploring the path of its revolution. No systematic programme of the revolution was ever announced. Cabinet Ministers – and newspaper editorial writers – had to gauge its aims and means by the public utterances of Gadafi. The isolation of the Cabinet from the RCC and the lack of confidence on the part of the Ministers led to a confusion of policy and direction. Administration slowed down to a crawl, in some cases to a halt. Apart from the leading politicians, the majority of the senior civil servants who had run the previous régime were in prison or under house arrest. The constant references to corruption made civil servants edgy. Rather than face accusations or make mistakes, they evaded responsibility and surrendered initiative. Every departmental matter, however trivial, came to rest on the desk of the Minister. But in the end the only men who were confident enough to act, sat on the RCC, which was not only all-powerful but inaccessible. Twice in three months the civilian ministers asked the RCC for permission to resign. Their differences were not so much over policy or principle as over their place within the RCC system of government.

In the reshuffle at the beginning of 1970, five RCC members including Gadafi joined eight civilians; eight months later the composition of the Council of Ministers was changed once again, to reverse the proportion of soldiers and civilians. There were four Councils of Ministers in two years,[6] but whatever the proportion of soldiers and civilians, and however the mixture was shaken, the problem remained the reluctance of the RCC to delegate power. From its outset the Libyan army revolution was firm in following the Nasserite precept of the hegemony of the military. Gadafi gave an interview to *Figaro*:[7]

'Why is the RCC confined to the military only; will this not lead to an indictment of the army for dominating the government?'

'Frankly speaking,' Gadafi replied, 'the officers have the conscience to recognise the people's claims better than others. This depends on our origin which is characterised by humbleness. We are not rich people; the parents of the majority of us are living in huts. My parents are still living in a tent near Sirte. The interests we represent are genuinely those of the Libyan people.'

In other words, army officers of humble origin equal the people of humble origin; the one can interpret the needs and will of the other; the one is the other.

The régime spent its early period in office trying to compensate for the deficiencies of an independence which had done so little to erase from Libyans the sense of contempt they felt at the hands of Italians and other foreigners. Vestiges of colonialism had to be eliminated, like the expulsion of the Italian community;[8] the conversion of foreign banks into Libyan joint-stock companies; the evacuation of the bases. Symbols of conversion were important: so all place and street names in Latin script had to make way for Arabic; cathedrals and churches were closed; foreign privileges cancelled and foreigners harassed by petty control regulations; and a ban placed on alcohol as a return to Islamic tenets of living. Royal projects were suspended, including the making of a new throne for the King, but more importantly, restrictions were placed upon the operation of the *zawiyas* and Sanusi religious education. The minimum wage was doubled; rentals reduced; contract labour stopped. Ministers were prohibited from carrying on private commercial enterprises or leasing state property, or borrowing government funds without approval.[9] This was part of the drive against corruption.

Within the first year, People's Courts[10] were at work. First, the King, members of the Royal Diwan, and former premiers went on trial;[11] then a large group accused of election rigging; and finally journalists and editors charged with corrupting public opinion. The trials were televised at peak viewing times, and the television station was besieged with requests for repeat showings. The judgements tended to be based less on any careful weighing of evidence and argument than on the political stance and position of the accused; some who expressed remorse got lighter sentences. It was not on the whole a vengeful régime; but the court findings were to legitimize what the soldiers' coup had already achieved. Oil companies were untouched, and it was uncertain whether the government would look into the way that they had gained and worked their concessions. Ten newspapers had their licences suspended, and soon, little remained of the Libyan press. In time even official organs like *Al-Thawra*, the official mouthpiece of the revolution, was shut down for unstated errors, and remaining publications came under the tight government supervision.

People's power was the recurring theme of Gadafi's frequent public speeches:

> The men of the revolution will not remain in their offices. They will go to the people ... to investigate their problems. The age of dealing with the problems which disturb the classes of the toiling masses by means of counterfeit promises from air-conditioned offices has now irrevocably ended.

Premier Maghrabi told a press conference that it was unlikely that party organization would assume any importance. The revolution stood for what benefited the people; 'as for subtle intellectual matters, we will study them later'. Gadafi said government hostility to 'groups supporting specific parties' was unlikely but it was hoped that these people would adhere to the revolution. It was intended to set up a popular organization 'to bring the working forces of the people together', and it would be formed by the RCC and the 'popular vanguards' which were 'conscious active groups faithful to the principles of the revolution'. A few weeks later Gadafi explicitly excluded 'party' politics:

> He who engages in party activities after today commits treason ... The revolution will pay no attention to the past on this subject. It will not call to account those who sought the road to deliverance by way of party activities ... But henceforth he who engages in party activities commits treason.[12]

This became one of the slogans displayed on banners for public occasions. Those who formed the core of opposition under the monarchy, who had been imprisoned for acts of opposition and also for adherence to the tenets of Arab nationalism and socialism now advocated by the young soldiers, were rejected. Gadafi went further. He announced that 'labourers and the revolution' are an indivisible entity, so there would be no labour unions which could take advantage of their position 'for their own ends'; and while there might be certain Labour organizations, they would be for 'ordinary administrative duties'. He added: 'We do not accept intermediaries between the revolution and its working forces.'[13] Old trade unionists like Rajab Neihum, the founder of Arab nationalism in the Libyan trade union movement, were ignored. When new unions were organized from scratch, this was done under the auspices of the Ministry of Labour. Within the first half-year the RCC scuttled what chance it might have had of enrolling into the revolution the tiny force of radicals, admittedly most of them intellectuals, that the country had produced.

Gadafi also produced a formula for united politics in the Arab world, which was one of the preconditions for pan-Arabism. The occasion was the first press conference he gave, in February 1970. His theme was the failure of Arab unity in the past. This was due to the great number of organizations in the Arab homeland which had hindered the unity of the Palestinian *fedayin* and had made Arab states victim to conflicts among themselves instead of achieving unity:

The Arab Socialist Union does not meet with the Baath Party and both organizations do not meet with the Algerian Liberation Front ... The objectives of the Baath Party are unity, freedom, and socialism, and those of the ASU are freedom, socialism, and unity, and those of the Arab National Movement are liberation, unity, and social justice. Thus the slogans are the same but we differ in their arrangement and enter into a Byzantine philosophy and a sterile ideological dispute as a result of the great number of political and ideological organizations. If we set up a new organization (he had been asked about the form of politics to be permitted in Libya) we shall add another problem and another obstacle on the path of convergence ... Discussion is going on to reach a unified formula and one Arab movement ... At a meeting with the Syrians, Egyptians, Algerians, and Iraqis we considered this question and all agreed that the delay in unity was caused by the many political and ideological organizations, and a settlement of this great problem should be reached.

This ideological regionalism, in Gadafi's view, was similar to the religious sects whose appearance had led to the collapse of the Islamic state after Mohamed.

In May 1970 the RCC organized a series of public discussions known as the Revolutionary Intellectuals' Seminar.[14] It was concerned with 'a definition of the working forces of the people who have an interest in the revolution'; the popular organization and its basis; Arab unity; the problem of democracy and revolutionary transformation; and the responsibilities of the government during the stage of the social revolution. The participants were hand-picked and included the RCC members, some Free Officers, the Mufti, the Rector of the Islamic University, and those described as 'Libyan Intellectuals' though not students. There was a handful of women. The proceedings were relayed by television. This was to be the forerunner of a series of public consultations, convened ostensibly to involve the masses or their spokesmen in policy-making, but whose scope was obstructed by the limits of Gadafi's own thinking.

As the proceedings opened, a participant asked that the slogans of the revolution (freedom, socialism, and unity) be included on the agenda for discussion. Gadafi rejected the suggestion out of hand. The slogans were taken for granted because the revolution was staged to achieve them. The central debate was an attempt to define the forces for or against the revolution, and what constituted the 'crushed' or 'mashed' classes (*mashruta* – powder) of Libyan society. Since this was one of the rare occasions when Gadafi allowed ordinary people to speak in public, the extracts below will give something of the flavour of the debate:

'ABD AL-MUN'IM AL-MUNIR MUHAMMAD: Before we define the working forces I think it would be appropriate to know which revolution we are talking about . . . if it was the Libyan revolution . . . we should in this case put some light on the revolution itself . . . whether it was a socialistic revolution or . . . (Before he ends his talk the Moderator interrupted him and said 'the aims of the revolution are clear and are not for discussion or questioning'.)

GADAFI: Pardon me . . . We are talking about the revolution that took place in Libya . . . and to be more specific the September 1 revolution . . .' (Laughter)

'ABD AL-MUN'IM: There are two kinds of revolutions: the revolution of the middle class; the socialistic revolutions. The September 1 revolution is a transitory event which will eventually turn into a socialistic revolution . . .

MODERATOR: Please come to the point . . . and if you cannot speak your mind . . . please give others the chance to speak.

'ABD AL-MUN'IM: Well . . . I believe that those who have an interest in the revolution are: labourers, farmers, revolutionary middle class people, intellectuals, and soldiers.

ABU ZAYD: In order to define the working forces we should know who are the enemies of the people . . . If we could do that, then we would reach the point where we would be able to define the working forces.

RASHID KATAYT: He attributes the problem from which the Arabs are suffering to the writers and the originators of imported theories.

JUM'A AL-FEZZANI: The upper middle class is the counter-category to the revolution. Because this category is tied up with the concerns of imperialism . . . [He continued that there are two classes of people: 1. The exploiters and, 2. the exploited class of people.] Toilers are the only class of people which form the real revolutionary working force.

GADAFI: [Asked the speaker, Jum'a al-Fezzani, to talk about the lower middle class of people since he talked about the upper class of people and also to define the category of toilers and to be specific in his interpretation of the roles of those categories.]

FEZZANI: The lower middle class of people are those whose monthly earnings do not exceed 100 pounds. Students, teachers and government employees are considered from the lower middle class.

GADAFI: [Talking to Mr Fezzani] You said that the lower middle class of people are the teachers, students . . . [Before Gadafi ends his question Mr Fezzani said:] The army officers are also from the lower middle class. [Laughter.]

GADAFI: Do you consider the student who lives in a shack to be from the lower middle class?

FEZZANI: Well . . . If he believes in the toilers' theory he will be considered a revolutionary element, but if he does not believe in that . . . he may still be considered from the revolutionary forces but should not assume a ruling position.

JALLOUD: [Talking to the speaker] Let's say that we improved the living standard of those toilers you talked about and they come to enjoy a good life and are not related to the category of toilers . . . In which category of people will you then attach them? [Laughter.]

FEZZANI: Mao Tse-tung, Castro, and Ben Bella are from the lower middle class . . . and they are still from the middle class because they adopted the toilers' principles.

GADAFI: [Asked the speaker how much money he makes per month.]

FEZZANI: I make 117 pounds per month.

GADAFI: [Said while laughing] Oh . . . you must be from the upper middle class. [Laughter. Gadafi continued] I make 192 pounds and 6½ piasters per month . . . this figure, of course, makes me one of the upper middle class.

MUHAMED MUSTAFA AL-MAGHRIBI: There should be no distinction between classes of people.

HUSAYN BASHIR 'UMRANI: Some of the speakers were of the opinion that we have no working forces . . . But I say yes, we have working forces, for example, the port workers, the workers of the electricity company, the municipality workers, the tobacco workers, etc . . . The intellectuals do not live with the workers or feel their problems . . . The labour force is made up of those who carry the burdens which can't be carried by the employers or the intellectuals. [Applause.]

MAHMUD ALI' AL-SWALI: It is not possible to define the working forces of the people . . . We have farmers who own 100 sheep and they get about 500 kilograms of barley from the government in addition to £200 a month given them by the government . . . and it is not possible to include them in the category of toilers . . . Also the monthly earnings of any government employee is known . . . but the amazing thing about them is that in four or five years of service they become owners of villas and stores . . . do we consider them from the category of toilers?

MODERATOR: You are asked to define the working forces of the people that have an interest in the revolution and not to talk about social corruption.

MUHAMMAD MABURK SHRAFA: I thank God because I am not from those who claim to be intellectuals. The revolution was staged for the people . . . Therefore the whole people have an interest in the revolution, and categories of people should not be segregated one from another, considering the fact that our socialism is a democratic one.

Whatever analytical trends were struggling to emerge were obliterated in Gadafi's summing up, which he presented as follows:

1 The proportion of those who were of the opinion that the whole people have an interest in the revolution was eight.
2 The proportion of those who were of the opinion that they are labourers, farmers, revolutionary intellectuals, the non-explosive national capitalists, and the army people was eleven.

3 The proportion of those who were of the opinion that they are faithful people, productive people, and those who support the revolution was nine and a half.

4 The proportion of those who were of the opinion that the people is divided into two categories represented in labourers and farmers was two.

5 The proportion of those who were of the opinion that the working forces of the people should be defined in the light of the circumstances of the community and the new social relations was two.

Suggested categories were:

1 Capitalists
2 Idle rich
3 Exploiters
4 Those who cooperate with foreigners
5 Corrupt people
6 The shepherds who consider the people as a herd of animals
7 Selfish people
8 Rumourmongers
9 Lazy people

When the gathering discussed Arab unity and the shape of popular organization, Gadafi encountered views in sharp conflict with his own. The great majority of speakers were of the view that the popular organization should be developed from the base to the summit by election:

(COL. GADAFI: Do you mean that the representatives of the popular organizations should be elected by the people? Do you think that the people have reached a degree of consciousness where they could have free elections? Have you thought of the old days where votes were bought at the rice and cous-cous parties?)

In the ensuing months RCC decrees dissolved women's associations and the lawyers' union.[15] Since the existing trades unions were said to be defunct, a new labour law[16] promulgated minimum work conditions and wage-fixing procedures and directed the Ministry of Labour to establish and supervise new unions. Union officials were named by decree on the recommendation of the Ministry after consultation with the workers; and, later, elections were closely supervised. A workers' education centre was established to teach principles of trade unionism. It was a curious system of firm Ministry guidance laid down by law but in part mitigated by the awareness of certain Ministry officials that official protection and control were no substitute for independent workers' organization. The unions were prohibited from affiliating to any 'foreign' trade union federation. Government employees other than labourers were not covered by the trade union law.

By the time that the newspapers were instructed to initiate a public debate on the shape of popular organization, the RCC had made up its mind. The model was to be the Arab Socialist Union. This was the only authentic political form of the Arab revolution.[17] It took a national form but was based on 'pan-national' experience. It abolished differences between classes peacefully and avoided the tragedy of class struggle. It did not depend upon secrecy and underground cells. It enabled the application of socialism, and so guaranteed that no capitalist government or society would appear. Transplanting the Egyptian model, the ASU Charter defined the forces of the revolution as peasants, labourers, soldiers, intellectuals, and national capitalists; and stipulated that at all levels of the Union, 50 per cent of the members should be peasants and labourers. The national or non-exploiting capitalist was defined as one who did not exploit others, who earned his money by lawful means, who could use his capital efficiently, and who was subject to progressive taxation.[18] Membership was open to all Libyans over eighteen unless disqualified by order of the RCC. There was a fairly conventional organizational pyramid, from basic unit to national congress, with the addition that army and police organizations were to be formed and run under the RCC, and that the RCC had perched itself on top of the pyramid as 'leading supreme authority of the ASU'.[19] The initial committees were hand-picked by the RCC and instructed to organize the first elections, during which, in the absence of the right to campaign on policy and ideological issues, it was not surprising that voters and candidates resorted, as in the past, to family and factional politics instead.

On the face of it, the ASU founding conference[20] placed no restraints on political expression; but once again it was most revealing as a gauge of Gadafi's thinking and his style of demagogic politics and ruthless control of the base. At times the conference was a debate among equals; at other times Gadafi played schoolmaster to a class of recalcitrant pupils. He defined socialism as social justice:

We want to progress and rid the people of poverty, hunger, backwardness, and ignorance. We call this socialism. A philosophical discussion on what constitutes socialism, communism, capitalism, society, and cooperative society can be carried on by philosophers and thinkers. They can write books on the subject explaining the various doctrines. The ordinary people like us must search for progress and that is all . . . We want to attain progress in the manner that suits us. Communism suits some, while capitalism or socialism suits others. Theoretically speaking, socialism means here that nobody should have a lot of capital and be very rich and able to exploit the people. Socialism does not mean the final elimination of class differences. Such differences are essential to society. That is the law of life . . . Briefly, socialism means social justice. It is the middle road. It is the way to close gaps between the classes.

Some delegates contradicted him boldly:

SPEAKER: True we need hospitals, schools, and a very quick revolutionary and social transformation. However we must learn how to build a sound edifice . . . How can we build a pyramid at the top when the foundation is unsound? One day the pyramid will collapse.

GADAFI: This is not the heart of the matter.

SPEAKER: The duty of the revolution is to build freedom and democracy; that is the duty now.

GADAFI: You are mistaken . . . Suppose we want to make a decision affecting the workers. We want to consult the workers. The workers are influenced by their own interests. They would produce decisions that are unfair for the other sections of the people's working forces. The larger the number of people consulted, the more it is done at the expense of revolutionary transformation.

SPEAKER: The Prophet consulted his companions.

ANOTHER SPEAKER: I say democracy is not a problem because it is non-existent in Islam. When the mission of Islam began on earth, Almighty God spoke thus to Mohamed: 'Consult them about the matter. When determined rely on God.'

Gadafi laid down the law on the role of trade unions and their relation to the ASU:

Today's topic is the ASU's relationship with the trade unions – all unions are not just workers' unions. We must determine the relationship of all trade unions and federations within the framework of the ASU. We fixed this day for discussion of this topic but so far no one has given pertinent points on the daily relationship between the ASU and the trade unions. If you have the answer to this question, fine. This answer should be given to the Congress secretariat, which in turn will hand it to a special committee to discuss your views. If the purpose is merely to speak over the microphone, we can bring 500 microphones so you can speak loud and clear. We are not entertainers, but representatives of the people. Our aim is to seek justice, not to speak over microphones. As I have already said, whoever has an answer, an opinion, or a solution to the problem should write it down briefly and present it to the secretariat.

Finally, the ASU is political work, a popular political organization. The trade unions have nothing to do with politics – at no time and at no place. Trade unions and federations are professional organizations. It is ASU members who engage in politics. It must be clear that trade unions and federations are professional organizations which tackle the problems of their members. Politics must be confined to the ASU. It is impermissible to conduct politics outside the ASU in any union or profession. Otherwise, trade unions and federations would turn into political parties. Consequently, there would not be a single organization for the people's working forces. There would be a group of political parties in the country.

The ASU was born dead. Shortly after its formation Gadafi made a speech at Sabrata of more than characteristic vigour and frankness. He disclosed that he had left the command for three weeks because the revolution had failed to make strides. (This was not his first attempt at resignation. Once before he had been persuaded by emotional crowds to continue as leader.) He wished to remain in the service of the revolution but as soldier not leader. The revolution was failing because 'pecuniary lust is rooted in the hearts of officials'. The Free Officers, he said, had been living on their nerves for ten years doing secret work inside the armed forces. After the revolution they had lost the right of private freedom. 'Nobody among us can go to a shop, sit in a coffee shop, mix with the people ... The ruling seats in the revolutionary era are not chairs but fire and embers.' He had resigned because his concept of the revolution differed from the revolution in its practice. The people were sunk in passivity. It was exactly what his radical critics were saying. The difference was that they saw the RCC and its view of politics as the cause of bureaucratic sluggishness and popular alienation and apathy. The structure and rules of the ASU made it less a popular political movement than a parallel administration, an adjunct to the machinery already run by the RCC and the ministries on the local government level. The rigid direction of the RCC had already suffocated all initiative in the civil service; the same fate awaited the ASU. And if despite all odds ASU groups managed to develop a dynamism or a policy contrary to the RCC conception, it would without doubt face dissolution. How could there, in any case, be participatory politics with such tight control from the top? This was to be the source of endemic strain between Gadafi and groups of urban, politically-minded Libyans.

During the ASU conference, he had delivered a fierce attack on the Libyan intellectuals educated before the revolution. Some had gone to Russia: 'Their case must be dealt with,' he said. 'They either convince us or we convince them; they either imprison us or we imprison them . . .' Others had studied in Arab countries: some in Damascus, others in Iraq, and still others in Lebanon.

At that time, the Baath Party, a nationalist party, wanted to unite the Arab world. Young Baathists used to say: Your country is reactionary and ruled by the Americans, the British, and the monarchy. Our party must operate in your country because some Libyans are Baathists. I knew the Baathists by name.

The peasants and workers, members of this congress, do not know anything about Baathists, Arab nationalists, communists or others. Only the intellectuals know them; those who have studied in the

United States, Britain, France, or elsewhere. Their culture became Western. Because they studied the capitalist economy, they defend Western liberalism and other ideas . . . We want to establish a group of educated people to be the backbone of the ASU. But this backbone must be purely Arab which has faith in and is loyal to the legacy of the Libyan Arab and the Arab nation. It must also be sincere in expressing the nation's requirements for its independent future and in preserving its character and nationalism. We shall not allow suspect elements with a black record to mislead the Libyan masses and to kick the ASU sometimes to the Right and sometimes to the Left.

The Moslem Brotherhood was not acceptable either, since it functioned conspiratorially.

The ASU conference was barely concluded when the RCC decreed a law[21] making the ASU the only legal political organization in the country and declaring that all party political activities were treasonable. Anyone who advocated or established a political group, whether secretly or publicly, would be subject to the death penalty. Anyone who had knowledge of such grouping and failed to report it, was subject to imprisonment for not less than ten years. The RCC would convene special courts to try offenders.

There was the fear that others would steal the army-made revolution; and the fear of radicalism. There was also the hangover of the frustration engendered by the factional disputes of Middle East politics; and the army's traditional anti-intellectualism and its contempt for civilians. The effect of this running fire directed at political groups and ideology frightened even nonparty adherents into withdrawal from public activity. The government's official organ, *Al-Thawra*, was shut down by Gadafi in a fit of impetuosity: it was badly written; its editorials were unsound; why did the intellectuals not write for it? he railed. But anyone not in direct or indirect government service had been intimidated into silence. Students who had started as enthusiasts for the revolution were disconcerted by Gadafi's stress on the religious content of the revolution. At the beginning of 1972 the RCC staged a confrontation with the student organization by refusing to admit certain duly elected delegates to the impending student conference and to permit any autonomous student organization. The students struck in protest. The dispute was conciliated but the anti-strike measure that followed affected students equally with workers in the public sector. Side by side the RCC encouraged a rival officially-inspired Nasserist student organization.

After the ASU conference, the civilian Ministers tendered their resignations. It took some months for a new Cabinet to be formed,[22] and some of its members were appointed without their prior agreement. Gadafi tried to turn this reluctance to enter government into a virtue. It distinguished them from the ministers of the defunct régime who had hung on to office at all costs. He revealed that every one of his ministers had submitted his resignation 'many times'. He read a letter from the ministers suggesting that the next crop be appointed from the ranks of elected organizations, presumably the ASU, seeing that this was the only legal political body. It was a case of ministers still carrying responsibility without power. They had seen the politicians of the previous régime on trial for actions and policies of a régime that they had been unable significantly to influence. Who could tell how permanent any régime was, and how close the day that they too might be called to account?

It was true that there had always been a political vacuum in Libyan politics, due in part to monarchical control but principally to the economic feebleness of the middle class, which constitutes the base of politics of other Middle East states. After independence, and especially after oil, the corporate-owning clans that had formed the basis of Sanusi social and political structure had begun to disintegrate into factional political and business groupings. Oil had been ushering in a new middle class. But the revolution interrupted the process and then froze the independent activities of this class, so that the army might control social development and generate its own legitimizing ideology. Since the Islamic ethos is essentially universalistic and egalitarian, preaching the equality of all believers regardless of differences in wealth or occupation, it deliberately ignores the economic structure and minimizes its social significance, inhibiting the emergence of politics as class-defined. This, of course, coincides unerringly with the 'middle' ideology of the petit-bourgeoisie which characterizes the army régimes of the Middle East, and whose growth is so stimulated by the expansion of the state machine and the state-directed economy. It was populism in the service of the army-run corporate state. To those who pressed for democratic structures, for institutionalized forms of parti-cipation, rather than Gadafi's style of guided democracy by public session, and for a political programme representing the needs of the people, Gadafi's riposte was 'You are imagin-ing the people. You talk about the people, but what do you know? *We* are the people. The Free Officers, the sons of poor families, were the embodiment of the people. Power that accrued to them meant power to the people.' It was the Nasserite form of populism as an ideology, as a political movement, and as a legitimation of the power of the RCC.

But Gadafi went further than Nasser, the grand exemplar of state-initiated politics, in seeing politics as true religion controlled by the religious state:

Question: You are a true Moslem, Mr President. What is the role played by religion in your private life ? What is the relation between your religious consciousness and the political decisions you have made ?

Gadafi: There is no contradiction between religious consciousness and political decisions.[23]

Gadafi's view of religion as politics meant that setbacks to the Arab cause were attributable to human corruptibility, to a failure of true belief, to a departure from the moral principles of Islam. This approach reduces social and political action to the level of spiritual commitment, and the pursuit of policy to a highly individual crusade. While few if any of the army officers around Gadafi shared his religious zeal, their notion of politics was likewise religious rather than secular. In Gadafi's view there was only one source of truth. 'Here,' he told the *Le Monde* correspondent,

read the Koran or re-read it. You'll find the answers to all your questions. Arab unity, socialism, inheritance rights, the place of women in society, the inevitable fall of the Roman empire, the destruction of our planet following the intervention of the atom bomb. It's all there for anyone willing to read it.[24]

Politics was reduced to revelation and fervour; and statesman-ship to canny reading and memorizing of the texts.

The Gadafi style of religious philosophical debate was next institutionalized on the Supreme Council for National Guidance, which, together with the principal planning body, fell directly under the RCC and under Gadafi's chairmanship. On this body, mufti from many corners of the Arab world joined Libyans, hand-picked as usual, in a search for a philosophy of the revo-lution and a universal theory. It was on this body that *shar'ia* law, its interpretation according to the Koran, and its applic-ability to the modern world, were debated. Following these debates, the RCC promulgated a group of Islamic laws, including one for the punishment of thieves and armed robbers,[25] by the amputation of hand and foot. The law contained a battery of qualifying and exceptional clauses which made its general application unlikely, but it observed the principle that the letter of the Koran is as relevant today as it was in the seventh century; though amputation, according to Article 21, was to take place by medical methods including anaesthesia. There had been debate, even mild dissension, but solely within the context of state and religion being interchangeable, and the Koran as the basis of law; which meant that all was reduced to religious semantics. Did cutting off the hand of the thief in fact mean 'interrupting' the hand, as some argued, by removing tempta-tion, social pressure, and conversion, or did it mean amputation? Judges, mufti, newspaper columnists, and linguistic experts debated the issue on television. The most literal interpretation prevailed.

Soon Gadafi was ready to launch his Third Theory. It steered an alternate, middle course between capitalism and communism, but had essentially to be based upon religion. He propounded it not only for Libyans but for the Arab world and, indeed, the world as a whole.[26] The failures of the 'isms' of both east and west had given rise to the need for a new outlook. This was based on religion and nationalism, since these are the paramount drives that have moved history. (Marx's economic interpretation of history, he said, had been caused by the conditions of poverty in which he and his children lived in London 'where his food was given to him by his friend Engels'.) Without religion, people and states had no moral obligation. Islam was the ideal religion, but all who believed in God could share the Moslem belief, and distinctions between those who believed in the Prophet Mohamed or Jesus or any other apostle should be abandoned. Gadafi invested a great deal in the exposition of the Third Theory that he placed before an international youth conference in Tripoli during 1973. Apart from some small delegations from African states beholden to the Libyan régime for aid, its only apparent converts were in the delegation of French Gaullist youth who equated it with De Gaulle's theory of a third force but who were howled down by delegations from Guinea and Dahomey when they tried to present De Gaulle as the liberator of Africa. For the rest, delegations including those from Arab countries dismissed the theory, in private anyway, with derision as the musings of a petty religious philosopher.

By the time that the Third Theory had become the official philosophy, the popular or cultural revolution had been launched. This came as unpredictably as most of the RCC's major policy initiatives, at a public meeting in Zwara to celebrate the birthday of the Prophet Mohamed.[27] The revolution was in peril, Gadafi said. Libyan commandos sent to take part in the struggle for Palestine had been held back not by Israeli but by Arab soldiers. The front-line states had given up the battle, but Libya would not. In spite of repeated appeals to Libyan youth, they had not enlisted in the army. Ideal agricultural and resettlement schemes had been set up, but Libyans were refusing to work in remote parts of the country. University 'perverts' were engaging in subversive activities. 'I personally cannot allow any more of this irresponsible behaviour.' He suggested a five-point programme:

1 All existing laws must be repealed and replaced by revolutionary enactments designed to produce the necessary revolutionary change.
2 The weeding out of all feeble minds from society by taking appropriate measures towards perverts and deviationists.
3 The staging of an administrative revolution so as to get rid of all forms of bourgeoisie and bureaucracy.

4 The setting up of popular committees whereby the people might proceed to seize power. This was meant to ensure freedom for the people as against bureaucrats and opportunists.

5 The staging of a cultural revolution so as to get rid of all imported poisonous ideas and fuse the people's genuine moral and material potentialities.

Within days of the speech, two overlaying waves of arrests took place. In some instances individuals were denounced by Popular Committees, but the majority of the arrests were carried out by the secret police. University lecturers, lawyers and writers, employees of government ministries including the attorney-general's office and the Tripoli Chamber of Commerce, younger members of prominent coastal families – most of them, seemingly, individuals identified in the past with Marxist, Baathist, Moslem Brotherhood or other such political circles – were seized. There had never been any suggestion that 'factional' organization existed; the persecution was aimed at those who had not succeeded in identifying with the régime's system of state-run politics. The cultural revolution was against people who 'propagate poisonous ideas' alien to the Islamic origins of the Libyan people. The political prisoners were held *incommunicado*. Unofficial circles calculated that there had been as many as a thousand persons arrested; this, at the rate of one in prison for every 20,000 Libyans, made the country the most politically confined in the world.

Side by side with the arrests, popular committees appeared, mostly in university faculties and other educational institutions, to remove bureaucrats and 'passive and obstructionist elements'. Their actions were to be confirmed by the RCC; but meanwhile a tussle for control of the committees seemed to be developing between the Ministry of Education and the Arab Socialist Union. Some observers saw in the cultural revolution the first expression of popular initiative and the first attempts of the lowly to bring down hierarchies of authority. But popular committees were precluded from operating within government ministries, the bastions of bureaucracy. Student committees removed staff, censored textbooks, and tried to revise their courses; other committees pruned the stock of a few bookshops and demoted men from executive positions in para-statal bodies. In Benghazi students waded into the congestion at the docks and claimed to devise a system that would clear the backlog; Tripoli agricultural students marched out of classrooms and towards agricultural schemes on the land. It was difficult to know how sustained this movement would be, and what results it would produce, within the system of RCC supervision, and proceeding as it did side by side with police repression, and as one of its instruments.

By now Libya's internal security apparatus, modelled on Egypt's and installed by members of Egypt's *mokhabarat*, comprised several overlapping but autonomously directed intelligence machines. After the arrest of one group suspected of counter-revolutionary plotting, there had been disclosures of torture by soldiers commanded by Free Officers. (It was considered too dangerous to bring them to book, for this might split the army.) Less sensational but more pervasive was the system of informers and the emergence of groups of organized government supporters who played a strategic if sycophantic role: carrying out the tenor of Gadafi's speeches to the letter, and reporting to him only what they knew he wanted to hear. The popular committees had both a positive and negative aspect: on the one hand they might very well succeed in provoking a response from ordinary people within the limits of manoeuvre allowed by the RCC; but on the other, they could be equivalent to the security apparatus, denouncing and rooting out any who had doubts about the methods of the army régime.

Postscript. August 1973 was the last date for the formation of the cultural revolution's popular committees. After that the committees tended to be incorporated within the ASU, or to fall away altogether.

No trials were held of detainees. Some though not all of the political prisoners were released towards the end of the year, some after televised 'confessions' – though all insisted, after explaining their political convictions, that they had been active only until September 1969 and the army revolution of that date.

In August 1973 Gadafi had told Libyans they had 30 days in which 'anyone who still belongs to any organization can come forward and surrender himself, write to me by post. After the 30-day period I do not want anyone to come.' After that anyone who disrupted national unity, 'who seeks to dominate the people or society through a class or party will be considered a traitor subject to the death penalty'.

Wall poster of the cultural revolution:

Listen brother – all that this employee knows is 'come tomorrow', 'come after tomorrow': exchange him with a revolutionary employee.

9 The Economic Environment

In the first decade of its independence, Libya's main exports were esparto grass, used in paper-making, and scrap metal salvaged from the debris of the Second World War. It was the poorest nation state in the world. The colonial period had neglected industry and training and brought so few Libyans higher education that King Leopold's régime could claim a better record for the Congo at independence. Such agricultural investment as was undertaken on Libya's inhospitable soil was for Italians in the settler enclave, with Libyans virtually untouched except by neglect; much of the traditional economy had been dislocated by the punitive policy against the resistance. The war had torn up what infrastructure had been built. During the British and French military administrations, there had been almost complete standstill: no one was prepared to spend money on a no-man's-land, except to distribute grain against the famine which raged during and after the desert battles of 1940/43.

The country seemed by any standards an impossible case for development. It was an immense (680,000 square miles) stretch of land; but with the greater part desert, and only 2 per cent arable. There were hardly any people.[1] Economic life was concentrated round Tripoli and Benghazi and the oases in the Fezzan. These centres of population lay hundreds of miles apart, each isolated from the other in its own poverty and underdevelopment. To the polarities of town and country so characteristic of underdeveloped economies, Libya contributed her own dualisms: between the oases and the coast; between the nomadic Bedouin and the settled farmers; between corporate clan ownership and private property of the market economy.

International experts and consultants threw up their hands in despair. Libya, economist Benjamin Higgins reported to the United Nations in 1953,[2]

> has only one major untapped resource: the latent skills of its people. Raising the productivity of the Libyan economy must consist largely of improving the productive methods used by the people in their present occupations. The emphasis in the plan is accordingly on teaching Libyans to do better what they are already doing.

The total budget recommended for the first phase of economic and social development in this desolate land was £2,300,000 in 1952–3, with an additional £2,800,000 to be spent over the next five years. It was a bare survival operation.

Libya balanced her modest books by foreign aid, for it was only the military bases which paid her faltering way (p. 143).

The first so-called development agencies functioned under the direct supervision of Libya's foreign creditors. Thus the Libyan Public Development and Stabilization Agency (LPDSA), set up in March 1952 under the Libyan Public Development and Stabilization Agency Law of 1951, was run by funds paid over by Western governments, and its powers were vested in a board composed of members appointed by these same governments. It was this Board which gave final approval to the annual economic plan. LARC (the Libyan-American Reconstruction Commission) was set up in 1955 to supervise projects paid for by American money; this was the period during which grants direct from the United States government shot up to outstrip not only British subsidies but the combined total of subsidies from Britain and international agencies.[4] The Libyan government was barely consulted by the aid agencies, perhaps on the ground that as Libya could pay for nothing herself her intentions could safely be disregarded.

The World Bank surveyed the Libyan economy in 1958–9. Its report placed special emphasis on the development of agriculture – though its recommended programme entailed expenditures of barely over £1 million a year. But although the World Bank report was presented several months after the first major oil find, it seemed unable properly to evaluate the likely impact on Libyan agriculture, and its recommendations were based on

Libya Foreign Assistance 1950-65 in million £Ls[3]

	1950	1951	1952	1953	1954	1955	1956	1957	1958	1959	1960	1961	1962	1963	1964	1965
UK and French grants	1·35	1·46	2·23	1·92	2·91											
LPDSA			0·44	0·72	1·12	1·05	1·02	1·47	0·25							
UK Grain grants			0·25													
US technical assistance				0·17	0·19	0·22	0·26	0·26	0·26	0·22	0·22	0·22	0·22	1·85	1·00	0·82
US grants			0·64	0·50	1·52	6·15	4·62	5·89	5·61	11·20	10·85	6·92	6·86	5·44	2·93	0·91
UK grants						2·79	2·75	3·00	4·63	3·25	3·25	3·25	3·25	3·25	3·25	
Totals	1·35	1·46	3·56	3·31	5·75	10·26	8·66	10·63	10·75	14·71	14·32	10·38	10·33	10·54	7·18	1·75

Source: Bank of Libya 'Statistical Supplement', *Economic Bulletin*, Tripoli, July 1967.
(Note the heavy increase in grants in 1959 and 1960; these were the years when oil exploration was getting under way.)
Apparent discrepancies in some totals arise through the rounding off of some amounts.

entirely unrealistic assumptions. No sooner had it been written than the massive report of 524 pages dropped into oblivion.

With the coming of oil, the bilateral aid agencies were dissolved and replaced by a Libyan Development Council. The first development plan was for 1963–8. (It was extended for a further year to 1969 when the second plan was inaugurated, to be interrupted by the September coup.) As pipelines coursed through the desert, government revenues rose spectacularly. By 1966 there was, for the first time in the country's history, a surplus of revenue over expenditure. The closure of the Suez Canal induced a still more sensational rise in oil revenues. Beside oil money, Libya's other sources of revenue were derisory:

Summary of Government Revenues (million Libyan £s)

	Actuals				1970–71	1971–2
	1966–7	1967–8	1968–9	1969–70	Budget	Actual	Budget
Oil revenues	268·5	191·0	279·4	363·4	468·7	469·1	560
Non-oil revenues, including customs duties; rates; public utilities	53·3	58·5	79·1	83·6	77·6	82·7	72·3

The Libyan pound was renamed the Libyan dinar in 1969. There was no change of value.

Libya's economy had become one of the fastest growing in the world. At independence the average income of the population was £15 a year. By 1970, it had risen to close on £600 per head. As in Kuwait and Saudi Arabia, it was a precipitate leap from rags to riches. Suddenly this state began to accrue such handsome reserves that, however profligate, the country seemed unlikely to bankrupt itself.

Until oil, eight out of every ten Libyans lived as nomads or by agriculture. The country's modern farms were largely owned and managed by Italians, and Libyan agriculture was mostly subsistence, except for cereals and livestock, which produced marketable surpluses in good years. Rainfall determined agricultural production, which was thus both limited and unpredictable: so that there was substantial seasonal unemployment, and often more like permanent under-employment. In spite of this, agriculture was the backbone of the economy. It engaged about seventy per cent of the active labour force and produced about sixty per cent of the gross domestic product. Exports consisted mostly of agricultural products. When oil revenues became available, ambitious plans were made to develop the agricultural sector.

The consequences of oil for the economy have been graphically described by Ali Attiga, then Libya's Minister of Planning and Development.[5] He has shown how money supply increased rapidly, with this increase concentrated in the main urban centres. Whereas agriculture had been the only means of livelihood for the great majority of the population, oil opened up easier and more lucrative sources of employment. There was a rapid wave of migration from the countryside to the coastal towns. The rush for the proceeds of oil attracted far more people off the land than the oil industry could absorb. The result was crowded urban centres, but deserted farmland in many parts of the country. A side result was the sudden increase in the demand for food in the towns, as a result both of the increased urban population and of the extravagant consumption by foreigners in the oil industry. This might have been a strong stimulus to agricultural production but the low state of technology in agriculture was one of a number of factors which made this impossible. In any event, there were higher profits on investment in the trade and service sector of the economy. So both capital and labour continued to move away from agriculture.

'With this movement' writes Attiga,

Libyan agriculture was left to stagnate in its low level of development and the consumer turned to the world markets for the purchase of his daily food. Oil-induced prosperity provided him with essential income for such purchases and it also provided the country with the essential foreign exchange for significantly increased imports. At the beginning of oil exploration the total value of imported food and food produce was about £L0·5 million. By 1968 it was £L27·6 million. On the other hand agricultural exports had declined from a value of £L1·23 million in 1956 to £L600,000 in 1961, and to only about £L32,000 in 1968. This was not enough to pay for Libya's import of food for one third of a single day.

145

From here on the circle grew even tighter. Imported food became an easy alternative to the development of domestic agriculture. Increased incomes and prices brought about by oil made agriculture even more inefficient by increasing the cost of labour.

'Such a situation' this account continued,

clearly called for strong government intervention to subsidize agricultural production and protect rural income. But unfortunately such a policy could not be followed at the proper time because of two basic limitations. The first was simply lack of public funds, with which to support a large-scale programme of agricultural subsidies. The second was the necessity to keep food prices as low as possible, in the face of an inflationary situation, created by the injection of funds by the oil companies. As the Libyan consumer became more and more dependent on imported foodstuff, tariffs became less and less applicable as a means of protecting domestic agriculture. Moreover the Treasury was at that time heavily dependent on customs duties as a form of indirect taxation. Thus between 1955 and 1962, a situation was created in the economy which led to a drastic decline in traditional agriculture. At the same time the introduction of modern agriculture could not take place ... because the level of agricultural skills was low and the level of earnings and profitability was much lower, even on efficient farms, than they were in trade, services, and real estate. The government was unable to play a significant role in dealing with the situation, because it lacked the necessary skills and funds, as well as the determination to use fiscal measures to favour agricultural investment and discourage relatively unproductive activities, such as real estate speculation. Politically this was not feasible ... and technically it was difficult to use modern fiscal and monetary instruments to redirect the allocation of resources towards agricultural development ...

The result was the abandonment of traditional agriculture and nomadic activities in many parts of the country. Although the more modern farms ... and mainly operated by Italians, remained in production, their relative position in the economy was rapidly deteriorating. Thus, during the period 1956-62, the economic forces released by the discovery of oil produced their greatest adverse effect on agriculture. The latter simply could not withstand the great pressure of economic forces generated by the injection of substantial funds in the urban areas.

In the view of Libyan planners the worst effects of the impact of oil on agriculture were over by 1962, when the trend of agricultural production began slowly to be reversed. Agricultural output crept up very slightly, but its importance was almost imperceptible beside the oil sector which grew so much faster. Oil was now laying down the characteristic patterns of the economy, as seen in the disproportionate contributions of various sectors to the gross domestic product. Agriculture had shrunk dramatically. Manufacturing, as small as it had always been, had declined in relative importance, though in absolute figures its contribution to gross domestic product had increased.

Sectoral Contribution to Gross Domestic Product in Percentages[6]

	(at factor cost)	at constant 1964 prices		
	1962	1965	1968	1969
1. Agriculture	9·7	4·9	2·6	2·4
2. Petroleum and quarrying	27·2	54·8	61·3	65·0
3. Manufacturing	5·6	2·6	2·2	2·0
4. Construction	7·1	7·0	6·9	5·6
5. Electricity and gas	0·5	0·3	0·3	0·4
6. Transportation	5·5	3·8	4·0	3·6
7. Trade	8·6	5·1	4·6	4·1
8. Banking and insurance	1·1	1·4	1·2	1·2
9. Public administration and defence	9·7	7·4	7·4	6·8
10. Educational services	3·2	2·6	2·5	2·5
11. Health services	1·3	0·9	1·1	1·0
12. Ownership of dwellings	17·2	7·5	4·8	4·5
13. Other services	3·3	1·7	1·1	0·9
Gross domestic product	100·0	100·0	100·0	100·0

This pattern was hardly to change in the ensuing years except to confirm itself. Thus the 1971 government forecast figures were 70·9 per cent for petroleum; 2 per cent for agriculture; and 1·4 per cent for manufacturing.

By the middle of the 1960s, oil was providing funds on a scale that could in theory pay for a modernized agriculture; the problem was if and how this could be achieved. For whether this was recognized or not – and talking to planners and ministry officials active both before and after the September 1969 coup, I would say clearly that it was not – Libya was up against the peculiarly skew form of underdevelopment induced by the oil economy. Like the Middle-East oil-producing economies, she was afflicted with the wealth but also the problem of the rentier state.

Rentier states, according to H. Mahdavy who demonstrates the case of Iran,[7] are countries that receive substantial amounts of external rents on a regular basis, paid by foreign governments or foreign concerns. Payments for the passage of ships through the Suez Canal (allowing for the operating and capital costs involved) are external rents. The same holds for payments to countries in the Middle East that have oil pipelines through their territories. Above all, oil revenues received by governments of oil-producing and exporting countries are external rents. The distinguishing characteristic of the rentier state is that 'the oil revenues received by the governments of the oil-producing and exporting countries have very little to do with the production processes of their domestic economies. The inputs from the local economies – other than raw materials – are insignificant.' The turning-point in the economic history of the Middle East was during the 1950s when Anglo-American rivalries to control Middle East oil enabled governments in the region to appropriate a larger share of the rents that accrued to the oil companies as profits. The public sectors in the rentier states began to receive rents on a scale that affected the pace and pattern of their economies to a degree previously unknown. These governments could thus embark upon large public expenditure programmes without resorting to taxation and without running into drastic balance of payments or expenditure problems. Since oil revenues typically increase at a spectacularly faster rate than the gross national product of local economies, the public sector of these countries expanded rapidly. The government became the dominant factor in the economy – and out of this, significantly, a special form of *étatisme* was to grow.

On its own, extensive government expenditure, Mahdavy writes, is not enough to generate rapid economic growth; for all expenditures do not have equal growth effects. If most of the oil royalties or rentals are used to import goods for consumption, all the productive sectors of the economy will remain relatively untouched by such expenditures, however large. Government expenditures paid for by oil revenues need not produce any related expansion in the rest of the economy. For

> the danger that faces the Rentier state is that while some of the natural resources of these countries are being fully developed by foreign concerns and considerable government expenditures . . . are creating an impression of prosperity and growth, the mass of the population may remain in a backward state and the most important factors for long-run growth may receive little or no attention at all. And this will produce social and political stagnation and inertia . . . If the country is to become more than a producer of raw materials, and growth is to be sustained, then the entire socio-economic framework of the country has to undergo a transformation . . . The level of education of the population and their technological sophistication has to be raised considerably. Also the necessary political and administrative mechanism for mobilising national resources has to be devised. The oil revenues offer unusual prospects for development precisely because they can make certain short-cuts in socio-economic transformation and long-range economic development possible.

But as Robert Mabro shows in his application of the rentier state model to Libya,[8] it is these very short cuts that pose the dilemma for the oil state. Libya the looted state suddenly became Libya the wealthy rentier state, but the economy remained dependent and underdeveloped. This is because the hallmark of the rentier state is the generation of an expensive product by an industry that employs very few people and very few local resources, so that popular participation in productive economic activity is extremely low. There is no nexus between production and income distribution, since revenues accrue directly to the government not through any production but from oil taxes which come from outside the economy. Government expenditures and development programmes become totally dependent upon oil revenues. Consumption patterns become geared to the use of imported commodities. There are no links between the proceeds of production, effort, and incentive. The rentier state can achieve dramatic rises in *per capita* income without going through the social and organizational changes usually associated with the processes of economic growth. With technology static except in the oil industry and with little change in the country's social structures and in standards of education and training, prospects for long-run growth and development are gloomy. A consequence of the rentier state is that government reverses the usual development process, for instead of the usual progression from agriculture to industry to services, oil provokes the growth of the third, services, sector only, directly in the shape of all the ancillary services that the oil companies need: accommodation, pipelines and storage tanks, supplies to the desert and provision for the army of workers, foreign and Libyan; and then indirectly, since this sector also expands rapidly as government revenues purchase the advantages of development: housing, infrastructure, education, and administration. Why bother with productive investment when revenues are already guaranteed, the rentier state asks itself? Agriculture and industry therefore tend to stand still.

Growth in the tertiary services' sector is clear evidence of wealth, but it is not a condition for development. It might seem that oil offers unlimited industrial use in the shape of fertilizers, plastics, detergents, natural gas, and the whole range of petrochemical products. But, writes Mabro, the paradox is that it presupposes from the start a certain stage of development; and wealth is not a simple substitute. Oil's potential use is invaluable, but it also makes it difficult to handle: the technology, the know-how, the organization necessary for the exploitation of this versatile product, are highly complicated for a backward economy. The rentier state cannot straight away steer its efforts towards the development of its oil industry, for it begins the wrong way round, with the tertiary services sector. Development for an oil-producing country must lie in preparing the way and speeding up the shift from the rentier state to the producer state.

The solution is for Libya, the rentier state, to use its oil to buy time for the training of human capital. How did the monarchy use oil and time?

Once oil money was flowing abundantly, it was decided that 70 per cent of oil revenues should be allocated for development projects. It was on this basis that the first Five Year Plan was drawn in 1963. The government overspent heavily on this Plan:

Development Expenditure under First Five Year Plan 1963–4—1967–8 in £L millions

	Original plan	Actual
Agriculture	29·3	37·7
Industry	6·9	14·9
Transport	27·5	52·7
Works	38·7	87·5
Education	22·4	25·8
Health	12·5	8·7
Labour and social welfare	8·7	13·6
Housing	—	29·5
Interior	—	19·8
Other	23·3	0·3
Total	169·3	290·5

The concentration was on infrastructural projects. Thus in 1964 teams of advisers made inventories and plans for housing, transport, and urban and rural development. No fewer than 150 master plans were compiled in a great spurt of preparatory work for decision-taking. Roads and housing were a pressing priority, and the Idris building project was budgeted at £L400 million. Popular low-cost housing and schools began to go up in far-flung parts of the country, but there were criticisms: the housing was badly sited, in areas already abandoned by their populations; it was clustered in centres far away from farmers' fields; it was not suitable for Libyan ways of living. There was the scandal of Beida, the Brasilia of Libya, built from nothing for nothing. New roads were necessary; but why four- and six-lane highways in a country where traffic density is absurdly low? There was wastage especially in the funds lost to ill-fated agricultural projects and in the speculation scandals. Nonetheless, much of the expenditure of the first plan laid down the basement of the infrastructure that had been missing. The government was less successful when it came to the use of human capital; in fact, it started on a

ruinous policy which is the temptation before every rentier state.
Robert Mabro writes:

> Wealth brings the temporal horizon closer. It persuades people to
> call for miracles here and now, and strengthens the political pressure
> for immediate distribution. A government, even a very sensible one,
> will not always know how to resist. It often gives in and offers every-
> one direct or indirect means of consumption. A classic method is to
> offer every citizen who wants it a job. The size of the payroll increases
> beyond all measure ... for in order to avoid dangerous political
> discontents, the state multiplies the posts in its own bureaucracy ... in
> Libya the government smothered the administration with useless
> civil servants, workers, orderlies and watchmen. A job created by the
> state is often 'disguised unemployment' and the salaries paid to
> employees who scarcely work a disguised handout.

Mabro argues that while the state is obliged to improve living
standards even as it seeks routes to a developed economy less
dependent on oil, this is not a sensible policy. In Libya it led to a
serious manpower shortage, particularly in the building industry,
but also in agriculture. The state absorbed manpower just when
new sectors of construction and transport began rapidly to grow;
so creating artificial labour shortages and forcing the import of
foreign manpower. Government also encouraged inflation by
offering salaries higher than those paid by the oil companies. It
spread education but it also killed incentive and initiative. One
instance was immediate translation of graduates into bureaucrats;
and underemployed and under-used bureaucrats at that. Mabro
argues that there were essentially two ways in which Libya
could use her oil to overcome the awesome disadvantages she
had carried through history. One was to get more out of her oil
(by extracting it more slowly; or perhaps faster but for larger
shares of the profits) in order to buy time for development; the
other was to concentrate on developing Libya's human capital as
the sole key to real development. The monarchy failed on both
counts.

The second Five Year Plan had just been launched when the
Revolutionary Command Council took over. For some months,
even the greater part of the year following, the economy marked

time. Government departments were being reorganized and were slow to become operational, and alarmed investors hung back, while the projects of the development plan were frozen for scrutiny in the general crusade against corruption. Any projects connected with the Sanusi family were cancelled outright. Corruption, it was said, had so eaten into the plans of the previous régime that there was interest in large and ambitious projects only; smaller projects did not surrender a large enough percentage for the middlemen wheeler-dealers. The accusations of corruption were loud, though not a great deal was subsequently proven in courts, even in the trials of the men who were the principal supports of the régime; however it was common knowledge that oil companies, like other contractors, had used politicians and civil services for business. For a while there seemed to be a paralysis in decision-making and spending, prompted in part by what appeared to be the régime's phobia of being cheated by corrupt international business.

In mid 1970 the new régime produced a transitional one year development budget which was increased during the course of the year, though actual expenditure did not exceed the amount allocated because so much time had been lost in getting the machine operational again. The 1971–2 development budget allocated a sixth of its monies to agriculture and agrarian reforms; a fifth of this amount to water and soil preservation, and loans and subsidies to farmers. Industry had the second largest allocation, mostly on projects of the state National Industrial Corporation. For the first time there was an allocation for a state oil industry. Most of the pre-revolution projects were resumed. After this, regular forward planning of expenditure was resumed. A three year development plan for 1972–5 was announced and then converted into a rolling plan: overall expenditures for the total period were unaltered but re-allocation within its framework was undertaken year by year. A year after it came to power and when the economy was flushed with prosperity from the new oil revenues following the successful 1970 negotiations with the companies, the RCC decreed that any amounts accruing from the adjusted prices paid by the companies for the period 1965 to 1970 should be deposited in the reserve account. Also into that account went 15 per cent of total oil royalties each year. Of the remaining 85 per cent of oil royalties, 70 per cent was earmarked for development.[9]

A summary of government expenditure from 1966 to 1971 shows the trends under the two régimes:

Summary of Government Expenditure (In million L dinars)

	1966–7	1967–8	1968–9	1969–70	Budget 1970–1	Actual 1970–1	Budget 1971–2
Ordinary expenditure	112·6	166·4	238·6	199·1	182·8	193·8	200·7
Defence	17·3	11·1	14·2	21·4	30·0	33·7	30·0
Interior and municipal	16·7	25·9	33·2	33·8	31·0	30·4	35·3
Transport and communication	10·1	10·3	15·7	15·8	15·0	15·1	7·2
Education	20·5	24·5	39·1	42·9	43·8	49·9	46·3
Health	10·2	12·3	13·9	15·9	15·0	19·1	19·3
Special allocations	—	38·7	70·9	n.a.	n.a.	n.a.	n.a.
Other	37·8	43·6	51·6	69·3	48·0	45·6	62·6
Development expenditure	82·3	119·7	140·4	113·1	200·0	146·1	300·0
Agriculture	10·0	17·4	14·4	13·2	50·0	23·4	50·4
Industry	4·9	7·4	7·4	6·3	20·5	15·2	32·0
Oil	—	—	—	—	—	—	21·6
Transport and communication	9·3	19·6	24·2	14·5	27·2	12·2	39·8
Public works and electrification	16·9	39·4	38·1	23·6	18·4	18·8	53·3
Education	9·1	9·6	13·6	7·9	11·4	6·6	30·2
Health	2·1	5·5	4·9	2·9	5·9	4·9	17·0
Housing	11·6	17·9	18·2	27·5	32·8	34·0	40·0
Other	18·4	2·9	19·6	17·2	33·8	31·0	15·7
Total expenditure	194·9	286·1	379·0	312·2	382·8	339·9	500·7

Beginning from 1969, expenditure totals are understated, due to the exclusion of 'special allocations' for defence aid to Arab countries.

Source: Ministry of Planning, Tripoli.

Expenditures, like revenues, rose dramatically, and by 1971 were getting on for double the amounts spent five years earlier. The increases in ordinary expenditure on health, education, and local government administration follow the rising pattern of expenditure in almost parallel lines. When it came to the development budget, the amounts provided by the post-coup régime were markedly higher than allocations in previous years. Thus for agriculture there was five times as much budgeted for 1971–2 as there had been in 1966, and seven times as much for industry. There was to be heavy expansion of public works, electrification, transport, and communication; as well as heavy spending on health (mostly large new hospitals) and housing.

Social services received increased expenditure; and so did defence. In 1965 defence expenditure was £L8 million; the following year it almost doubled. But expenditures on defence were considerably understated, due to the exclusion of special allocations. Concealed defence expenditure was, of course, nothing new. From 1966–9 the transfers account showed growing deficits, accounted for principally by grants to other Arab countries. These were mostly payments made by Libya under the Khartoum Agreement of 1967 which rose from £L27 odd million that year to over £L42 million in 1969. In 1970 there was a slight decline in this amount, as a result of stopping the payments to Jordan; as again in 1971. In 1969 and 1970 Egypt received £L31 million, more than three quarters of the total paid out for these grants. It has been estimated that special allocations, mainly in the shape of aid to Arab countries, totalled £L71 million by 1968–9 and £L76 million by 1969–70. In addition to the special allocations, Libya's balance of payments data showed a rapidly increasing outflow under the item 'net errors and omissions'. This rose from £L6 million in 1967 to £L23 million in 1969, and then to £L65 million in 1970: or a tenfold increase in four years. There are no recent official data available on expenditures to Arab and African countries or for the purchase of special military hardware like Mirages.

By the time that the three year plan for 1972–5 had been launched, new sounds were being heard about development strategy. The plan projected an annual growth rate of 10·7 per cent. It might have been 20 per cent, said the official press release, but government policy was aimed at limiting oil produc-

tion so as to preserve the national oil wealth. (By now oil production had been cut back from daily production of 3·3 million
barrels a day to 2·2 million barrels; but the lower production
level was more than compensated for by the price rises
achieved in several rounds of bargaining with the companies.)
Since oil was a wasting asset, the Libyan economy had to be
induced to reach conditions of self-sustained growth independent of the oil sector, within a period of twenty years. Pride
of place was to be given to agriculture and to the building
of a modern industrial sector. The combined allocations for
industry, a petroleum industry, and electrification, totalled close
on £L400 million, or more than 34 per cent of the total planned
expenditure. This was a 50 per cent increase compared with the
amount allocated for industry and public works in the second
1969–74 development plan of the monarchy.

Development Plan
Allocation of £L millions

	1972–5	Percentage total
Agriculture and agricultural reform	165,000	14·2
Industrial and mineral projects	174 456	15·0
Petroleum	122,000	10·5
Electricity	103,000	8·8
Transport and communications	163,780	14·1
Education and national guidance	107,572	9·2
Public health	47,000	4·0
Labour and social affairs	16,125	1·4
Housing and utilities	124,762	10·7
Local administration	99,000	8·5
Tourism	8,600	0·7
Information and culture	15 410	1·3
Planning and management	4,600	0·4
Project reserve	13,690	1·2

Source: Ministry of Planning, Tripoli.

In the three year 'rolling' development plan which is to
spend £L1,200 million over three years, the productive sectors –
industry, agriculture, and electrification – are expected to grow
by 15 per cent. Petroleum's growth, on the other hand, has been

limited to 7 per cent, so that other sectors will replace income from oil in the shortest possible time. Libya is to be made self-sufficient in food and animal production. The Ministry of Agriculture is responsible for production on existing farming projects, but a newly formed Ministry of State for Agriculture has been given £L95 million over three years to reclaim and establish new farms on 550,000 hectares of new land. The country has been divided into four regions for purposes of agricultural development: Kufra and the area to the north of Ajdabiya; the Jebel Akhdar hill area and the Benghazi Plain in the east; the Jefara plain in the west and the Fezzan area. Each region will boast a complete regional development programme. Water supplies are a top priority. A series of ambitious projects are investigating re-routing water from the Nile into western Libya; a desalination project; a pipeline from the underground water supplies of the desert in the south. The Development Plan has also budgeted for a number of factories, to produce cement, shoes, glassware, cables and electric wiring, batteries, fish and tomato canning. There are 30,000 houses under construction and a scheme for 30,000 more. Eleven new hospitals are to be built and 28,000 classrooms. The Industrial and Real Estate Bank has been allocated £L28 million towards private construction loans. Under this Plan, Libya is to launch her petro-chemical industry with two refineries, one for home and one for export consumption; there is to be a government complex for gas processing; and the nucleus of a commercial and oil shipping fleet.* There are large harbour extension works at Tripoli, Misurata, and Derna; also projects for dams and public works. It is, once again, open season for foreign contractors.

If intention were decisive, Libya could be well on the way to becoming a developed country, as well as a rich one. But no one in government, save perhaps an odd harassed Planning Minister

---

* In April 1973 an increased development budget of £L1,965 million was announced for the period until the end of 1973, an increase of nearly 50 per cent over the revised three year budget issued four months earlier. The allocation for agriculture rose from £L240 million in the earlier plan to £L416 million. Allocations for industry and mineral developments were raised from £L174 million to over £L238 million.

and a handful of his experts, have grasped the need for, or been able to formulate, a concept of development to precede the expenditures.

Much that is characteristic about the styles of Libyan planning emerges from a broadcast live by Libyan Radio of a meeting between Colonel Gadafi and agricultural specialists. This was in October 1971, when the first year of parsimonious conservation of reserves was well over and spending was in full flood, especially on agriculture. Counting the recesses in between, the meeting lasted ten hours in all. Here, according to the report, is what happened:

The meeting was characterised by lengthy explanations by Qadhafi who began the proceedings by recommending that the object was to have a useful exchange of ideas. He impressed upon his listeners his own ideas about Libyan agriculture touching on such subjects as scientific soil studies, studies on potential sources of water, optimum use of cultivable land, agrarian reform, poultry raising, production of honey and bee-keeping, modern agricultural storage facilities, fodder, irrigation and portable water supplies, farm machinery, agricultural institutes, agricultural loans, farm manpower, farm co-operation societies, veterinary centres, animal husbandry and vineyard cultivation.

Agricultural specialists then put forward their proposals during an interlude of about four minutes after which Qadhafi resumed speaking until the recess at 11·16 GMT.

The second session, which began at 12·40 GMT, consisted of questions put by Qadhafi to various specialists and their answers on specific agricultural subjects, the emphasis being on the need to develop agriculture on a scientific basis, with Qadhafi frequently interrogating the speakers on how their proposals could be put into practice. The discussion continued on its way until 16·50 GMT.

In the last session, which began at 19·15 GMT, the problems of water and how to get it, well drilling and forestry were discussed. Qadhafi then listened to complaints from various people, and wound up the meeting, which ended at 22·36 GMT, by saying that the material discussed would be analysed by a committee and a report submitted to him for action.[10]

Every ministry has its shelf of expert reports commissioned by one or other or both of the régimes. Advisers are falling over one another; consultants swarm all over the country. Expertise and consultancy hire is often an adjunct of foreign policy; where this is to give each of the big powers a showing and also to spread good relations and business between a scatter of small states and so-called neutrals, the expertise in the field has this same patchwork quality. At one point several different teams were investigating underground water resources,[11] some working the identical region, and each apparently ignoring previous work done in the field. Some advice is good; some bad; most of it goes uninterpreted and uncoordinated. There have been experts on long-term secondment to ministries who have tried to evaluate the advice of consultants and to impress on government some over-arching concept of long-term development. But they are told that the analysis of expert advice and projection of planning priorities falls into the realm of policy-making. So the experts are herded off to their calculating machines and their blueprints and the Council of Ministers, but effectively the RCC, once again, takes over. In this body there is neither conceptualization of the development process nor the technical expertise to measure one set of proposals against another. If experts have no power of decision, neither do the trained planners in the ministries. At various times Colonel Gadafi has convened sessions of the planning departments of his economic ministries, and international experts have even on occasion been invited to meetings of the RCC devoted to planning, but his presence and his style have turned these encounters into a political forum. In any case long-term planning needs to be undertaken consistently and at working level, and not in fits and starts to suit the political exigencies of the day.

The story of how the 1970–71 budget was produced shows how makeshift much of the planning has been. Each government department was instructed to outline its projected activity for the following year, together with its estimate of manpower and budget requirements, the relationship of one project to another, and to sources of raw material. The intention was that the individual plans would then go to the central planning authority for study and coordination. But the individual ministry plans were delivered too late for the central planners to do more than superficial pruning and to list them in sequence. In this condition, the draft plan was forwarded to the RCC, which reduced the budget by 15 per cent and sent it back again. The previous budget had run its term on a surplus of cash and a crippling shortage of technicians; its successors will probably do the same.

This style of planning has encouraged every ministry to flex its spending muscles over as many projects as it can reach. Anywhere else but in an oil-rich state, the planner's dilemma is to squeeze projects to fit the budget; in Libya ministries go in search of projects on which to spend their money. The legal requirement for the percentage of revenue to be spent on development now serves not to guarantee minimal spending on development projects but to stimulate already feverish spending to new heights. If development means spending, the race is on. The pattern of ambitious ministries fostering ever more ambitious schemes is now institutionalized procedure in Libyan planning.

One of the technical obstacles to long-range planning in Libya is that there is as yet no complete inventory of national resources. Agriculture remains the principal employment sector, yet those planning for it lack the most basic information. The only agricultural census (conducted with the doubtful assistance of the Food and Agriculture Organization) in 1960 presented a detailed count of every goat, camel, and crop, region for region, in that year. But in a climate where harvests rise and fall dramatically according to the rainfall, one year's findings are useless. Virtually nothing is known of the contribution made by the subsistence sector of the economy. The relation of outputs to inputs in a heavily subsidized agriculture is crucial: and except for the university team survey in 1968, of which no official notice was taken, nothing is known of this for the country as a whole. A large part of agricultural extension planning depends on underground water resources, but these are only beginning to be assessed. The experts are in the field but their prognostications on the effects of deeper drilling and new resources should surely precede and not follow the extension plans and budget allocations. The second Five Year Plan which fell away when the new régime arrived had included a long section on manpower. Its projections were made totally invalid after 1969 by the expulsion of the Italians, who had monopolized capitalist farming and much of commerce, and supplied the majority of the skilled artisans in the cities; by the evacuation of the bases (Wheelus alone employed over 5,000 men); and by the influx of foreign labour to staff the projects that mushroomed once the new development plan was in operation. Subsequent manpower surveys were based on partial samples only. Planning was being done without any close knowledge of the manpower situation.

Pressure from the ministries caused the census due in 1974 to be brought forward a year. This census will at least enumerate all employment establishments and not only those listed as 'large', for the vast majority are anything but large. Meanwhile the condition of the private economic sector is virtually unknown. Retail trade statistics have covered Benghazi and Tripoli only; the rest of the country has gone unassessed. Such statistics as are available are incomplete. Often definitions and sampling methods have changed from year to year; which makes comparison difficult. It is virtually impossible to discover what has happened to the expropriated Italian businesses. The census department battles against a backlog of incomplete statistics, and many hopes hang on the new census. But even here, impatience and technical incomprehension at the top force unrealistic targets on those below. It is feared that the date for the census will be upon the country before adequate preparation for it has been made. Yet in other respects there is meticulous attention to detail. Ministries are now using accounting procedures for keeping the RCC posted with periodic progress reports of every single project in the Plan. Thus in six-monthly follow-on reports, a factory is recorded as having made 12 or 24 or 57 per cent progress; but such merely means that this proportion of the allocation has been spent. There is very real concern about the rate of growth, and a great impatience to speed it up.

It is said, perhaps apocryphally, of the complaint by a Minister of Planning under the previous régime, that in the country's expectancy of miracles after oil wealth there was no time to plan. Ministries were under constant pressure to spend and had neither time nor strength to prepare properly. Spending had to be seen to be done. This is probably even truer under the army régime. Major Jalloud, then minister in charge of production, now Prime Minister, told a press conference of foreign correspondents the reason why. It was natural, he said, for any military group to produce economic and social plans for a radical change: so as to convince the people and the world at large that it was not a movement aiming only at a seizure of power. This was the way army leaders could prove that they had led not a military coup d'état but a revolution. But such is really the central issue: has there been a radical change? is it a social revolution? are the economic policies of the new régime a departure from the economic strategy of the previous government or a continuation of it, however accelerated?

Every extravagant planning decision has committed the country to long-term spending and helps to skew its growth in a certain direction. Yet there is as yet no clear overall perspective for long-term planning. On paper there is a rich range of options. Agriculture or industry? Import-substituting industry or a petro-chemical complex? Horizontal or vertical agricultural expansion? A hydrological and technological revolution for mechanized agriculture? Or a concentration on the provision of jobs in the towns, since a reversal of the rural–urban drift is unlikely? Should Libya's economic development, in Robert Mabro's terms, follow the sequence of oil revenues – services – manufacturing, rather than the usual progression of agriculture – industry – services? If some or all of these issues have been discussed at top level, the outcome has been to opt for all directions at once: which, in planning terms, is no direction at all. The idea seems to be that money can buy anything, and that more than enough money can buy everything. Often, though, one gets the uneasy feeling that these young men of the new régime have not got to grips with the problems of their own country.

By 1970 agriculture's contribution to the gross domestic product had fallen to less than 3 per cent, though a third of the labour force was still living on the land. The stagnation in agricultural production precipitated by the oil boom, when labour and capital fled to more profitable sectors, continued as this decade opened. Less than five per cent of the country's arable land was under irrigation (only 165,000 hectares in all). Many land holdings were below the optimum size for effective economic exploitation.[12]

Unlike most Arab countries under the Ottoman empire, when the Land Code of 1858 abolished collective land ownership and began the registration of land on an individual basis, Libya did not experience the emergence of large private estates, and of a tenant, sharecropper, or agricultural class working for absentee landlords. Intermittent and unstable Ottoman administration over Tripolitania meant that the transition from communal to individual ownership did not start until the end of the nineteenth century and was carried out on an egalitarian basis, with the consequence that the area presents a picture of excessive fragmentation and dispersion of land holdings. Hilal[13] considers that the absence of extensive irrigation works such as exist in Egypt and Iraq, and the economic and political weakness of the urban centres (by 1911 less than six per cent of the population lived in Tripoli) probably discouraged investment in land.

Under the Italian occupation, land seizure and usage were carried out strictly for purposes of Italian settler colonization and not by any native urban or political élite as happened elsewhere, where rural populations were transformed by the extension of market relationships and by the replacement of subsistence farming by production for the market.[14] By 1968 about half the Italian farmland had been bought, mostly in small lots, by Libyan farmers, with the assistance of a government agricultural reclamation authority.[15] But many of the government's agricultural projects were less farms than subsidized housing settlements in the countryside. The majority of family breadwinners on some schemes were government officials commuting to their work in government offices. Many who had made money in the oil boom bought former Italian farms, but they bought them not to farm but to beat inflation. Large sums were spent on subsidies and schemes that proved unproductive.

In the mid sixties, Libya and London universities combined

to conduct a detailed research project into Libyan agriculture and the changes that had come over it since oil. The report shows that given even optimal conditions, farming in Libya remains strongly inhibited by nature. Scanty rainfall is only in part compensated by drawing on underground water reserves; and while some new water is being located, this is remote from agricultural areas. Climatic and soil conditions mean that a great deal of investment is needed for any expansion of agricultural output. The government had paid out generously. In this period of heavy expenditure on agriculture, there was some development. It was a slow, almost imperceptible, 1 per cent growth rate a year, but it was a move forwards rather than backwards. (This contradicts the cry of the revolution that all was neglect under the monarchy.) But this agricultural improvement, the report showed, had been achieved at the cost of declining water resources. Water levels had dropped most steeply since oil revenues had paid for loans to farmers for irrigation equipment. There thus arose a twofold danger of water being driven down to uneconomic underground levels; and, equally important, of the balance of salt and fresh water being disturbed and coastal water resources permanently impaired. These were rather unpalatable findings, since they suggested that any overall development perspective would find it necessary to scale down agricultural extension.

Declining underground water levels were thus likely to prove a serious constraint in the most rewarding agricultural areas. (The new régime has recognized the fact of declining water resources in the Jefara, especially round Tripoli, and is directing development elsewhere. But there is no water law, and private exploitation goes on as before, with many new wells being drilled.) Another constraint, the report said, was the shortage of labour. Agricultural labour had become increasingly scarce, and agricultural wage rates so high that few farmers had been able to pay them. Libyans had found more rewarding occupations in the towns and Tunisian workers had to be called in for peak seasonal activities and also for regular cultivation. Perhaps, one of the researchers suggested, the rising cost of labour would be in the best interests of the long-term development of Libyan agriculture. High labour costs would force farmers – and planners – to develop only those areas which had a long-term potential, and which were without important physical limitations. It is at this point that government changed.

One of the first acts of the new régime was the expulsion of remaining Italian settlement. The RCC promulgated a decree restoring all property usurped during the colonial period, whether agricultural land, real estate, livestock, or machinery. This was placed under sequestration to the state. A decree also banned the issue of licences or permits to Italians to practise commerce, industry, or professions in Libya. Within a month the Italians began to depart: leaving behind a number of small businesses and workshops which were put up for purchase by Libyans, and 368 farms spread over 38,000 hectares. This land was placed under the authority of a body for Land Reclamation and Reform. The same department was already responsible for the acreage that had been the concern of NASA, and it was charged with managing and developing all agricultural lands under government control; with reclaiming and developing desert land; and with developing rural communities and agricultural cooperatives. The government was flooded with applications for the Italian farms, but they were divided into sixteen projects and allocated to the control of Libyan agricultural managers. The first graduates of the College of Agriculture had just qualified; their postings in charge of the farms were announced over the radio. The plan was to prepare model settlement schemes for Libyans, as Italy had once done for her nationals. Once it had been decided which farms were economic, for they varied in size from half a hectare to 1,500 hectares each, and how they would be subdivided, the lands would be planted, the farmhouse built and made ready, and only then would the farmers be invited in to reap the crop and qualify for the range of subsidies and agricultural assistance. The quip about ENTE's settlement schemes in the colonial days had been that the settlement farms were complete even to the box of matches on the kitchen table; Libyans would receive no less. For the first fifteen years government would retain title to the land; after that, it would be available for purchase. Cooperatives were talked about, but there was no strong policy favouring them; more likely a class of farmer proprietors would be encouraged.

The debate about the place of agriculture in overall development planning took place within a small circle of Ministry officials and university agricultural specialists; the latter gravitating from Ministry to their faculties and back again, depending on the shifts in both agricultural and academic politics. Some Libyan agriculturalists are fanatical advocates of farming at all costs. 'If we worship God,' one told me, 'next to religion is agriculture.' Gadafi clearly feels the same way. Agriculture is a duty. The other side argued that it was a romantic notion for people to be kept on the land at all costs. It was, in any case, too late. Services taken to the countryside required enormous social investment; it would be cheaper to have piped water and electricity in expanded towns than spread over thousands of villages. It was essential, they said, to clarify priorities for agriculture, since there had always been yawning gaps between planning and performance, with the budget for agriculture consistently under-used, and there were important reasons why. It was all very well plotting settlements on the map; but would there be farmers on the spot to man them? The sons of farmers who had migrated from countryside to towns were unlikely to return as farmers, for the cash rewards were so much less. The graduates of the agricultural colleges were not farmers but administrators.

It was important not to make unrealistic assumptions about agricultural potential. The debaters ranged themselves into the vertical and horizontal schools. The verticals argued, on grounds of manpower shortage, for raising the productive level of land already under cultivation: concentrating on proved areas round Tripoli, Wadi al Ajal in the Fezzan, and the Jebel Akhdar; on pilot schemes for better use of seed, pest control, fertilizers, and mechanization. The horizontals advocated the extension of agriculture in all possible directions at the fastest possible pace, in order to spread investment to the farther-flung regions for social – and no doubt political – considerations.

Of the grand new agricultural schemes, Kufra is the most prestigious. The Kufra story goes back to 1966, when Occidental

Oil Company tendered for the country's most promising oil concessions and won them with its related promise to plough back 5 per cent of its profits into the economy: through developing the water deposits in the Sahara whose discovery seemed as felicitous as the company's prolific oil finds. In fact the existence of this huge body of underground water had been known for some time. All experts agree that, as fossil water, it is not recharging and cannot be replenished. Some say, however, that this deep underground reservoir in the Nubian sandstone is so vast as to provide supplies for centuries. Others argue that the level of water has fallen in recent decades, that an isotope test to establish more exactly the age of the water is necessary before long-term development projects are initiated, and that none of the feasibility studies thus far undertaken have answered the crucial questions about the life and supply of the water. Having drilled the wells to reach the underground water, Occidental's pilot project was an exercise in hydroponics. The soil is devoid of organic matter, but careful balancing of soil, water, and chemicals by highly skilled imported technicians, some from desert 'miracles' in Arizona, grew several hundred acres of lush green alfalfa. Sheep were flown in by the Libyan air force to feed on the crop, and the desert agricultural project seemed launched on an experimental basis at least.

By the time that the Gadafi régime came to power, it was known that Occidental was not eager to continue with the Kufra scheme. The future of foreign capital seemed uncertain, and though excited estimates of the watery miracle had appeared in the world's press, the economics of the scheme had always been vague, and no accurate estimates for commercial exploitation had been made.

The first official visit to Kufra was six months after the RCC seizure of power, when the Minister of Agriculture came to see if the scheme looked as good as it was described. He was doubtful about the economic feasibility of the project. But by the end of the weekend Occidental management was told that the project was to be nationalized by the government. That week the Minister of Agriculture was not available for clarification; it was clear that this decision had been taken at a more elevated level.

For five months the future of the scheme hung in the air. The Ministry of Agriculture did not want to inherit the ambitious scheme without a comparable budget. Indeed, it was aghast at the prospect of having to tackle the scheme at all, and as the ministries of Agriculture and Petroleum bandied finance issues from one to the other, Occidental executives had to force the pace so as to get a follow-up to the original nationalization decision. The government take-over became official in mid July. Occidental bowed out except for two senior experts seconded to the government, and the project was put in the hands of the Kufra Agricultural Project Authority, a newly formed state agency under the Ministry of Agriculture. The period of indecision was over. It emerged that the key role had been played by a young army officer and close associate of the RCC who had been stationed in Kufra. He had persuaded Gadafi himself to visit the project. The visit had been the turning-point. From this time on, agriculture in the desert became central to development plans. Large sums were voted for the Kufra scheme, and ambitious expansion plans demanded; when these were delivered, the RCC pressed constantly for their still further expansion.

Irrigated by an advanced system of pivot sprinkler units, this mechanized farming deep in the desert is to serve as a huge-scale lamb breeding and slaughter factory, with the aim of making Libya self-sufficient in meat. Western expertise called in on contract to scrutinize the project – a feasibility study was undertaken when it was already operational – has called it 'unique', 'remarkable', and 'technically feasible': though desert agriculture of the magnitude contemplated for Kufra has never been undertaken in a comparable environment. Are there no problems? Indeed, there are, say the experts. The project must be allowed to operate with minimum hindrance – in procuring personnel, equipment, and supplies, and contracting for construction and services – from other echelons of government; otherwise the delicate logistics operation involved will surely fail. Thus wrote one report:

Under present conditions of industrial and agricultural development in Libya all production inputs for irrigated agriculture including fertilisers, pesticides and improved seeds must be imported largely from Europe and North America. The same goes for all farm machinery, sprinkler irrigation equipment, spare parts and supplies including even baling twine. Any interruption in supply would mean massive crop losses and would disrupt the sheep production programme.

As for skilled personnel, in principle the recruitment of qualified management and expertise provides no insurmountable problem. At a price, that is. The experts have cautioned government that costs of training and recruitment will appear exorbitant compared with costs for other development projects in the country; but without the right personnel, the project could prove a complete failure. In other words, given enough money and the readiness to purchase foreign skills and supplies at any cost, the scheme might work.

Critics have likened the Kufra project to shooting pigeons with rockets. Push-button mechanized farming in the desert is excellent for prestige; but, they ask, has anyone worked out the price to the Libyan housewife of a pound of mutton? Will the project pay in ten years, or fifteen? And meanwhile what effect will this massive sheep-breeding project have on livestock husbandry in the rest of the country? The strongest argument against the project is its inaccessibility. For two thirds of the journey from the coastline to the central Sahara, there is no road or marked track. Huge trucks shuttle between Benghazi and Kufra, but at heavy cost and with heavily reduced working life, over the desert route. Refrigerated trucks could travel along a road if there were one; but construction costs would be prohibitive. Air freight is the alternative, but equally costly; though the scheme's advocates argue that Libya flies imported meat from Bulgaria, so why not from Kufra? The decisive factor will be the flow and cost of expertise and labour. Libyan graduates look to executive posts and professional life in the towns and are not coming forward to live in desert trailers with leave at the coast only once or twice a month. Like the oil industry, Kufra will be a slice of technology inserted into a backward economy and, like oil, run by foreigners. Those who make policy believe that cost is no object and that the country must break dependence on food imports at all costs. But this dependence is being exchanged for a new dependence, on the West's advanced technology. In the Libyan desert, oil is being traded for agriculture on a scale that only oil revenues could afford. It is a combination of the extravagant spending momentum of the oil economy together with the army cult of management and technology. Since Kufra became a priority of the development plan, a second and similar scheme, but twice as large again, has been projected for the Sarir area 200 miles north of Kufra; a hydrological study is now in progress.

Under the latest Plan almost 3,000 farms are projected for allocation to farmers. Farmers would be eligible for long-term loans and subsidies. The Agricultural Bank purchases surplus products – like groundnuts during 1972 – to stop the price from falling. There are ambitious plans for afforestation and pasturage improvement. Milking cows have been imported from Denmark, and Danish experts with them to begin a cow-breeding programme; two dairy plants to process milk products are to be established. Two new agricultural colleges are being opened, one in Sebha and the other near al-Marj, and students have been sent for training to Egypt. Meanwhile there are plans for thousands of miles of agricultural roads to link agricultural regions with marketing centres. 'All this,' the Ministry says, 'is bound to result in increasing production and income of farmers, and the creation of new incentives to farmers to remain on their lands, which is one of the main objectives of the development plan.'

Libya has virtually no industry. By the time that the Gadafi régime came to power, there was a tobacco factory in Tripoli employing 500 workers; two textile factories in Benghazi; a gypsum factory in Tripoli, with barely more than fifty workers; small plants for the processing of macaroni, olive oil and fizzy drinks, detergents (on foreign patents), and tomato canning. There was one cement factory. The construction industry, like the rest of the economy, relied on imports; and a sack of cement grew perhaps four times in price on its journey from coastline to interior.

The new government's industrial policy was outlined in a

decree of April 1970. Large-scale and medium industry, especially in the fields of oil, gas, agricultural processing, and construction materials, was to be reserved to the public sector. A state-run Industrial Corporation was put in charge of the public sector projects. Under the Three Year Plan, eighteen new factories are under construction. These projects are considered beyond the capacity of the private sector to finance, and in any case their timing is crucial to the progression of the development plan. (Ministry officials complain that it took four years for private capital to establish a cement factory, although government had provided 80 per cent of the finance.) The private sector is expected to concentrate on small industry, possibly some medium-size, and on retail trade. Foreign minority participation is permitted in industry which needs or uses the latest technology or produces for the export market.

Lest the reservation of a sector of industry is not considered inducement enough by private investors, large sums have been allocated to the Industrial and Real Estate Bank for interest-free loans. The private sector is also offered generous tax exemptions, protective tariffs, and exemption from duty in the import of machinery and raw materials. But in a year (1969–70) in which government allocated £L3·5 million in the form of subsidies to private investors in industry, less than a third was spent. The private sector remains hesitant about its place in an economy run in the name of a revolution, and confused about the relations between the private and public sector.

Public- or private-sector emphasis for Libya? Both, according to Premier Jalloud.[16] A decree stipulates that in the transport sector, no private owner should operate more than three trucks. Yet in the construction industry, private capital is being given a free run. Contractors and real estate investors are offered generous government loans, and control has been lifted so that they may recoup capital in record time. Some taps in the private sector are turned off; others on. On the land the expropriation of the Italian farms, many of them highly productive, offered an opportunity for the development of large-scale cooperatives or public sector farms, but even the larger farms are being divided into plots for private ownership. Policy towards the public and private sector is haphazard and *ad hoc*: demonstrating once more absence of a comprehensive development strategy. Meanwhile private capital hesitates. Businessmen watch to see which way government will blow over industrial projects and the control of private enterprise. Some, it is said in Tripoli, no longer deposit their money in bank accounts, for the memory is still fresh of the frozen bank accounts of those suspected of doing business with the previous régime.

Until 1969 the public sector did not extend beyond the government tobacco factory, a cement factory in which the Ministry of Industry had a share, and an oil processing factory run by the Agricultural Bank. The new régime's first nationalization measures, in November, were directed against foreign-owned banks. These were two Italian banks, one Egyptian, and Barclays. The latter had established itself in the footsteps of the Eighth Army as the armed forces' bank, and had successfully withstood the pressure under the monarchy for Libyanization; by 1970 it held over a quarter of the assets in Libyan banks. Rather than offer majority control to the Libyan government, Barclays preferred to pull out altogether. The bank nationalization law stipulated that no Libyan could own shares exceeding £L5,000. The government became the majority shareholder in all the banks.

In 1970 insurance companies were placed under government supervision and control. The Libyan National Insurance Company, which was completely Libyan-owned, had to cede 60 per cent of its holding to government. Branches of foreign insurance companies were given a year to liquidate their operations and to convert, like the Libyan companies, into joint-stock companies with majority Libyan and part government holdings.

In the same year, government nationalized – without compensation – all petroleum distribution facilities within the country There was also the BP nationalization,* undertaken as a political reprisal for the British government's role in the Gulf.

Major infrastructural projects of the Development Plan are supervised by the public sector but have been contracted to foreign firms. Kufra's well-drilling is being carried out by a Libyan contracting firm, the only one of its size, but the consult-

* For later nationalizations see the chapter on oil.

ancy firm supervising the drilling and carrying out further technical studies for the expansion of the project is American. The contract for the supply of turbine pumps and petroleum engines was won by a Libyan–Syrian company. The hydrological survey in the Sarir area to the north of Kufra is in the hands of a British company. In the Ghadames area the search for water is being conducted by a French part-government consortium. Egypt's state land-reclamation authority is in charge of a government model farm project in the Jefara plain, and an Egyptian company is searching for underground water in Fezzan. Tripoli's £L20 million harbour extensions have gone to a Turkish contractor; the Zawia oil refinery to an Italian firm. West German interests are involved in desalination and electrification projects. Yugoslav contractors are building dams. It's a recognizable international division of labour, with Libyan oil paying the bills and international firms supplying technology and reaping the profits.

By 1972 Libya had an estimated labour force of just over half a million.

	In thousands		
Total labour force	557		
Libyan	477		
Foreign labour	80		
Employment by sector:	*Total*	*Libyan*	*Non-Libyan*
Agriculture, forestry and fishing	163·5	154·8	8·7
Petroleum and gas production	11·5	7·8	3·7
Other mining and quarrying	6·9	6·0	0·9
Manufacturing	38·8	30·2	8·6
Electricity and water	7·3	6·6	0·7
Construction	60·5	29·6	30·9
Trade, restaurants and hotels	38·3	35·8	2·5
Transport, storage and communications	51·9	50·3	1·6
Financing, insurance and business services	5·7	4·9	0·8
Public administration	88·7	85·8	2·9
Educational services	40·5	33·1	7·4
Health services	21·3	17·1	4·2
Other services	22·1	15·0	7·4

This shows that for every six Libyans in the labour force there is one non-Libyan; and the figure for foreign labour is considered to be a strong under-estimate.

It has proved impossible to get figures for Egyptian labour in Libya, despite – or perhaps because of – the projected unified state. A Labour Ministry estimate of Tunisian labour, mostly agricultural and seasonal, was put at 40,000 during 1973, but this is probably an over-estimate.*

It is estimated that of the total number in employment, 62 per cent are wage or salaried employees and the rest farmers, proprietors, tradesmen, craftsmen, and family workers.

There have been two recent (1972) census reports of government employees. One provided a total of 104,000; and the second, conducted by the Civil Service Department's Control Bureau and probably the more accurate, 134,560. But because neither the army nor the police force are included, the total of those on the government payroll is far higher. The break-down of government employment into professional, technical, semi-skilled and unskilled labour is revealing for the dependence of the administration on highest grade foreign skills:

Professional	8,980	of which	3,890	are non-Libyans
Technical and supervisory	33,307	,,	6,333	,,
Clerical	17,500	,,	478	,,
Skilled and semi-skilled	31,981	,,	495	,,
Unskilled	38,694	,,	18	,,
Non-specified	4,098	,,	86	,,
	134,560		11,310	

Source: Labour Survey UNDP–Libyan government 1972; preliminary results

Is there an industrial working class? The Census Department produces quarterly statistics on production and employment in 'selected large manufacturing establishments'. 'Large' means any establishment engaging twenty or more persons: and there were just over 200 such establishments in the country.[17] Many

* An estimate of 250,000 foreign workers, or one eighth of Libya's total population, is given by Ragaei El Mallakh, 'Industrialization in the Middle East: Obstacles and Potential'.

of these offer seasonal work only, as in canning factories. By 1970 there were 7,306 workers in manufacturing, most of them operatives. (The figure included 155 working proprietors and unpaid family workers.) Of this total, 1,550 were in food processing factories, and 1,135 in tobacco factories. Other industries in which a total of more than 500 persons were employed were textiles; chemical products; cement; and fabricated metal, though not machinery. The 1964 census reported that the average number of workers employed per enterprise was 1·7. This is family production rather than manufacturing.

Additionally, 13,701 were employed in construction: the majority (7,451), non-Libyans. (Of Libya's sixty-eight construction firms that year, twenty-four were foreign-owned.) As in the economy as a whole, the majority of professional, technical, administrative, executive, and supervisory workers were foreigners, and the majority of Libyans worked as unskilled workers.

The oil industry employed just under 13,000 persons in all; 6,478 employed by the oil concession-holding companies, and 6,391 by companies providing services to the oil industry. In the oil companies proper Libyan workers constituted 66·5 per cent of total manpower, and this figure is being pushed up in the government drive for Libyanization.

Manpower remains the straw that could break the back of the government's development plans. There is a large and growing shortage of skilled and trained labour. A third of the trained posts in the civil service are unfilled. Every new development project compensates for the shortage of Libyan manpower by recruiting foreign labour. Yet paradoxical as it may seem, a hidden surplus of labour does exist in Libya. Its reallocation to crucial sectors where workers are in demand could contribute to economic growth, except that the labour bottleneck is a consequence of deliberate government policy, begun by the old régime but continued by the new, as one of the peculiarities of the rentier state.

The recorded labour force at the time of the 1964 census was slightly less than 26 per cent of the population, which is low. The participation of children was smaller than in most developing and Middle East countries, though in part this was due to the expansion of schooling. The participation of women was almost negligible. But the labour force itself was not fully employed. This, Robert Mabro shows,[18] meant that institutional forces were interfering with the proper functioning of the labour market. In most oil-producing countries of the world, it is the oil industry – whose wage bill is tiny in relation to profits – that is the wage leader. Not so in Libya. Typical hiring rates for un-skilled labour in the oil sector are lower than in agriculture and than in all other sectors of the economy. Before the oil era, wages in agriculture were very depressed, and the rural–urban wage differential, though small, favoured the slowly emerging modern sector. In 1956, when the oil companies started exploring, they offered employment at wages substantially higher than the rates prevailing elsewhere. The rural surplus of labour was trans-ferred to the towns. But neither oil nor manufacturing could absorb the surplus, and the private sector could not expand sufficiently either; furthermore the state was not in a position to satisfy these demands, not yet having received any substantial revenue from oil. When oil revenues started to flow into the treasury, the government had no option but to create new jobs in its own departments. Salary scales were revised and adjusted upwards in 1964, and again in 1966; and official employment expanded. Family and housing allowances were granted. Recruit-ment to government services was not restricted to the towns but extended to the rural areas, too. From 1964 the oil industry ceased to be the wage leader of the economy. The role was taken over by the government. Workers were leaving agriculture to find employment not in productive sectors of the cash economy but in non-productive government activity where jobs and wages were the most convenient means of distributing oil revenues. It was a disguised welfare state, better by far than a flamboyant shaikhdom, but an economy cushioning unproductive labour through the distribution of benefits.

Mabro's study of the composition and stability of the labour force showed that the towns were breeding a generation of workers lacking industrial skills and reluctant, in the context of oil wealth and rising expectations, to take unskilled jobs. The provision of employment on easy terms in government service had raised the marginal price of effort: it was difficult to recruit Libyans for irksome tasks in construction and agriculture. Though it was recognized that economic development depended on agricultural progress, on the growth of an infrastructure, on the emergence of new activities in manufacturing and services, the government's strong interference in the labour market hindered the process.

Within days of taking power, the new régime doubled the minimum wage and lowered rents by decree. The oil companies were obliged to follow suit. In the years following there were further wage increases.[19] Graded civil servants were the exception. Their last increase, of 60 per cent, had been given in late 1964, and they had received housing subsidies in 1968. The new régime thinned out civil service ranks by offering pensions for early retirement: this was partly to shrink this overstaffed sector but partly also to weed out the politically suspect. But further than this the government dared not go in cutting disguised unemployment.

By 1970 government-employed messengers in Tripoli were taking home £L70 a month. There was a chronic shortage of trained workers; yet unskilled wages were often not far below those paid to the semi-skilled and the skilled. This was an attractive policy of egalitarianism but it meant that there were few incentives to train. In the schools and on vocational courses, there was a high rate of wastage, due to the ease and security of government employment. Libya was producing an ever larger population in unproductive employment, even as development schemes grew more ambitious. Above all there was no more appalling waste of labour potential than the condition of women. A manpower projection conducted in 1970 estimated that by 1985, Libyan women would comprise only 7 per cent of the country's total labour force.

Few studies in depth have been conducted into the effect of oil on the village economy and social structure in the countryside. An exception is the investigation by Jamil Hilal[20] into a group of villages in north-west Tripolitania in the district of Msellata, where olive cultivation was the traditional basis of livelihood. In this village society, two economic sectors coexisted by the mid sixties: the agricultural or traditional sector, which included those whose main income derived from farming; and the modern sector, of those whose basic source of income was non-agricultural. Of the adult men in the villages, 37 out of every 100 were living and working away; and another 15 in every 100 worked outside the village in wage labour, government employment, or trade.

Within the agricultural sector there was a good deal of differentiation. Over a quarter of the households in four of the villages had no or very little property: less than a hectare of land or less than five olive trees. About a fifth of the households had larger land areas: more than thirty hectares and over 200 trees. The usual sharecropping method of working the land had persisted: land was leased to a sharecropper who was required to provide the labour, half the seed and half the expenses of ploughing; landlord and sharecropper then shared the proceeds. This system turned large landowners free for other occupations. But whereas traditionally the poor and the landless had to depend for their livelihood on the larger property-owner, with the arrival of the oil economy, working on the land was no longer the only possible source of employment. Share-cropping, seasonal and day-labouring work was still available, but there was now a great shortage of such workers. A new labour market had opened for permanent wage labour and even salaried occupations in the non-agricultural sector. For the people living on the land, a dry year no longer meant famine or extreme hardship, and there was no longer total dependence on an unreliable and hostile nature. Better-off landowners were quick to make use of generous government subsidies, loans, and credit facilities; large landowners in any case had ways and means of diversifying their income by investing capital in the modern sector of the economy. The consequence was an increase in the economic differentiation between individuals in the villages. Traditionally men had invested surplus income in land or livestock; now it was likely to be invested in buildings and shops in Tripoli.

The village thus came to accommodate distinct categories of

people with radically different work conditions. Economic differentiation was most pronounced within the non-agricultural group.

The market situation and the work conditions of the village shop-keeper, the unskilled manual workers, the teacher and the administrator differed significantly. The government official obtained – or expected – a range of benefits from pension and medical facilities to housing allowances and paid holidays. A government official could earn an income several times higher than an unskilled manual worker. But some farmers had also turned into traders because farming was seen as a less and less viable source of livelihood, and of course numbers had migrated to the urban areas.

Of the emigrants 15 per cent had become traders or pedlars; 25 per cent were in manual jobs as building or dock workers or porters; another 25 per cent worked as messengers, guards, waiters, or ushers in government offices; and the remaining 30 per cent were teachers, clerks, policemen, or did administrative jobs in government. The poor were more likely to emigrate; for the wealthier could afford to live in both worlds, remaining land-owners and committed to agriculture, yet investing capital in non-agricultural resources.

Despite these many changes, important aspects of village life retain their traditional and conventional character. There had been little change in the position of women. In the villages, though economic differences had grown, these were not specially displayed or organized. Residence continued to be based not on class differences but on kinship. Economic differences were not even conspicuous in people's style of dress, food, or housing. As for ideology: 'It was not possible to discern any political ideologies that can be said to reflect the incipient class divisions in these villages' ... Hilal asked why the presence of permanent wage labour in a cash economy, together with considerable differences in wealth and occupations had not led to the perception or articulation of different interests by distinct social classes. There seemed to be several reasons. Very large landowners were rare: partly because of the system of fragmented land holdings; partly because of adverse agricultural conditions, which made the rise of a professional class of farmers extremely difficult. It was common for landowners to work alongside the labourers in their employ. The relationship between landlord and labourer was seasonal and thus temporary. There was no stable group of people who worked as agricultural labourers throughout the year. Above all, village society was characterized by the many bonds that held its members together as kinsmen, co-worshippers, and neighbours; even men who formed the nucleus of a new middle class nonetheless retained ties with manual workers and landless peasants.

People did not conceptualize their economic position in class terms. Hilal points out that words like *fellah, amil* (manual worker), or *muwadhef* (salaried) were used to indicate sources of income, not class position, or an exact position in any economic structure. A *fellah* could be landless, a sharecropper, or a farmer working his own land. *Muwadhef* did not differentiate between clerk or highly paid administrator. Men were grouped depending on whether they were urban, rural, or nomadic. Informants asked to classify society into a hierarchy put into the highest strata men who ate beef, lamb, and bread made of wheat; used butter; had running water, electricity, and modern-style furniture; and employed servants so that women did little housework. This is the way of life of the city dweller. The middle group ate camel and goat meat, and bread made from barley; used cistern water for drinking, and paraffin for cooking and lighting; and their women worked inside the home. This style of living typifies the rural settled areas. The third group ate oats for bread, dates and figs; lived in caves and tents; used wood for cooking; and their women worked outside the home. These are nomads or communities in semi-settled areas. This view of society ignored stratification within cities like Tripoli, or the degree of differentiation already present in rural areas. It was revealing, said Hilal, not for its accuracy but for the attempt to fit the society into a traditional framework of stratification, where incomes and their source did not qualify as a basis for differentiation.

Hilal's study was done in the early years of oil and in one part of the country only. In the more densely settled areas closer to Tripoli in more recent years there has grown an even larger population of rural residents commuting to the city. In the countryside in western Libya the most notable stratification is that between the landowners and their non-Libyan, mostly Tunisian, farm labourers. Observers have calculated that on some of the small farms, five out of seven farm workers are Tunisian, and on others two out of two. Non-Libyans are filling more and more of the jobs at the lower ends of the salary scale which Libyans do not, and have no need to, fill. In this dependence of 'patrician' Libyans on 'plebeian' foreign labour Libya is beginning to resemble Kuwait.

Libya's interdependent role in the international capitalist system is firmly established with her export of oil in exchange for manufactured goods and even the most basic foodstuffs. The insertion of an advanced capitalist mode of production in the oil sector has caused a dramatic acceleration of economic growth; yet the only direct impact of the petroleum sector on the rest of the economy is through the government's expenditure of oil income and the local purchases of goods and services by the oil companies. There has been almost no industrialization. There is no financial or industrial bourgeoisie; only a dispersed and fragmented commercial class that sells to the internal market.

The new régime's measures temporarily froze the growth of a speculative and commercial bourgeoisie; though for political rather than economic reasons. And the result was not a dismantling of this class, but a certain redistribution within it. On the other hand, Libyanization of commerce – only Libyans are allowed to register companies and hold partnerships – provided new avenues for this class, as did the open season for private real estate contracting. The new régime's policy towards an emergent capitalist class is expressed in the Charter of the Arab Socialist Union. 'Non-exploiting' capitalists will be tolerated, perhaps even encouraged, depending on how the policy towards the private sector is elaborated in the coming period. What distinguishes a capitalist from a non-exploiting capitalist? Taxation will place limits on his size, and his activities will have to be synchronized with the needs of the economy.

A strong nationalist capitalist sector is unlikely to develop.

What is striding ahead is a form of state capitalism; for all the major projects of the development plans are being undertaken by state-run corporations, although these in turn are contracting to foreign firms and technology.

In a country like Libya the state is not an instrument of specific class interests of, say, an established bourgeoisie, for the state does not rest on a social basis of advanced capitalist relations but, for the most part, on socio-economic structures of a pre-capitalist type. So the form of state-run capitalism inaugurated does not entrench the property rights of a bourgeoisie, but the state itself functions as an independent owner of the principal means of production. The managers of the state – army men and bureaucrats for the most part – are not spokesmen of clearly defined class interests, but form a separate social community, even assume the role of a group proprietor, but one which serves as a link in the chain of complex international economic and political relations.[21] As the government sector grows, and its state-run projects increase, there is created an ever larger body of government and state management employees linked in symbiotic relationship with the oil revenues and their continued flow, and whose thinking is inspired by the ethic of the rentier state: heavy government protection, easy living and unproductive labour for a large part of a very small population.

The single significant structural change introduced by the new régime has been to decree that land not in use must revert to state ownership. This was aimed at the eastern region where the major tribes, shaikhs, and families of Cyrenaica had been the economic and political under-pinning of the Sanusi régime. While tribal land was communally owned, it was allocated by shaikhs for use to commoners, and this system of land patronage by a score or two of powerful tribal heads had produced a system of client politics. The ministry of Agriculture hit on a subsidiary technique to whittle away the influence of the large tribal landowners: a regulation on subsidized fodder stipulated that no more than twenty tons would be sold to any individual farmer, and he had to produce proof of his holding. This was directed against the speculator who had bought up fodder in quantities though he had never fed a sheep in his life.

The effect of these attempts to undermine the big men of Cyrenaican tribes has been difficult to evaluate; since apart from the inner condition of the army, there is probably no more sensitive subject in Gadafi's Libya than the post revolution reaction in the eastern region.

In the countryside there is a growing yet uncertain class of small landowners heavily dependent upon state loans and assistance. The growth of a class of capitalist farmers will be slow if not impossible because of the capital cost of machinery, labour, and expertise. Within the subsistence economy, there has been a steadily falling rate of productivity on the land and a flow of unproductive rural labour to the cities. The class of propertyless day labourers appearing in the heavily state-subsidized agriculture as well as on private farms, is largely non-Libyan: Tunisian and, more recently, Egyptian. (Likewise the private contracting industry will re-coup much of its capital at the cost of the Libyan state, since housing for most Libyans is a state undertaking, but also at the expense of new immigrant non-Libyans.) The urban petit-bourgeoisie of Benghazi and Tripoli and smaller coastal towns – a scattering of professionals, public officials, and small shopkeepers – is a large heterogeneous class, shortly to be made more varied still by Egyptians, now invited freely into the Libyan economy. The preponderant layer of this class comprises those employed in the public sector. But while Libyanization of the senior posts in the oil industry and large allocations for post-graduate training will build an upper technical élite and administrative class, the lower levels of the public sector brim with a large pool of unskilled labour. The urban working class is tiny still, as under the previous régime; and concentrated in the oil industry, on the docks, in construction and in small import substitute factories. The petroleum workers produce immense surplus value; but this is mediated between state and corporations, with the government refusing to permit the workers direct action in the oil industry. In March 1972 stevedores and dockers at Tripoli harbour staged a week-long strike for higher pay and better working conditions, but in the same year the government forbade strikes and sit-down protests, as well as stoppages by students in educational establishments.

Disputes are to be settled by the Islamic practice of 'consultation'.[22]

It is still too soon to know the outcome of the great majority of projects undertaken by the new development plans; most are still merely on paper. King and Colonel have proved equally susceptible to the blandishments of high-powered salesmen for arms and highly capital-intensive projects. Both régimes have accepted and deepened the rentier state economy. It allows large public expenditures without taxation; it disguises poverty and the underdeveloped population. There is a quick road to ostensible development, and this is the road Libya is taking. In the first instance the development is being carried out by foreigners. In 1964 there were 17,000 non-Libyans working in the economy. By 1973 this figure had jumped to 80,000. In the last quarter of 1972 foreigners were coming into the economy at the rate of 5,000 a month, and this looked like becoming the steady rate of increase. The union with Egypt was imminent, and the common labour market was already operating. Gadafi's vision of a unified Arab state posed many imponderables but none as critical for the domestic future of Libyans as the way in which the massive influx of non-Libyan labour would obscure the real problems of development.

Each year about 22,000 newcomers join the labour force. A ministerial committee on employment found that fewer than one in three have been educated above the elementary level or have any vocational skills. By the end of 1972 this affluent society had fewer than 150 in-plant trainees for industry. The annual shortage of skilled labour was estimated at 6,000, even without any replacement of non-Libyan workers. The society was thus accumulating a large reservoir of unskilled and deprived young labour. On top of this untrained and ill-used mass is an élite, larger than before and growing fast, of secondary-school and university graduates, some trained to technology and executive positions. Any gaps in the labour force are filled by the importation of foreigners. The more grand projects are added to the development plans, the more this pattern is confirmed. On the surface there is spectacular development, of huge projects bought abroad. Oil pays for imported hospitals and hotels, expertise and technology; but meanwhile the mass of Libya's people are unchanged, even if they are well paid in disguised under-employment. Libya has no construction industry and no plans to build one; for while there are new cement factories, there is nothing of the organizational and training infrastructure that must lay the domestic base for the first stages of industrialization. Many of the projects could grow into white elephants as those of the previous régime did, for international capital is certainly no more scrupulous about the wastage of Libyan oil resources than the Libyan government. There is as yet no evidence that Gadafi is prepared to use his power and his prestige to drag Libyans screaming into a productive economy.

It is one thing to point to the deficiencies of Libyan planning policies; it is, admittedly, another thing altogether to cure them. For the point must be made emphatically that the faults are not always the result of ineptness – though some undoubtedly are, in a society struggling to adjust to massive change – but that they have grown inevitably out of the constraints placed on the Libyan economy by the nature of the rentier state. And if the latter constraints were not serious enough, there are also the peculiarly difficult conditions imposed on the country's economy by nature: geography and climate and the vast desert distances between population centres. Like Libya, Kuwait is a rentier state in the desert. But she has far fewer problems, for Kuwait is less a country than a large town built on oil, with none of Libya's problems of building an infrastructure to link widely dispersed centres, with no possibilities at all, and thus no dreams, of agriculture, with even fewer people and thus more extravagant oil wealth to spread between them. If Kuwait has development problems – as distinct from wealth – they pale beside Libya's.

The problems have been constant between monarchy and RCC régime, but has there been no difference at all in their planning conceptions? Many of the schemes of the new régime are difficult to judge because they are still on paper. But wasteful expenditure is clearly not a thing of the past. At the same time the new régime has distributed generous amounts on social services. By the end of 1969 there were 3,000 Libyans enrolled in university courses; by 1972 the total was 8,220. New schoolrooms, hospitals, and clinics are going up; incomes, especially of the lower-paid groups, have risen. Government protects the employed in their jobs and subsidizes their housing; it also subsidizes the un- or under-employed. Since oil began to flow, government in Libya has indulged the population in a large portion of the cash benefit; this régime has more money and is spending even more than the previous one did. Whatever the criticisms of a régime for planning and spending without an overall development conception, rather a welfare state than a government run by millionaire shaikhs squandering their riches in Hilton Hotels. Nonetheless it is the conception of planning and of development which is the seminal issue. There is evidence in the new régime's sectoral figures of expenditure that the government is trying genuinely to increase investment in the productive sectors. The difficulty is that not all productive sectors can be productive in Libya, since natural disadvantages have to be taken into account, and there are no signs of the ruthless calculation of development and planning priorities that a rentier state economy demands if it is to break the sequence of its own peculiar underdevelopment. There is no sign that the country's planners are coming to terms with Libya's inadequacies, natural as well as manpower. There is no criticism voiced about wastage, about inertia, about senseless extravagance. The indictment may well be that this generation is squandering resources needed for the next, and for long-term development as distinct from mere economic growth. It is no easy problem for Libya to restructure a badly balanced economy so as to relieve her dependence upon oil, but it is made even more urgent by the fact that oil reserves have been calculated at only thirty years of future production.[23]

10   The Oil State Beyond the State

Though they started with the advantage of British control during the military occupation and British influence afterwards, British oil companies were no match for the American oil industry.[1] The early drafts of what became Libya's petroleum law were prepared by a British law adviser, and there was an attempt to make provision for concession rights to companies which had carried out previous exploration, like Shell and BP. But when the draft went before a government Petroleum Commission, which in turn consulted all the oil companies, this provision was deleted. By then ESSO was well in the field; geologists of the parent company, Standard Oil of New Jersey, now Exxon, had carried out preliminary reconnaissance in 1947 and 1948, and once independence arrived exploration work began in earnest. Italy, which had started the search for oil in the 1930s, was frozen out altogether.[2]

Libya promulgated its Petroleum Law, Royal Decree No. 25 of 1955.[3] It laid the basis for an oil industry very different in structure from Aramco's monopoly of Saudi Arabia's oil fields or Basra's of Iraq, where a single giant cartel exercised control over the entire oil concession, though without necessarily working it. Libya was trying to break into the oil business at a time of plentiful supply, and United States oil fields were operating at only part capacity. Oil companies had to be seduced to new fields: and Libya's oil law accordingly went out of its way to offer favourable inducements to smaller and competing oil interests. The 1955 oil law was drafted by a panel of oil economy experts including N. Pachachi, later secretary of OPEC, the Organization of Petroleum Exporting Countries, and a Dutch petroleum consultant attached to the Ministry of Finance; with government advisers and company representatives sitting together. Anxious to break into the oil industry, the independent oil companies played an important role in the casting of the law. A ceiling was set on the maximum number of concessions and the total areas to be held by any one interest; concession holders had to surrender unused concessions after a stipulated period of time, and the government was free to offer a relinquished concession for competitive bidding once again. (Spectacular strikes were to be made on more than one relinquished area.) The law thus ensured rapid turnover of concessions and maximum competition between oil companies. The idea was to induce the largest possible number of competitive bidders to enter Libya in search of oil, and the plan worked. In the first year after the law was passed, fifty-one concessions were granted to seventeen companies. The rush to find oil was on.

The Libyan oil industry grew at an unprecedented rate. It was the first oil-producing country to surpass production of a million barrels a day in less than five years from the start of production. By 1968 Libyan oil production was 6·7 per cent of the world's total. It had taken Venezuela 40 years, Iran over 30 years, and Kuwait 24, to reach the same level of production.[4] Libya was supplying more than a third of Western Europe's oil imports. By the end of 1967 forty companies were operating in the country, seventeen of them exporting oil.[5] Instead of having a group company, operating as a unit, to deal with, as in the older oil-producing areas of the Middle East, Libya had a flock of individual firms, for the competitive conditions had induced both Majors[6] and Independents to enter the country. By 1965 the Independents were extracting just under half of Libya's total oil production. ESSO, the world's largest oil company, which is a third owner of Aramco, was the largest producer among the Majors; but a group of three Independents combined in Oasis (Amerada, Continental and Marathon) produced almost as much.[7]

For nearly ten years, Western Europe had been the scene of a tremendous price war in the oil industry. The Majors dominated the Western European market and had their refineries and marketing organizations there. The Independents used price-cutting to nudge into the European market. Some of the Majors retaliated by cutting posted prices and consequently revenues per barrel paid to Middle East producers; and this led directly to the formation in 1960 of OPEC, the Organization of Petroleum Exporting Countries, when the oil-producing countries came together in combination to lessen the bargaining position of the Majors. The Majors charged the Independents with being responsible for the rapid deterioration of the European market. A Royal Dutch–Shell chief executive claimed that, as a result of the disruptive influence of the independent oil companies, quantities of 'uncommitted oil overhung the market'.[8] He defined uncommitted oil as oil from Russia or oil owned by the independent or non-integrated oil companies, much from recent Libyan discoveries. The Majors decided on a strategy to edge the Independents out of their Libyan advantage. Libya thus became the battleground of the price clash between the Majors and the Independents, one of the combatants in the clash, but also the instrument of the Majors.

Oil prices paid by consumers, and the share allocated to the oil-producing countries, have never been based even remotely on the cost of producing oil. From the outset the oil industry maintained a monopolistic pricing system which rested on the basic structure of the dominant American-controlled industry. The feature of this system was the complete integration within each of the major companies of all phases of the industry: exploration, production of crude, refining, transport and finally marketing. Competition between the major oil companies, at each point in the industry and for the industry as a whole, was thus virtually eliminated by the integration of the companies with each other at various phases of the oil-production and selling process.

By 1949 the seven major oil companies owned 65 per cent of estimated crude reserves in the world, and 92 per cent of crude reserves outside the United States, Mexico and the Soviet Union. They controlled 88 per cent of crude production outside the United States and the Soviet Union, and 77 per cent of refining capacity outside those two countries. In addition, the majors controlled directly at least two thirds of the tanker fleets and all the major pipelines of the Middle East. Because of the concentrated and integrated nature of the major firms, they could set the price of crude oil with an arbitrary relationship to cost: how profits were distributed among the various phases of the oil operation was a book-keeping operation of the companies.

The immense profits of the international oil industry in the Middle East rested on the difference between the extremely low cost of producing Middle East oil and the artificially high price structure maintained by the industry with the assistance of the United States government.[9]

In the late 1940s Venezuela pioneered the agreement whereby producing countries and the international firms 'shared' profits according to duly negotiated formulas on royalty allocation. In later years the same system was introduced into the Middle East. By 1960 the monopoly price structure of the industry was under challenge from two directions. There were the attempts of producer states to gain more favourable terms and a larger share of profits; and at the same time the independent oil companies were trying to nudge into the immense profits of the international oil industry. OPEC had been formed as a response to political changes in the Middle East and to this inter-industry competition, and it was at this point that Libyan oil began to flow into the international market.

In 1963 OPEC adopted a new royalty expensing formula more favourable to the producing countries. It provided that the royalty paid per barrel by company to government should be treated as cost instead of as part of the tax on profits paid to the oil-producing governments. Libya had joined OPEC in 1962. And no sooner had she done so than the Majors offered to apply the OPEC formula to Libya – on condition that the Libyan petroleum law was amended, so that the same conditions were imposed upon all companies, Majors and Independents alike. Until then the Independent producers had computed their oil price on the basis of prices realized, whereas the Majors paid on posted prices, which were prices unilaterally published by the producing or trading affiliates of the major international companies. Taxes were levied at 50 per cent of the price. ESSO, the largest and most successful Major in Libya, had fixed the posted price of Libya's oil at \$2·21 a barrel; the Independents led by Oasis were realizing prices of between \$1·30 and \$1·40 per barrel; so that this meant a substantially lower government revenue per barrel from the Independents than from the Majors. Libya's adoption of the OPEC formula meant that she would be paid half not of the realization from actual sales but half of the higher posted price. It would bring Libya's oil costing and pricing system into line with that of the Middle East, and considerably increase the Libyan government's oil revenue. It would also rock the profits of the Independents, which worked on smaller profit margins because their production and marketing costs were higher and which, without integrated markets and a selling organization of their own, had broken into the European market only on the strength of their much lower prices.

The announcement by the government that it was preparing to revise the petroleum law in line with the Majors' proposals stunned the Independents.[10] They argued that they had taken no part in the OPEC negotiations in the Middle East and were not bound by its terms. They argued that Libya was reneging on contractual agreements; that this was tantamount to enticing oil companies to undertake the risk of exploration and then, after exploration had yielded success, to stiffen its concession agreements. They argued that they were selling at the maximum possible prices to independent buyers in Europe and could not sell Libyan oil any higher in view of the sharp competition of lower-cost Middle East crudes. They pointed to the role that they had played in finding large oil reserves in Libya and in developing outlets for Libyan oil in Europe which would not otherwise have been available since it was in the interests of the Majors to keep out Libyan oil. They objected to a price settlement negotiated on their behalf by their rivals.

The struggle had just begun when Libya announced that she was ready to open bidding for new oil concessions all over the country, including the highly sought areas in the Sirte basin. Until then the government did not seem to have made up its mind about the royalty offer from the Majors, and the Independents were still hopeful. As the companies prepared to bid, the government announced seventeen items which would determine preference. These included posted prices as a basis for determining royalties; a profit split to exceed the standard 50 per cent;

the availability of markets; and the readiness and capability of companies to establish refineries and petro-chemical industries in Libya; with bonuses and other 'benefits' to government. Independents took hope from a rumour that the government had decided no new petroleum law would be necessary, since its requirements would instead be incorporated in these 'suggested' terms of bidding for new concessions.

When the bidding opened, several dozen combinations of companies from seven different countries submitted their offers. Among the new bidders were European state-backed firms, especially West German, and a swarm of new independent operators fresh to the international oil scene. About a hundred top oil executives flew in for the formal opening of six crates of bids. Over great stretches of Tripolitania and Fezzan there were few contenders; but there was a heavy concentration of offers in an area where Oasis, Mobil-Gelsenberg, and Esso's biggest fields had been found. This was the first major bid for concessions since 1961, when the oil boom had really got under way.[11] The *Petroleum Intelligence Weekly*[12] tipped as likely winners European bidders (like Hispanoil and France's CFP) which have markets and 'tend to dilute the feeling of being under the thumb of the international majors' as well as a couple of Majors 'to be on the safe side'.

The bids were no sooner lodged, than the Libyan government reopened the issue of prices. Increased revenues were needed for the development plan, not least for a prestigious and ambitious housing programme to which the King had pledged his name. A Royal Decree incorporating the OPEC formula was drafted in readiness to be rushed through parliament: government was anxious to collect extra taxes for that year, and its partners in the battle, the Majors, were stepping up the pressure. The Majors appeared first before the government committee and indicated their acceptance of the new formula. A deadline was set for the Independents to state whether they would voluntarily amend their existing deeds accordingly. Complaining that at 'sales price levels the new deal will give us zero profits', the Independents tried to mount a counter-offensive. By then they were collectively outproducing the Majors by 15 per cent of oil production. A group of the Independents went direct to the Prime Minister to argue that there had been no negotiations and no chance to present their case.

If Libya loses the independents, the seven companies told the Prime Minister, then the majors holding low cost Arabian Gulf production 'could drastically reduce Libyan production by substituting the Arabian Gulf oil'. The majors 'could then determine Libya's revenues by regulating oil production. This threat is so powerful that these companies could conceivably in time put enough pressure on Libya to reduce their oil taxes.'

The seven-company group cited Abu Dhabi and Oman as illustrating the 'reality of major international control'. They claimed the major internationals held an exclusive concession in Abu Dhabi for 25 years with practically no exploration effort, and started production there only after the dispute between them and the Iraq Government in 1964. They also declared that the Oman concession has been held 25 years and is not scheduled to come into production until 1967. By contrast, the group noted, in Libya where the independents were active, production has increased at a rate many times that of the Arabian Gulf.

Turning to the OPEC tax and royalty upon which Libya's proposed law is based, the independents said it would give Libya 'a short term gain but a long term loss'. The OPEC formula, the companies admitted, would give Libya a high revenue per barrel but would 'impair the levels of future production . . . and not give the highest ultimate revenue to Libya'.[13]

This plea notwithstanding, the new petroleum law was decreed in mid November 1965, and the government served notice on the companies that it intended to compel quick acceptance of the new terms. The Independents continued to hold out. The government announced that the granting of the new concessions was postponed for a month and that the new law permitted companies not only to maintain their original offers if they conformed to the new law, but to add 'certain conditions more favourable to the Libyan government'.[14] Shortly before the expiry of the deadline, the Independents capitulated. The four-month blitz by the Major internationals to force the Independents into conformity had succeeded.

All eyes now turned to the concessions awarded. When they were announced, the Oil Minister Fuad Kabazi agreed that it was 'a peculiar list' in many ways.[15] But it showed 'where our interests lie and which way we intend to go'. Five West German companies won awards to highlight the drive by Germany – already taking 38 per cent of Libya's crude – to secure North African crude oil. German sources said that the Bonn government had exerted influence on behalf of national firms.[16]

Apart from Union Rheinische and the Wintershall–Elwerath partnership, both of West Germany, the Spanish–French–American Hispanoil group, with French and American interests, and Italy's ENI were the successful state oil companies; winning their bids by virtue of their direct relationship with consumer governments in the European market area.

Among the successful bidders there were fourteen newcomers to Libya with no prior oil experience abroad. The oil industry expressed its puzzlement at some of these new concessions. 'When the winners were announced,' wrote the *Oil and Gas Journal*,[17] 'Libya-watchers were shocked to learn that only three awards went to the major companies who had pioneered Libyan exploration . . . On the winning list appeared some strange new names and companies unknown to the industry: Circle Oil, Lion Petroleum, Mercury, Libya Texas, Libyan Desert, and Bosco Middle East.' They were described by the journal as 'paper companies'. 'There were a few whispers of hi-jinks in high places but these were quickly quashed in Tripoli,' the journal added. But not before three of the non-ministerial members of Libya's Higher Petroleum Council which had studied the offers, submitted their resignations. This was when the King's private secretary issued an unprecedented press statement denying as 'baseless rumours' certain allegations by 'certain officials' that the King had recommended two companies in the bidding.[18] The statement said:

The truth is that when His Majesty studied the list of bidders together with the recommendations made by the Higher Petroleum Council he noticed that certain companies had offered very good terms for the public interest, notwithstanding that the Petroleum Council had recommended that they should be disregarded on account of their not being qualified. It should be pointed out that the King did not recommend that any oil concessions be granted to a particular company but was of the opinion that those companies whose bids were more advantageous to the state should be permitted to prospect for oil.

The newcomer that raised eyebrows highest in the oil world was the California-based Occidental Petroleum Company of Dr Armand Hammer, which was given one of Libya's most coveted concession blocks, ex-Mobil acreage in the Sirte basin. It was Occidental's first oil venture outside North America. Its management had bought up Occidental as a moribund company nine years earlier, and its total assets at the time of its Libyan bid were said to total no more than $5 million. Not long after its entry into Libya it floated a large financial loan. It was a maverick firm, an oil company without a lineage by the standards of the others. Occidental's bid was apparently wrapped in the ribbons of Libya's national colours and it included a handsome file of offers. It agreed to nine of the government's preferential factors. It agreed to devote 5 per cent of its net profit before tax to an agricultural development project in the Kufra oasis, and it offered to join the government in building a gas-fed ammonia plant. This and the Kufra proposal fell under the category of 'special benefits', and there were others in the package. Occidental started drilling four months after the agreement was signed and struck oil just over a year later. Was it luck; or Occidental foresight in acquiring the report of geologists from a rival company that was retrenching at the opportune moment? The Occidental concession proved to be one of the world's major oil deposits. Dogged by rumours that it had sold a share in a lucrative field to acquire working capital and then not honoured its commitment, the company trebled its earnings in four years thanks to its Libyan finds.

In 1972, six years after the granting of its lucrative concessions, documents on file in the New York Federal District Court showed some of the influences that might have been brought to bear in Occidental's winning of the prize. The breach of contract suit against Occidental was filed by Allen & Co., the Wall Street Investment banking firm. Involved in the hearing were an agreement by Occidental to pay $200,000 to one Ferdinand Galic, described by the *Wall Street Journal*[19] as a *bon-vivant* European businessman and promoter; the financing by Mr Galic of a documentary film written by Fuad Kabazi, Libya's Oil Minister; alleged payments by Occidental to Taher Ogbi, the company's Libyan representative, who became Minister of Labour and Social Affairs, and to General de Rovin, described as a 'notorious international swindler' whose real name is François Fortune Louis Pegulu, and who had disappeared from sight by the time the suit started. No one, said the *Wall Street Journal*, had even intimated that Occidental did anything illegal in its successful effort to gain the big oil concessions; but Occidental's activities provided an insight into how huge companies sometimes operated in far-off lands.

The story, wrote the *Wall Street Journal*, as pieced together from the court documents, began in 1964, when 'General de Rovin' came to promoter Galic in Paris with a proposition: if Mr Galic could line up an oil company willing to spend millions of dollars on the project, he, General de Rovin, could obtain lucrative concessions in Libya through a highly placed Libyan. Mr Galic phoned Mr Allen of the Wall Street investment firm, who contacted Occidental. The Libyan businessman turned out to be Taher Ogbi, who became Occidental's representative in Libya and, later, a Cabinet Minister. Through Ogbi, Mr Galic cultivated Fuad Kabazi who, according to Galic's sworn testimony, began to exert his influence to induce the government of King Idris to favour Occidental with two of the best of the concessions that the government granted in February 1966. Mr Kabazi's own deposition reported how he had pressed Occidental's case before the Cabinet; and how, with the King's approval, Occidental had got the concession being vied for by oil companies from all around the world. Mr Kabazi's deposition insisted that his efforts in inner circles to help Occidental obtain choice concessions, had been strictly for Libya's good. But he revealed that he had known from the start why Mr Galic was becoming friendly with him. 'The whole purpose of his contact and close relation was to get this done.' It was an offence punishable by a jail sentence for a government official to give out confidential information prior to its official release. Mr Kabazi claimed that he had divulged secret information because Mr Galic was Occidental's envoy, 'the man authorized to talk and the man to whom I should tell everything.' Kabazi had checked on Galic with Omar Shalhi, who had 'recommended Galic highly'. Galic and Kabazi had met in Europe; they had written to one another in secret code; and once, when they discovered that they were on the same plane together, had pretended not to know one another. When it came to the concession allocation, Mr Kabazi said he had faced 'stern resistance' from others inside the government, but he had viewed his promise to Mr Galic as a commitment. Kabazi had confided to the Italian film-maker who had directed the documentary film that Mr Kabazi had written (and which was never shown commercially):

There are many, many interests involved. Imagine, it's as though there were a large dish filled with all little bones and around this dish are many, many dogs that are trying to edge each other out to grab a hold of the contents of the dish, but in view of the fact that Galic is a dog larger than the rest, he will eat the bone that he has asked to eat.

When Kabazi had achieved the support of the Prime Minister, the Cabinet had accepted his recommendation that the concessions go to Occidental.

The companies had been scrambling over one another for the same concessions. 'You could go into the Libya Palace Hotel looking for a concession,' an oil man said, 'and a bell-boy found you a man to bribe.' It was said to be a matter of who bribed the highest and who bribed the most influential man in government. A month after the fall of the régime, the *Los Angeles Times*[20] delivered a verdict on the government's management of its oil industry. 'The former Oil Minister,' it said, 'was considered both corrupt and a hopeless alcoholic. The leading Shalhi family was said to be the conduit for millions of dollars in payoffs. Oil men say that Shalhi demanded five million dollars from oil company concessionaries before their applications were even considered.'

The newspaper's article was entitled 'Will New Libyan Regime Put US Oilmen Through Wringer?'

As 1967 opened, Libya began to stake a claim in the fixing of
the posted price of its oil. The issue arose out of a wrangle with
four companies that had, as usual, unilaterally fixed a lower
price for Libyan crude on the grounds of its high wax content.
The Oil Ministry charged the companies with infringing the
law's regulations: though it was conceded that the relevant
Regulation 6 contained gaps and needed tightening. This time
Majors and Independents were united. What bothered them,
according to one source,[21] was: 'that once a government becomes involved in price-posting decisions, participation might
easily end up tantamount to complete control before long'.
Libya was reminded of what had happened to Venezuela when
earlier that year she had tried to seize direct control over export
prices. The issue, said the companies, ran to the root of the
whole per cent concept of company management: 'the right to
determine what price is needed to win a customer'.

The closing of the Suez Canal after the Six Day War put
Libya, on Europe's doorstep, at an enormous geographical
advantage. But the régime was reluctant to take advantage of it.
In the Oil Ministry the technicians were pressing for tough
government action to assert its right to take part in price-fixing,
but the Cabinet was in awe of the companies and felt beholden
to them. Eventually the companies agreed to pay Libya and
Saudi Arabia (for the oil which went by Tapline to the Lebanese
port of Sidon) an allowance as a 'temporary' measure, and the
government was conciliated. The price issue was never brought
to a head. The government accepted the company's oil royalty
payments 'under protest'; but these periodic protests were
casually treated as annual *pro forma* complaints by the companies.
The timid gestures and conservative thinking of a régime
chronically dependent on Britain and the United States died
hard. Apart from the régime's dependence on the West, the
government was indebted to some of the oil companies for
loans to make up deficits in the budget. In 1965 it had taken
six extended Cabinet meetings to persuade the Cabinet that
the amended Law was necessary. 'We were struggling against
the inertia of our own government,' an official of the Oil
Ministry told me. By 1967 the need for an adjustment to the

price was glaring, but the régime was reluctant to press for one.

During 1968 a Ministry committee had been pressing ESSO and Occidental about the flaring of gas: Occidental in particular was pushing production heavily to meet her financial obligations and was notorious for the raping of fields and the flaring of gas. (The more slowly oil is pumped the more total the recovery of resources: this is an ever-present conflict between companies pressing for the speediest possible exploitation and government regulatory attempts to nurture resources.) The members of the committee heard on the radio that their committee had been dissolved; it had been doing its work too well. Four replacements were appointed to the committee, but it never met. The Oil Ministry prepared a consolidated regulation on the conservation of flaring gas resources to conform with the OPEC decision, and this had already been proclaimed and produced by the government printer when the Oil Minister, Khalifa Musa, told oil companies that the issue was still negotiable. By August 1969 there was reputed to be a draft of an amended petroleum law in the offices of the Ministry, prepared by technicians and advisers: oil companies, said the Ministry's under-secretary, Mr Ibrahim Hungari,[22] had either to step up their posted price or face stringent legislation which would make them comply with the government's demand. The government, he said, would demand a price of $2·31 a barrel. Negotiations with the companies were to open in September, and the government was hoping for a mutually agreed arrangement of a higher price. There was no time to test the general scepticism that the government would lose its nerve when finally faced by the companies; a fortnight later there was a new régime.

From one government to another, the flow of oil down the pipelines was uninterrupted. The new régime's early statements on oil were caution itself. The governments of the United States, Britain, and France were notified that Libya would respect all agreements in force. The companies put on a bold international face. But inside their Libyan offices, confidential memoranda alerted executives that 'the normal processes leading towards nationalization of the oil industry in Libya have been accelerated by the September Revolution'. The companies should expect demands for wage increases for locals, restrictions on the employment of expatriates, and the increased use of the government oil organization (LIPETCO) as a 'tool to exercise greater influence on actual operations'.

Once the regime is stable it will launch a frontal attack on the oil industry. Driven by missionary zeal of secure absolute economic sovereignty, the regime will use every possible means of 'persuasion' but it is unlikely that it will resort to outright expropriation.[23]

However, the example of Iran under Moussadeq, where production was interrupted for more than three years after nationalization in 1951, would surely serve as deterrent. 'In any case,' the oil companies comforted themselves, 'unity and solidarity have not been characteristic of the modern Arab world', and 'outright expropriation is impractical when negotiations are the means to reach a settlement'. The month after the régime came to power, it was announced that the battle for a higher posted price would be resumed. A government committee was hard at work on tactics.[24] By January 1970 it was ready to meet the oil companies. They had worked out a strategy too. If the Libyans raised prices to a level higher than Gulf or West African oil, Royal Dutch–Shell and BP would substitute Gulf and Nigerian oil for some Libyan. But Occidental, which accounted for nearly one third of Libya's output, could not shift its production, which was all in Libya. As the negotiations got under way, the Trans-Arabian pipeline (Tapline) was blocked by a Syrian bulldozer. At more or less the same time, the Libyan government began to impose production cutbacks on several of the operating companies. These, said the ministry, were conservation measures in no way related to the price issue.[25] But the timing was scarcely fortuitous. The direct effect of the cutback and the closure of Tapline was small, but large enough seriously to affect tanker rates. (In 1970 small cutbacks of Mediterranean oil had a large impact on oil prices through tanker freights because by that year alternate sources – like Venezuela and the United States Louisiana fields – had reached their capacity. There was still oil from the Gulf but it takes six times the tanker capacity to ship one ton of oil from the Gulf to replace one lost from the Mediterranean. The total reduction in oil exports from Tapline and Libya was about 50 million tons a year, or a million barrels a day. This would have required additional tanker capacity of 300 million tons which was not then available.) Then Libya struck at the companies one by one. Occidental came first, as the most vulnerable. And Occidental capitulated. Oasis was called in next; but Shell, which has a sixth interest in the consortium, refused to take part in the settlement. Libya ordered the Shell terminal to shut down. The series of ultimata split companies down the middle. BP raised the prices of Libyan and Iraqi crude but insisted she was not influenced by events in Tripoli, in an attempt to reassert that the sole responsibility for price-fixing lies with the companies. But meanwhile BP's partner Bunker Hunt was prepared to settle, as was Gelsenberg of West Germany and another of the American Independents. The Foreign Office, studying Middle East supplies, dropped broad hints to BP and Shell that their stand would be awkward. When Shell found herself the only company standing out, she settled too. The new Libyan price at $2.53 a barrel was the highest outside the United States. But far from being a final settlement, Libya announced that she regarded it as a rectification of past injustices for the price paid until then, and not a new price.

Assisted by Algeria, Libya's conduct of the negotiations was adroit. She was Western Europe's biggest single oil supplier at a time when the closure of the Suez Canal had hampered deliveries east of Suez and had sent oil tanker costs round the Cape soaring. The repair of Tapline took a prodigiously long time and in the event not only earned higher transit fees for Syria but also gave Libya extra bargaining advantage. Libyan oil was not only on the Mediterranean side of the Canal, a few days' delivery from Europe's ports, it was excellent quality, low-gravity crude, with good viscosity and a comparatively low sulphur content.

Libya's success prompted OPEC-directed action by all producing countries for an increased tax payment. Four months after her victory, Libya gave notice of her own next set of demands for a tax increase along with a freight and proximity allowance. The oil companies prepared to fight the 1971 round collectively. The United States Department of Justice authorized an unprecedented waiver of anti-trust legislation so that oil companies, Majors and Independents, could sign a secret mutual aid pact, and negotiate as a bloc with producer nations.* At a New York meeting, thirteen oil companies, eight Majors and five Independents, called for centralized negotiations with all ten oil-producing countries (six Gulf states, Libya, Algeria, Indonesia, and Venezuela). This cartel combination then sent a memorandum to OPEC offering a five-year price stability pact, and set about enlisting European support in this company line-up, with the direct diplomatic intervention of the British government. The oil committee of OECD (Organization for Economic Cooperation and Development) convened a restricted and high-level meeting of four Western governments in whose territory the eight international Majors were based; the USA, Britain, Holland, and France. From Paris there was a company announcement, like the one already issued from New York, of global negotiations with oil-exporting nations to fix prices for five years to come. This time the divergence in company interests was expressed by the Italian state-owned ENI Corporation, which under Enrico Mattei had built itself by offering more favourable joint ventures to producer countries. ENI dissociated itself from the combined company initiative. France's ERAP too, part of a Libyan government joint venture which had just found oil in Libyan coastal waters, also did not subscribe to the common front: it drew almost half its total oil supplies from Libya and Algeria, and was locked in its own bilateral negotiations with Algeria. Meanwhile the Nixon administration had more publicly than usual dispatched American diplomats to intercede for a package deal with the more conservative rulers of OPEC countries. It seemed that the companies had adjusted them-

* This extraordinary action of the cartel was to be an augury of the future pattern of oil relations with Libya's government: thus when Bunker Hunt was threatened with nationalization it was reported that this firm had obtained supply guarantees from the other companies.

selves to price increases.* In a situation of oil supply shortage and an inelastic demand for oil, the companies were able to pass the full price increase on to the consumer, whether through higher crude oil prices or through higher prices of refined products – for oil is refined in company refineries and sold through their marketing channels. Price increases continued to benefit the companies – and the balance of payments position of the United States. What the companies did seek were stable and predictable prices and assurances that what they accepted would not be changed for five years. And despite their wish to conclude a single arrangement for all oil producers, the price negotiated at Teheran by the six Gulf producers was unacceptable to Libya. That government was also insisting on a freight differential for its short haul oil, an allowance for its oil's low sulphur content, and clauses on re-investment and retroactivity.

Libya had begun to use the tactics which had succeeded so well the previous year, and to pick off the companies one by one. Occidental was singled out once again; but so was Bunker Hunt, in a canny move to embarrass its BP partner and prevent the Majors from achieving their united front. The government expected the companies engaged in separate negotiations not to reveal the terms to other companies: 'forbidden to talk to one another, in an industry like ours!' an oil executive fulminated. The warning notwithstanding, the ESSO computer in Tripoli was put at the service of the companies, which fed information to it for their executives in London and New York.

During the negotiations Libya announced that she was studying a project to sell oil directly to foreign state companies. She also called a conference of the four producer states whose oil is exported through Mediterranean terminals – Libya and Algeria, Iraq and Saudi Arabia – and though their statement was ambiguous, and hinted at different agreed price levels, they declared that they would jointly embargo their oil if the companies did

* The *Economist* ('The Phoney Oil Crisis', Survey, 7 July 1973) has voiced the suspicion that the United States capitulated only too readily to OPEC demands because they saw increased oil prices as a quick and easy way of slowing down the Japanese economy, 'whose exports were bothering Americans mightily at the time and which would be more hurt by rises in oil prices than any other nation'.

not agree to the Libyan terms. Libya's master-stroke was to call Amoseas in for early negotiation. Though by definition Amoseas is an Independent existing only in Libya, it comprises two Majors, Standard California and Texaco; and this was the Majors' soft under-belly. A few weeks later a settlement emerged. Libya somewhat slightly moderated her demands – under Egyptian pressure it was suggested – and there were last-minute dramatics which caused the oil executives to up their offer. The companies accepted retroactive payments, and committed themselves to re-investing some of their profits.[26] The result of the negotiations was an immediate gain to Libya of $800 million. After a second round of bargaining, the price of Libyan oil was set at $3·47 a barrel, or an increase of 35 per cent. In 1971 and again in 1973, contracts in dollars were re-negotiated to compensate for the fall in the value of the dollar, and the price went up again.

Libya had started by pressing for terms more in line with those offered elsewhere in the oil world; she ended not only leaping ahead of these, but also acting as a prod to generalized price increases for all producers. OPEC, formed for self-help when the price was plunging, had up to Libya's entry been able to produce no collective action on the part of the producer states, except for the 1965 royalty expensing formula; in 1971, when the Gulf states in OPEC bargained together as a group against the oil companies, this was a major break in the historical pattern of individual deals between countries and cartels. The producer countries had gained enormously in confidence and experience.

Libya's tough tactics had been fortified by huge reserves. There was the psychological advantage held by a régime that had just nationalized banks and whose chief spokesman was announcing that Libya could do not only without the oil companies but even without oil. Oil-producer policies in this decade, it might be argued, were devised less by revolutions than by the oil consultants spawned by the industry, skilfully reacting to the new bargaining possibilities within the changing structure of the international oil industry. Libya's case was based on already available OPEC studies on oil price fixing, and some of it had even been prepared by the Oil Ministry under the monarchy. What was needed was a régime with a blazing sense of persecution at the hands of foreign oil monopolies, and the reckless abandon with which Gadafi and his colleagues entered the fray.

Libya's revenue from oil grew spectacularly, although her annual production dropped after the cutbacks ordered from 1970 when she decided that she would preserve resources and aim for increased revenue rather than increased production:[27]

Libyan Oil Revenue[28]

	Million Libyan dinars	Million barrels	Average daily production
1968	357·8	1,012·5	2·77 million
1969	370·0	1,196·6	3·28 million
1970	363·0	1,211·1	3·318 million
1971	469·0	1,007·686	2·76 million
1972	580·0	815·201	2·2 million

Libya's gold and foreign reserves have grown from $917 million at the end of 1969 to $1,590 million in 1970, $2,665 million in 1971, and $2,929 million in 1972.

Yet these figures give only a partial picture of the finances of oil. American oil companies alone made about $5,800 million in profits between 1963 and 1968 from their oil operations in the five major Middle East oil-producing countries, including Libya; according to a recent study.[29] Taking goods bought by these countries in the United States, dollar deposits by their central banks in the United States, and repatriated profits of American oil companies, these five oil-producers made a positive contribution of nearly $2,000 millions in 1968 to the US balance of payments. While United States markets directly draw very little oil from the Middle East – perhaps only about 3 per cent of domestic oil consumption – the impact of American oil operations on the US balance of payments has been increasing significantly over the years. Over the six-year period 1963–8, the realized profits of American oil companies operating in Iran, Iraq, Kuwait, Saudi Arabia, and Libya more than doubled – from $657 million to $1,430 million. American exports to these countries increased from $315 million to $667 million in the same period. The increase in the balance of trade, always favourable to the United States, rose from $102 million to $401 million. Official reserves belonging to the central banks of the five States, invested in securities and bank deposits in the United States, and in US stocks and bonds bought by individual Arab investors also weighed in the balance of payments calculations, again to the advantage of the United States. According to this study in this period, when the US balance of payments ran in the red by an average of $1,900 million a year, these five Middle Eastern states were making a contribution that averaged $1,700 million.

One of the study's most telling disclosures is the enormous increase in profits drawn by American oil firms from Libya. Profits there amounted to only 4·5 million in 1963, a tiny sum compared to the four richer oil-producers. But the figure rose to $35 million in 1968; and by that time, Libya was second only to Saudi Arabia as the most profitable source. By 1968 the combined total investment of American oil companies in Libya was calculated to be more than $1,500 million. Stated profits are, however, only part of the picture. Multi-nationals drain even higher proportions of foreign exchange than the bare profit figures suggest, for profits reflect what is over after the company has met costs, foreign and local, and has made payments to parent multi-national companies for management services, licences, components, raw materials, and machinery. And these company deals can be almost as expensive to the producing country as the remission of profits. The oil companies re-invest hardly any of their profits;[30] and their local expenditure and thus their contribution to the domestic economy is minimal. In 1971 oil company expenditures in Libya amounted to £L88 million; by the following year they had declined to £L70 million.[31]

By 1971, despite the impressive results of two rounds of bargaining, the producing countries' 'take' of the final selling price of a gallon of petrol was 12·5 per cent compared with the share of consuming governments, which were taking an average of 45 per cent in taxes for themselves.[32]

In other words, the high cost of petrol in the West – and in the underdeveloped world – is not majorly the result of increased OPEC taxes.

It is the United States which dominates the international trade in oil. One third of total US investment abroad is in oil. The industry remits vast sums into the American economy. More than 70 per cent of American investment in the countries of the Third World is accounted for by oil. The close integration of the oil companies and Washington is central to the politics and the economics of oil. An oil company employee in Libya told me: 'We have a director in Washington who does nothing but kick Under-Secretaries of State; you can't beat an oil company.' Despite the extra millions paid out to producer countries after the 1970 and 1971 negotiations, 1971 was an even better year for company profits than 1970. The multi-nationals producing the oil were amenable to tax increases, because they used the occasion to increase their own profit margins and their returns on investment in both crude oil and refined products. The best summary of the results of the 1971 agreement for increased prices was made by a well-known oil financial analyst, who called it 'truly an unexpected boon for the world-wide industry'.[33] And when the producing countries made fresh demands later in the year, an American investment advisory service remarked that tax increases were actually favourable to oil company profits.[34] In 1971 American oil companies produced about 6·5 billion barrels of oil outside the United States. It has been calculated[35] that for every cent of increase in prices above that paid in tax, there is an additional $65 million in profit.

Arguing the case for the consumer countries – he was delivering his lecture[36] in Japan in April 1972 – M. A. Adelman, of the Massachusetts Institute of Technology, described what he saw as the convergence of interest between the multi-nationals and the oil-producing countries at the expense of the consumer states.

The 1960s marked one long slow advance in the power of the producing country governments at the expense of the companies. The original price erosion of 1958–60 spurred them into the development of OPEC. The principle became established that posted prices and thus taxes were not to be reduced, whatever might happen in the market place.

According to this view, oil cartels and oil-producing governments are in collusion to push taxes and thus prices upwards. A former OPEC secretary is quoted as having said 'truly there is no basic conflict between companies and producer nations'.[37] The head of Shell called it a marriage of companies and producer governments.[38] The multi-nationals, declared Adelman, are centrally the agent of the United States, without whose active support OPEC might never have achieved so much:

> When the first Libyan cutbacks were decreed (after the start of the first round of negotiations–RF) the United States could have convened the oil companies to work out an insurance scheme whereby any single company forced to shut down would have crude oil supplied by the others at tax-plus-cost from another source ... Had that been done, all companies might have been shut down, and the Libyan government would have lost all production income. It would have been helpful but not necessary to freeze its deposits abroad. The OPEC nations were unprepared for conflict. Their unity would have been severely tested and probably destroyed.[39]

The multi-national oil companies, operating the greatest monopoly of history, can pass the burden of higher taxes on to the consumer countries because the multi-nationals are the producers of oil and also the sellers of refined products. The problem, in Adelman's opinion, is to get the multi-nationals out of crude oil marketing. He is content to let them remain as producers under contract and buyers of crude for transport, refining, and marketing of products. The real owners, the producing nations, 'must assume the role of sellers and they should be assisted in compelling the price of crude oil down'. The only way to unmake the monopoly is to 'remove the essential gear wheel from the machine, the multi-national companies'. In his opinion, the consuming countries, notably France, are doing their best to get their own companies into the machine, and are thus themselves developing a vested interest in high oil prices. Meanwhile, the less developed consuming countries suffer the most.

The higher price agreement gains of 1970 and 1971 were

within the framework of the oil industry as it had always operated. Arguments about posted price or realized price, raising or lowering the price, bonuses for quality and freight advantage, were moves within the same circle. The companies continued to manipulate the market, to control all downstream including refining facilities, and company profits continued steadily upwards. It was in the interests of the United States companies, which had control of the market, for the price to rise. Higher prices also made marginal fields in the United States itself more economic. In part the United States oil control explained the trend in OECD countries – the largest consumers of Libyan oil[40] – towards oil deals between producer and consuming state companies. Libya's interest in joint ventures coincided with this move. The previous régime had initiated some joint ventures[41] – though most of their discoveries had not been of commercial value. The 50–50 participation agreement signed between ENI and LINOCO, the Libyan state oil company, in September 1972, made the Italian company responsible in the final analysis for the marketing of the crude at a price which included a marketing commission for the Italian partner and provided a half-way price if the crude had to be sold at less than the current price. According to those who knew the side-letters of the agreement, it gave the Italian partner a favourable deal.

There were good reasons for choosing an Italian partner: Italy was near by, and Libya had a strong trade balance with her. ENI also signed a contract for the training of Libyan oil engineers and personnel.

In the long term LINOCO was intended to be a fully integrated oil company operating exploration, drilling, transport of crude oil, and processing through a petro-chemical industry. Any future participation by foreign-owned oil companies would take the form of partnership agreements with LINOCO. And in addition to these, LINOCO was assigned all concession areas relinquished by foreign companies, including small wells in western Libya. Until the nationalization of BP, LINOCO had marketed Libya's 12·5 per cent share of company production, mostly to Yugoslavia and East European countries, and on the advice of Arthur D. Little. The nationalization of BP's £L70 million holding in March 1972 was Libya's first serious attempt to solve the marketing problem. BP's half share in the Sarir concession, operated together with Bunker Hunt, was handed over to the government's Arabian Gulf Petroleum Company. In June 1973 Libya nationalized the other half of the former BP-owned Sarir field which belonged to Bunker Hunt, an independent American company. Britain's legal and diplomatic attempts to prevent the sale of BP oil on the international market failed; but Libya's attempts to market the production were not eminently successful: some Libyans concluded that the United States and the Soviet Union had a tacit agreement not to stir one another's oil barrels. Whatever the reason – perhaps because among others these economies operate on a taut supply–demand balance system for at least a year ahead, especially for imported commodities like oil, and planning is inflexible – initial negotiations with East Germany, Czechoslovakia, and Hungary about sales of Libyan oil were inconclusive. Eventually the Soviet Union, Bulgaria, Rumania, and Yugoslavia bought small quantities of Libyan oil, principally by barter agreement. China was not purchasing oil in any quantity. Nationalization of the sophisticated technology of the oil industry thus presents enormous problems to Libya, which is far behind Algeria in skilled manpower and expertise and leans heavily on her training programme;[42] the acute problem for a national oil company is to break into a market monopolized by the giant cartels.

Will the battle around concessions and participation agreements which opened during 1971 transform the oil world? The *Economist* wrote:[43]

The concession system, with all its objectionable colonial overtones and a history dating back to when Turkish sultans still ruled the Middle East, is the obvious target ... Concessions are the treaties under which the oil companies can explore for oil and then market it in return for royalties agreed on every barrel pumped. The new policy of the oil-producing countries is that all of them should be scrapped by 1979 when the present concessions in Iran expire. Saudi Arabia and Iraq now plan to revoke their principal concessions then, although they were supposed to run respectively to 1999 and 2000. The full terms for Kuwait's concession is supposed to be up to 2026. Arabs laugh at the idea that any Middle East country will tolerate such a delay.

An OPEC meeting set up a committee to investigate ways and means of increasing the producer-country's share in the management and property of oil companies. By September 1971 Libya announced that she would shortly demand the changing of concession agreements into participation. OPEC might ask for 20 per cent, but Libya would demand at least 51 per cent. By August 1973 participation agreements had been signed with both Occidental and Oasis, the largest independent and major group producer respectively, and the turn of the remaining companies was clearly not far off. The agreements gave the state sector a 51-per-cent share, and compensation was on book, not updated, values, which meant that Libya had stiffened her terms considerably against those offered in the Gulf.*

The participation achieved by Saudi Arabia – and also by Kuwait, Qatar, and the United Arab Emirates – is an utter misnomer, according to Adelman.[44] He calls it pseudo-participation (or non-participation). It does not mean that the government actually sells any oil or transfers it downstream for refining and sale. The cartel continues to act as crude oil marketer, paying the excise tax before selling it as crude or refining its products. It is simply an ingenious way of further increasing the tax per barrel without touching price or nominal tax rate, and so apparently respecting the Teheran agreements. The concession company and host government need to determine four items; Adelman told the Tokyo Institute of Energy Economics:

The government owes the concessionaires a certain sum per year to cover the amortised cost of the equity share.

The government loses the taxes it formerly held on the share it now 'owns'.

The concessionaire owes the government the 'price' of the oil which the government owns, and which it now 'sells' to the company.

The concessionaire owes the government's pro-rata share of the year's profits.

* There were further part-nationalizations of oil companies in September 1973 and February 1974.

Once the paper work is finished, Adelman adds 'the same oil is still lifted on board the same ships to be sold or transferred by the same companies'.

Libyan spokesmen have said that she will not be satisfied with the Saudi Arabian type of participation agreement. Iran's way was to establish ownership of the oil consortium's assets and formal control over its operations in return for long-term guarantees at a privileged price. But even this agreement simply distributed a number of nationals through the management at board levels and left the operating companies virtually intact. In any case Iran's agreement was the product of the virtual denationaliza-tion of oil in 1957 after the overthrow of Moussadeq. The new agreement leaves most of the marketing to the oil companies and is not really an improvement on the past. It is Adelman's case that the OPEC countries, militant or not, cannot function without the multi-nationals, cannot raise prices without them, and would risk losing all by expelling them. Experts retained by OPEC have argued that participation must not interfere with the marketing of the oil through the companies. For finally the multi-nationals could simply say: 'The oil is yours; when you want to sell it, look us up.' The way out was for producer countries to try to make long-term bilateral deals with consumer countries, as Libya was clearly interested in doing with both Italy and France.

Meanwhile Libya was calling stridently for the use of oil as a political weapon, and the most powerful sanction the Arab world had against the industrialized powers, led by the United States, on the Palestine issue. Would Libya have to go alone into such a boycott, with the risk that the oil companies would find ways to play one oil producer off against another? The use of oil as a political weapon was tightly linked with the state of politics in the Arab world as a whole.

11 The Search for Arab Unity

By the time of the Libyan revolution, the Arab world, though it echoed as resonantly as ever the rhetoric of pan-Arabism, was sadly divided. Only on the eve of the 1967 war with Israel did these quarrels drop to the ground. When King Hussein of Jordan flew to Cairo and a joint Egyptian–Jordanian defence pact was signed, Nasser could declare: 'The world will see that in the hour of need, the Arabs will unite.' Within a week the war was over; the Egyptian air force destroyed on the ground; great stretches of occupied territory under Israel; and Arab forces and morale in tragic disarray. This defeat on the battleground was mirrored eighteen months later at the fiasco of the Arab summit in Rabat. Precisely what went on in the closed meetings at Rabat is not known, but differences between the Arab states were such that they could not even produce an agreed communiqué. Plans for an Arab oil embargo which would produce Western pressure for a quick Israeli withdrawal were soon dropped; it was only after a walkout by the Egyptian delegation that Saudi Arabia and Kuwait agreed to step up their aid for the purchase of weapons to replace Egypt's shattered arsenal. At Rabat President Nasser made some hesitant attempts to demand a candid assessment of Arab strength and the recognition that the Arab states were unable to defeat Israel militarily; so that greater Arab strength should be used as a diplomatic weapon against Israel and only as a final resort in battle. Algeria demanded an absolute commitment to war: (as did Saudi Arabia, seeking to embarrass Egypt in her weakness). Nasser's talks with Boumedienne after the summit did little to heal the breach between them, for Nasser could not dispel the impression that he was putting Egypt's own security before the Palestinian and thus the Arab cause. But if Algeria was reproaching Nasser for defeatism, Gadafi's Libya presented Egypt with an option that suggested fresh revolutionary-seeming departures. Nasser and Gadafi, together with Nimeiry who, earlier in the year, had also come to power by military coup, flew from Rabat to Tripoli to announce a Tripartite Pact, an Arab Revolutionary Front to consolidate three progressive revolutions.

The Tripoli Charter set up a supreme planning committee and even a common security system under the Egyptian security boss Fath al-Dib, who was already supervising Libya's security and through his agents exercised a heavy hand on the Sudan's. The agreed communiqué was circumspect. It made no reference to any eventual political union and contented itself with setting up joint ministerial commissions to pursue coordinated policies. The three leaders were to meet at regular intervals. Cairo's interpretation, indeed Nasser's insistence, was that economic integration would involve some limited concrete initiatives such as joint agricultural projects, the formation of a joint development bank, and unification of the airlines. The ensuing year was punctuated by a series of meetings between the respective ministers of Finance, Foreign Affairs, Education, and Information and the governors of their banks; with announcements of agreements for technical cooperation, relaxation of customs duties, and the free flow of labour between the states.

In between the committee work, there were unceasing speeches by Gadafi about Arab unity. He flew from one Arab capital to another with his plan for the pan-Arabization of the battle for Palestine. It was surely the simplest of issues. To Arab nationalists of Gadafi's cast of thinking, the Arab world, from the Gulf to the Maghreb, is a single homogeneous whole; and the Arab nation, a single unit bound by common ties of language, religion, history, and the loss of Palestine. Since every setback to the Arab cause arose from Arab disunity, the Arab world had to be united; from the kernel of an enduring Arab union among like régimes.

Shortly after the Tripoli Charter was signed, the Libyan army leaders began to press for full constitutional unity of the three states. Nasser, still bruised by the collapse of the Egyptian-Syrian union, made clear his reservations. It had been the

Baathists in the Syrian army who had been insistent on a unified state; and when Nasser had agreed, on certain conditions, there had been jubilation in several Arab capitals. The ideal of Arab unity 'which had previously floated somewhere between heaven and earth like some Platonic idea or Hegelian concept was finally incarnate upon earth'.[1] But the Baath, which had pressed for union, had been undermined by Nasser; Egyptian authoritarian rule and Egyptian business had turned Syria into a subordinate province, and general discontent had finally exploded in September 1961 with a military coup in Damascus which arrested the Egyptian pro-consul and proclaimed Syria's secession. Yemen's association with this union had ended shortly afterwards. The federation of Jordan and Iraq, founded to counterbalance the Syrian–Egyptian union had lasted only a few months. In 1963 a proposed federation between Egypt, Syria, and Iraq had failed to clear the first triangular hurdles of disagreement between Nasser and the Syrian and the Iraqi Baathists. It was above all the Six Day War which illuminated all the contradictions and limitations of the Arab régimes of the Middle East and the paradoxes within the search for Arab unity.

The Middle East harbours more than half the oil reserves of the world, and Middle East oil is the cheapest and most profitable. Despite political independence, the ties that bind this area to the imperialist market are stronger than ever; preserved predominantly through the political control by patriarchal oligarchies of Saudi Arabia and the Gulf states, together with the dependent Jordanian kingdom (which lives on American aid and subsidies). At the other end of the political spectrum are the Arab nationalist régimes, Nasserist and Baathist, which despite their endemic and deep-running ideological disputes have much in common. Both are predominantly the movements of the petit-bourgeoisies in the urban centres of the Middle East. Indeed, even when these movements have attracted substantial mass followings, their slogans have remained those of the petit-bourgeoisie, and the interests of workers or landless peasants have been subordinated to it. They are movements that rely on the military coup d'état as the means of political change, for the coup allocates to the masses a subsidiary role and reflects the constant feature of this political style: a distrust of mass action as a means of social transformation. Palestinian writer Fawwaz Trabulsi[2] describes these as 'régimes of an embourgeoisified privileged minority of petit-bourgeois origin which has merged with the remnants of the old social order (like bureaucrats, for instance) and which appropriates the national surplus ... through its control over the bureaucratic–military machinery of the state'. Once in power, the minority controls the means of production in agriculture, construction, small and medium industry; it also controls internal trade and services, public works, indeed the whole public sector through its power of economic decision over it. But, Trabulsi argues, because it is unable to revolutionize productive relations, especially in the countryside, this privileged ruling group fails in the task of internal accumulation of capital. In underdeveloped countries, this is the precondition of development; a drawing upon the abundant human labour power of the country. But such is essentially a political question; requiring the mobilization of the masses in whose interest socialism is to be built. The new class builds mainly consumer industries, geared to the satisfaction of its own needs; it aspires to social prestige and identifies with the old bourgeoisie and the aristocracy of the old order. It thus not only retards the process of capital accumulation for social purposes, but it produces a drain of social wealth in hard currency remittances to the world capitalist market outside. The result is the essential inability of this type of régime to break loose from the economic domination of imperialism; and, hence, to wage systematic anti-imperialist struggle. Because of their very nature as the régimes of privileged minorities; because of their mistrust of the masses of people as the lever of change; these régimes waver between struggle at some times and at others a search for coexistence with imperialism and the reactionary Arab régimes linked with it.

Trabulsi argues that in the Six Day War this wavering posture towards imperialism resulted in an erroneous view of the enemy which brought catastrophic results. The error was to see as the enemy of the Arab world not Western imperialism as a whole but the so-called Jewish-Zionist world conspiracy; and it was a hardly avoidable error, given the class position of those in power in the Middle East. But the Six Day War was part of a general imperialist offensive against nationalist régimes of the Third World; and though waged by Israel, it was war by proxy for imperialism. Israel struck in the conviction that she was acting in concert with State Department policy. Although only a few weeks before the war, Trabulsi writes, Nasser was repeating his famous slogan 'Israel is America and America is Israel', it was precisely when the onslaught was upon him that he sought to dissociate the two and appeal to the United States to act in Egypt's interests. When the war was lost, Nasser interpreted the Arab defeat as the duping of the Arab leadership by the United States, which had guaranteed that Israel would not be the first to attack. This view of the role of the United States as mediator was begun by Nasser, but was to be used to the limit by his successor President Sadat.

The defeat tipped the balance in the Middle East heavily towards the reactionary Arab régimes. With his acceptance of the Rogers peace proposals, Nasser exposed himself to the reproach that, like his neighbours, he was abandoning the sacred Arab cause for the sake of Egypt's own security needs. More than ever his régime, and reactionary and nationalist régimes alike, needed to outflank their critics by militant cries for the battle. For, as Maxime Rodinson has shown,[3] Arab hostility to Israel arises from the most profound needs of the Arab world, since concessions to popular feeling on the Palestine question are easier to make and more agreeable, being mainly verbal and symbolic, than decisions to institute economic changes or review fundamental alignments with the major powers.

The only way of turning Israeli strength into weakness would have been protracted popular war. Nasser's last speeches showed some awareness of this. But popular war means relying on the masses; organizing and politicizing them; above all, arming them. These are régimes that survive by depoliticizing the masses; by using endless demagogy in search of popular support; by using the army and the state to conduct the 'revolution' on behalf of the masses, lest their independent intervention assault the privileges and policies of the military–bureaucratic régime.

After the 1967 débâcle it was the Palestinians who in part at least began to recognize that the Palestinian issue would have to be tackled not by conventional Arab armies but by popular struggle, and who began to confront the issue of how to free themselves from the patronage and control of self-serving Arab régimes, opposing popular struggle lest it lead to their own undoing.

These issues of the deep divide between, but also within, Arab politics; the wavering strategy that arises from them; and the problem of how to mobilize a subjugated but largely dispossessed people against a powerful state with international links reaching into the heart of the Arab world, were convulsing the Arab world at the time that the young army officers captured power in Libya.

Whereas by the time that he died, Nasser's capacity to paper over the cracks in Arab unity – and within Egyptian society – was exhausted, Gadafi's response to the death of Nasser was faithfully to repeat his policies, and his errors. In many parts of the Arab world, Gadafi's practice of repeating virtually verbatim many of Nasser's speeches regardless of changed time and circumstance, became a standing joke. But then, the policies by now outworn in the Middle East, were, to a Gadafi and Libya come late on the scene, brand new. Seemingly blind to the weighty problems of tactics and strategy facing the nationalist Arab states, the young soldiers of Libya's RCC reduced policy to several simple expedients: above all, immediate Arab unity, and readiness for the battle.

Even as he established his reputation as the most combative Arab leader in the Palestinian cause, however, Gadafi also became the first Arab leader publicly to voice sharp criticism of the guerrillas, by casting doubt on their readiness for battle. The timing was significant; for Egypt was feeling her way towards negotiation, and the *fedayin* organizations were the sharpest obstacle. Far better for Egypt's reputation as leader of the Arab camp that Gadafi throw doubts on them ostensibly in their own interests. For even as the Libyan leader played his gadfly role in Arab capitals, his Egyptian advisers were well placed to use Libyan belligerence to cover the flank of Egypt's more compromised manoeuvres. In between Gadafi was purging the ranks of

Palestinians in Libya of those whose ideologies were considered divisive: a large contingent of militants from the Popular Front for the Liberation of Palestine was expelled from the country. There was no battle cause more indispensable to Arab régimes than the Palestinian; but the Palestinian liberation movements had themselves to be the creature of the Arab régimes.

As their response to the death of Nasser, the November 1970 summit of Libya, Egypt, and the Sudan translated their projected merger into a union. Syria's request to join the new federation was negotiated on the telephone the same month by General Hafiz al-Assad, who had come to power by coup d'état against other factions of the Baathist Left wing a few weeks earlier. In April 1971, at a meeting begun in Cairo and adjourned to Benghazi, the Union of Arab Republics of Egypt, Libya, and Syria was founded. It was founded on the principles of no negotiated peace agreement with Israel; and no slackening of support for the Palestinian cause. The admission of the Sudan, Major Jalloud announced, would be a formality after General Nimeiry had put his house in order and dealt with the troublesome Communist Party.

The statutes of the new Union[4] placed it somewhere between a federal and a confederal system. Member states retained powers to maintain their own diplomatic relations with foreign countries and their own armed forces; but the federal structure was directed to lay the foundations of a common foreign policy, to decide issues of peace and war, and to supervise a combined military command. The supreme authority was a presidential council of the three presidents, each of whom would serve as Federation President for two-year spells. Initially this supreme body of three was to function on a majority vote; and though the clause had already been ratified by Libya and Syria, trepidations within Egypt's Arab Socialist Union that the wild men of Libya and Syria would lead Egypt astray, had this changed to the principle of unanimous vote. There was to be a federal parliament, composed of an equal number of representatives from each state and entrusted with federal legislative functions. Pending the achievement of a single political structure, each state was responsible for organizing its own political activity, but political groups in any one state were forbidden to operate in the others except through the recognized 'political front command'. This seemed calculated to prevent Syria from exporting her political groupings to her partners. Clause 7(a) of the statutes established the right of the Federation to intervene in member states to maintain law and order. It stipulated that in the event of a threat, internal or external, to the government of any member state, the Federation should immediately be notified so that it could take security measures. If, however, the government was not in a position to seek aid, the federal authority could intervene without being invited. It was clearly a power calculated to legitimize and garrison the incumbent régimes against any and every challenge.

In the Sudan, reservations about an Arab–Islamic Federation were prompted both by the provocation that this would offer the insurgent forces in the south and by the explicit objections formulated by the forces of the Left then represented in the Nimeiry government by the trade unions and the mass popular organizations, including the Communist Party. For close on a year the Sudan took part in Tripartite and federal summits, but she tried to stress the peculiarity of her own condition: unity was the ultimate goal of all Arabs, but it should be achieved step by step; and national unity was surely a logical precondition of Arab unity. The fourth congress of the Sudanese Communist Party at the end of 1970 stressed that unity had to grow out of the democratic movement and the fulfilment of the democratic revolution. Relations between Egypt and the Sudan had always been close; but unity built in the struggle against imperialism should not be allowed to turn into a unity of intelligence services. In the Sudan there were democratic mass organizations with an independent policy and mass support. In Egypt there was only an organization under the control of a bureaucratic state.

As for Libya we do not believe it has yet won its independence, for oil is still in the hands of the monopolies, and there are no ideas of social change. There are no trade unions, no political parties, only the Arab Socialist Union, a shadow of its Egyptian counterpart. It would be impossible to weld these countries together because of their different levels of development, and the anti-democratic nature of the

Libyan and Egyptian states could be used to interfere in the development of the revolutionary movement in the Sudan.

'Moves towards unity in these conditions would, we fear, put a weapon in the hands of internal and external counter-revolution,' the statement concluded with some prescience.

In Libya, *Jundi*, the organ of the RCC and the army, published a blistering attack on the Sudanese Communist Party, and, implicitly, on the Sudanese régime for harbouring it. During 1971 the Federation's pressure on the Sudan coincided with a mounting conflict inside the country; between the forces contesting for the hegemony of army-and-bureaucracy through an Egyptian-type Arab Socialist Union, and a mass-based Left-oriented political front including the Communist Party. The struggle culminated in a putsch from the Left in July 1971, but the régime that it installed lasted only four days before Nimeiry was once again reinstated in power. The exact sequence and sources of internal counter-revolution and external intervention have yet to be analysed in detail. But if the Libyan–Egyptian intervention was not solely responsible for the restoration and the white terror that followed it they certainly prompted the circumstances which made it possible: by the Libyan forcing-down of the BOAC plane and the handing over for execution of the two leaders of the new régime; the dispatch post-haste of loyal troops from the Suez Canal zone to the Sudan; the emergency planning for escalating intervention conducted by Sudanese, Egyptian, and Libyan army commanders together.[5]

But Nimeiry's return to power, far from consummating Sudan's membership of the Federation, threw her towards the other Arab axis that had formed, between Saudi Arabia and the Gulf states, under United States protection. Having eliminated his popular base, Nimeiry's survival was conditional upon his healing the breach within the Sudan with the South. At this critical juncture the West came to his aid, trailing in its wake Kuwait and Saudi Arabia with their aid and investment offers. Fighting, and paying, to keep the Arab world cleansed of Leftist doctrines, the oil shaikhdoms headed by King Feisal found in Nimeiry, who had physically exterminated such forces in his country, a convenient instrument in the moves to weaken and isolate the aggressive nationalist Arab states. The Federation, with its simple and inflexible formula for Arab unity, found itself hoist by its own petard: once Arab unity was based on national-ism and religion but devoid of ideology, so that the destruction of the Left was an inevitable corollary, the Saudi Arabian side could only too easily beat its rival at the same game. Gadafi was to discover this not only in relation to the Sudan but in his drive through Black Africa, too.

King Feisal had advanced the idea of an Islamic summit as early as 1966 and had tried to use Islamic solidarity as a counter-blast to the calls of Egypt, Syria, and Algeria. Gadafi made Tripoli host to an Islamic Preaching Convention which autho-rized Libya to call on Islamic governments and peoples 'for action to liberate Arab lands from Zionist aggression'. Soon both Saudi Arabia and Libya were combing Africa for governments that would respond to an appeal based on Islamic opposition to Zionism. The half-dozen régimes that severed diplomatic rela-tions with Israel were testimony to the reinforcing effect of these combined pressures.

Libya's African policy began tentatively with diplomatic missions to Libya's Black African, largely Moslem neighbours: Niger, Mauritania, and Cameroun. Israel's presence in Africa was behind the Arab battle-line, 'sapping our strength at the back door'. Since Islam united Arabs and Moslem Africa, it was surely no more than a short step from being Moslem to becoming pro-Arab and anti-Israel.

An anomaly in the region was Chad. Governed by the Sara people of the south, it was not only unconquered by Islam but hostile to it for it was engaged in prolonged counter-insurgency – under French military direction and with French armed forces – against a rebellion in the north, fuelled by the discontents of a largely Moslem minority and led by a movement, Frolinat, which was supported from the rear by Algeria and also Libya. The Libyan border, as the border with Sudan to the west, was in-dispensable to Frolinat for the infiltration of arms into Chad. Additionally there was a long-standing dispute between Chad and Libya: a hangover from Sanusi expansionism in the nineteenth century, when the Sanusi claimed part of Chad as the Fezzan, and Chad launched counter-claims dating from the French colonial administration of the area. Accordingly Tripoli was only too willing to harbour both refugees from the rebellion and members of the insurgent leadership, and between the governments of Chad and Libya there was a state of vicarious war. If confirmation were needed of their incompatibility, Chad had close relations with Israel. In September 1971 the Tombalbaye régime was charging that Libya had supplied arms and trained conspirators for an abortive coup d'état against the government in Fort Lamy. (This was a few months after Gadafi had announced premature support for the failed coup in Morocco.)

There was a series of devious negotiations to heal the breach between Libya and Chad. France's Machiavellian Arab policy was now equalled by Gadafi's success in using France as his principal arms supplier and at the same time aiding and arming a rebellion aimed at overturning one of the most dependent of France's former African colonies. President Senghor tried to conciliate Libya and Chad. Niger's President Hamani Diory accepted the role of mediator only to have Gadafi announce Libya's official recognition of Frolinat even as talks with the Tombalbaye government were due to begin. Libya was transmitting a radio programme, 'beamed to our dear neighbours the heroic people of Chad', which began with readings from the Koran.

In September 1971 M. Foccart, France's Secretary of State for Afro-Malagasy affairs, arrived in Fort Lamy for talks with President Tombalbaye. This was shortly after the French Ambassador to Tripoli had been summoned by Colonel Gadafi to discuss 'the seriousness of the situation in view of the presence of French troops in Chad'. Somehow France had to reconcile her politics of oil and the North African Mediterranean with her politics for Central Africa, where even if her direct defence commitment was shrinking – French troops began to be withdrawn from Chad during 1971 – the former colonial power could not be seen to be abandoning one of the most loyal and dependent of her former colonies and disturbing the neo-colonial equilibrium of the region. The formula was produced shortly after the visit of President Pompidou to Chad and Niger in January 1972. Chad's government would end her relations with Israel. (By then she was in the company of Mali, Uganda, Congo–Brazzaville, and Niger; for in the intervening period both Libya and Saudi Arabia had stepped up their offensive in Africa.) Libya, in turn, would quietly jettison her support for Frolinat. Shortly before, *Le Monde* had publicized Libya's commitment to France not to aid Frolinat as long as France guaranteed the delivery of Mirages. Mauritania's President, and then also president of the OAU, Ould Daddah, had been principally instrumental in healing the breach. Libya's Foreign Ministry explained the reconciliation by alleging that Mobutu, under United States encouragement, was planning to post paratroopers to Chad to support Tombalbaye when the French troops had gone. Attempts had been made in Tripoli, it was reported, not to make Frolinat the price of the reconciliation.[6] But there were larger state interests at stake. Soon Gadafi was giving a banquet for Tombalbaye in Tripoli and announcing that Libya would finance development projects in Chad. France had not only balanced both ends of her policy, but had diverted some of her aid responsibilities from her own coffers to Libya's.

In the case of Uganda, the rules of the game had been improvised in Tripoli, and it was largely their success with General Amin that made Libya susceptible to the Foccart–Pompidou–Ould Daddah formula.

Idi Amin's coup d'état in January 1971 was a bid to pre-empt his removal from the army command by President Obote. The Israeli presence in Uganda dated from the first years of independence, and was prominent in military training projects of which Amin himself was a product. During the Amin coup, there was some considerable evidence of both British and Israeli complicity, especially in the shape of Israeli security liaison with the coupmakers. Without strong convictions or an ideology of any kind; isolated in Uganda and also in East Africa, except for a small constituency of soldiers from his home and neighbouring areas in the north of Uganda bordering on Sudan and the

Congo, Amin pursued policies calculated for their efficiency in helping him and his lumpen-militariat – in Ali Mazrui's graphic phrase – remain in power. Not long after he came to power, General Amin went travelling to West Germany, Chad, and Libya. The visit to Libya was arranged from Bonn, though by whom remains obscure, and the Libyans claim that the visit was at Amin's initiation, not theirs. A meeting between Amin and Gadafi produced a joint communiqué which rejected dialogue with South Africa, opposed the illegal Smith régime in Rhodesia, affirmed their support for the 'Arab People's rights' and struggle against Zionism and imperialism and agreed to keep their two governments in touch. In Kampala Israel's Ambassador asked President Amin for an explanation of the communiqué; and to his astonishment,[7] Amin answered that his country was not taking sides in the Middle East conflict and hoped to enjoy good relations with both Israel and the Arab world. These explanations apparently did not satisfy Jerusalem, which was pessimistic at reports that Amin had received a promise of economic aid from Libya. The first instalment materialized shortly after in the shape of two small hospitals, one of them for the army, and a Libyan offer to train air force pilots and technicians and army personnel. In Israel there were strong reactions to intelligence reports that both Egypt and Libya had offered to train Ugandan pilots on Mirage aircraft. Behind the severance of Uganda's relations with Israel, there lay the Israeli refusal of Amin's request that Uganda's debts be re-negotiated for payment over a longer period, and the belief that if Israel were out of the way, Libya would step in to fill the gap.

Libya's adoption of Amin was born of even simpler logic. RCC inquiries about Amin in the Libyan Foreign Ministry elicited the information that Amin was a Moslem but that he was an army protégé of Israel. 'But if he was trained by Israel, who invited Israel to Uganda in the first instance?' a member of the RCC pressed. After all, he argued, Libyan cadets were sent to Britain for training by a government whose foreign policy they rejected. So Libya made her overtures to Amin on the strength of his attachment to the Moslem religion, and this coincided with Amin's need for fresh allies. By mid 1972 Amin, travelling in a plane provided by Gadafi, had visited nine Arab countries and was even an observer at a Mersa Matruh session of the Federation's presidential council. The same month a Libyan delegation laid plans for the opening of a Libyan commercial bank in Uganda, and Morocco offered to build a mosque at the head-quarters of the Uganda Supreme Council. When Amin announced the expulsion of Asians from Uganda and the confisca-tion of their assets, Gadafi hailed this as equivalent to Libya's expulsion of the Italian colonial remnant. Yet, while the deporta-tion of the Asians broke the monopoly on commerce of an imported commercial community, deliberately introduced in colonial days to keep Africans out of trade, Amin's policy was calculated not to inaugurate policies of social and economic reform but to feed haphazard property allocations to his sup-porters in order to build an economic base for the fragile power structure of the army.

In September 1972 Amin was claiming that attacks by opposi-tion Ugandan guerrilla groups harboured on Tanzanian territory constituted a full-scale invasion by Tanzania. And if this version were not tendentious enough, it was laced with the information that Israeli mercenaries and Chinese tanks were also part of the invasion force. Furthermore, Britain (and India and Zambia) had sent troops to fight alongside the Tanzanians so as to install a régime that would rescind the expulsion of Asians from Uganda whom Britain had been obliged to harbour. Amin's defeat and Obote's return would thus bring Israel back. This fevered version was told by Amin to the Libyan Ambassador in Kampala who promptly relayed it to Colonel Gadafi. In an urgent telephone call to Amin, Gadafi promised to place the entire Libyan armed forces at the disposal of the Ugandan people if they were needed. Meanwhile five aircraft carrying troops and arms were dis-patched. By then the Sudan was plotting a course in African and Arab affairs that dispensed with the need for immediate bonds with Libya and Egypt and that was preoccupied with healing the breach in the south and thus with some of her African neighbours. The Libyan aircraft were refused facilities in Khartoum, though they reached Uganda nonetheless. For a few precarious days it looked as though Uganda backed by Libya – and supported in the background by some of the most obscurantist Islamic states in the world, together with some African states bemused by the garbled presentation of the issues – might unleash full-scale war against Tanzania, objectively the single country in Africa with both an unequalled commitment to the Southern African liberation struggle and a policy for radical, if incomplete, social change from within to break the pattern of neo-colonial dependence. Then Somalia offered mediation, and more sober counsels prevailed.

If the myth of a grand conspiracy between Tanzania, Britain, and Zionism wore thin this time, it continued to inspire Gadafi's spurious diplomacy. On the anniversary of the expulsion of the Italians from Libya, he set out the grounds of his policy towards Uganda and Africa. Soon after Amin's appearance on the scene Libya had sent an envoy to judge him:

We do not want to go along blindly with other people. We know that Arab diplomacy is blind. And . . . that the Arabs are unsuccessful in international stands. We must know things for ourselves because we adhere to the Koran 'O ye who believe, if there come to you a sinner with information, then discriminate, lest ye fall upon a people in ignorance and on the morrow repent of what ye have done.' Those who accused Idi Amin of ignorance repented on the morrow. [Applause.] Why did Zionism plan to control Uganda? Because before Israel existed in Palestine they had chosen it for several places where the Jews could live. One of these places was the Jebel Akhdar, one was Rhodesia, another was Palestine, and another was Uganda. Their plan was that if they left Palestine they would emerge in Uganda one day. Therefore they were constantly tightening their grip on Uganda . . . Amin expelled the Israelis, because he saw the Zionist . . . [plan was] to make it into a substitute for Palestine even in 100 years . . .

According to the same speech, the Moslems of Uganda numbered 70 per cent of the population; though he conceded that other statistics showed 25 per cent. Gadafi had his own version of the reasons for Tanzania's alleged invasion of Uganda. The matter, he told his audience, had a religious background. In Zanzibar the Moslems had been annihilated and African rule developed. Moslem Zanzibar had then been annexed to Tanganyika to form the state of Tanzania.[8] Tanzania was apparently set on further anti-Islamic campaigns.

It was a grotesque travesty of contemporary history and politics, but nothing was to stand in the way of the Islamic assault on Africa for the ousting of Israel. Between them, religious propaganda and financial aid, or promises of aid, paid off. By 1973 eight African heads of state had visited Tripoli; six had severed relations with Israel; and King Feisal himself had been on a flying visit to African capitals, including Kampala. It was an unaccustomed setback to Israeli diplomacy. But Israel's role in Africa had from the outset been part of imperialism's Third Country technique – channelling aid through a third party acceptable to the donor. Israel was no longer so acceptable. Saudi Arabia was, and though she could replace Israel with funds but not with trained civilian and military personnel, she would seek to play the part of satellite to United States interests with a finesse born of oil-rich experience. Libya saw herself as diametrically opposed to Saudi Arabia in the Arab world; but imperialism could be understood for seeing Libya, for all her nuisance value, as an agent for combating radicalism, fostering obscurantist ideology in Africa, and dividing the continent by its religious politics.

Towards the monarchical Arab régimes, Gadafi's blend of religion and politics was slightly more discriminating. Heykal has written of Gadafi's revulsion in Rabat at the sight of premiers, ministers, and generals bowing to kiss the hand of the monarch: to him Hassan was Idris, and in Morocco it was overdue for the Tent to confront the Palace. Libyan radio tried to remedy the deficiency, and Libya's relations with Morocco were in a continuous state of radio war, especially after Gadafi's premature jubilation at the Palace coup that failed. Rabat replied in good measure twice a week: reviling Gadafi as the mad clown, the imbecile tyrant; and regaling its listeners with an account of how Gadafi had ordered the detention of a football club which had planned to muster larger crowds at the stadium than Gadafi's political rally during the visit of the Somali president. Sometimes it was fact, sometimes fantasy. It was Rabat that announced in March 1973 the formation of an opposition movement inside

Libya of workers, students, intellectuals, and some army officers in the Libyan National Rally Movement. Once again it was an exaggeration, but leaflets questioning the régime had appeared in the streets, and soon afterwards the government was to crack down with large-scale arrests.

As a monarchy Morocco was an outcast to the Arab Federation. But an embarrassing absentee was clearly Algeria. Approached more than once to join, Algeria declined. There is no indication that Gadafi and his RCC understood Algeria's reservations about unity by fiat. On the seventeenth anniversary of the Algerian revolution, which uniquely in Africa and the Arab world had resulted from a long war of national independence, Gadafi upbraided the Algerians for having lost a million martyrs in a domestic (Arabic *wataniyah*) battle, which could bear no fruit unless it became an instrument for achieving the national (Arabic *Qawmiyah*) goals of the Arab nation. How Gadafi subsequently retracted this tirade of ignorant and offensive political judgement at the hurried meeting insisted on by Boumedienne in a Saharan oil town is not on record. Algeria continued to go her own way: trying to build an independent statist economy from a suffocating colonial past; insisting that non-alignment meant not complicity with imperialism but total commitment to those struggling against colonial aggression; and castigating Arab states for trying to disengage from the Palestinian conflict. Algeria's approach to unity – building from the bottom through concrete projects – eventually showed in the terms of an agreement for Algerian–Libyan cooperation. A Gadafi–Boumedienne summit communiqué from Constantine in February 1973 talked of moving their joint relations 'into practical spheres through which the two peoples will feel that the day of unity is coming nearer'. The Foreign Ministers of the two countries were to chair a joint committee which would give priority to cooperation in the fields of energy, especially oil and gas, joint industries, and joint companies.

In the Maghreb, closer to Libya in history, geography and economics than Egypt, there remained Tunisia. In December 1972 Gadafi went on a state visit to propose that as 'like-minded régimes, both republican, both embracing socialism, and both with a popular political organization, the road to unity was open'. President Bourguiba arrived at the public rally as Gadafi was half way through his speech, and then delivered a blistering rebuff. Gadafi's honesty, sincerity, and genuineness were beyond question; Bourguiba personally might be prepared to hand over power so that Gadafi could be president of the two republics. But Libya needed to link Tripolitania and Cyrenaica: 'those people in the desert are still living in the Middle Ages, even in the days of Adam and Eve'. There was no disagreement on the distant target of unity; until its moment arrived 'let us prepare for it by cooperation'. The gates of Arab nationalism would open once narrow concepts of nationalism had disappeared. The Libyan–Tunisian cooperation agreement was for specific projects: the joint exploration of the continental shelf and fishing areas of the two neighbours; cooperation in the fields of education, information, and defence; and above all, the enlargement of the agreements under which Tunisians entered Libya freely for work and contracting.

It was in the Yemen that Gadafi made free play of his notion of unity. Two Yemeni delegations arrived in Tripoli to solicit Libyan support: one from the north, which was run by tribal shaikhs and was a protégé of Saudi Arabia (and behind it the United States and Britain); and one from the south, committed to a Marxist-influenced régime. Gadafi made aid conditional on their achieving a unified state. Yemen was the Berlin, the Korea of the Arab world, Libya argued; an instrument divided by the policies of the Big Powers. North and south equally were being manipulated. However distant the purposes of the two régimes – Gadafi was as usual disinclined to recognize either ideology or internal social structure – Arab unity demanded that they combine. In Tripoli a conference of both sides tutored by the Libyans hammered out the ten bases for a single Yemeni state, and appointed a joint committee to draft the basic law for a political organization guided by the recently formed Libyan Arab Socialist Union.

Unity professions came from all sides; but one state of two regions with such distinct class and international alignments seemed impossible, unless one smothered the other. Libya had

visions of mediating the differences between north and south
to achieve a somewhat more 'liberal' government in the north
and a less 'extreme' one in the south. Meanwhile it shipped arms
to both sides, depending on Gadafi's pragmatic judgement of
events. (He sent guns to the north Yemen when it tried to invade
the south; but had turned temporarily against the north for
intercepting Libyan arms shipments on their way to Eritrea's
Liberation Front.) Consistent with his policy of obliterating
Marxist influence, Libya was also arming Sultan Qabus of
Oman's counter-insurgency assault against the Dhofar guerrilla
movement.

In the Middle East proper, Libya's relations with other states
were prickly and growing more so. There was bitter enmity with
Jordan. When at a meeting of the Arab Armed Forces Chiefs of
Staff conference in Cairo, the Jordanian Chief of Staff raised the
question of Libya's suspension of financial support to Jordan,
the Libyan Chief of Staff, Lieutenant-Colonel Abubakr Yunis,
retorted that Libya supported fighters not butchers.[9] Gadafi
repeatedly urged Free Officers to arise in Jordan to topple the
throne.

Iraq staged a revolution but she was suspect because Baathist;
and though she nationalized part of her oil industry, she also
built close relations with the Soviet Union. When Iraq called for
unity with Egypt and Syria but left Libya out, there was under-
standable irritation. Syria was a member of the tripartite Federation, but she and Libya drifted ever further apart. When she was
left out of the Libyan–Egyptian merger, the Syrian President
passed this off as due to 'the geographical factor'. It was
Gadafi's attempts to goad the Syrians into belligerency that
probably produced his first inklings of how difficult were the
tactical problems of the Palestinian battle. Under the previous
régime the Syrians and Saiqa, the commando group it supported,
had been preaching popular war. On his first visit to Damascus
after coming to power, Gadafi had announced his belief that the
defeat of Israel by popular liberation war was a non-starter:
conventional warfare was the only way. Gadafi's attack was
designed to push the Syrian armed forces into taking their place
along the eastern front. One consequence of the subsequent

seizure of power in Syria by the Assad group was a noticeable toning down of Syrian belligerence. This was said to be due in part to the aftermath of 1967 and Nasser's death, and to Syria's fear of being exposed to Israeli retaliation in front-line battle.[10] Gadafi tackled his Federation partner about why the *fedayin* were restricted on Syrian soil. The Palestinians, Assad replied, would be better advised to work out how to infiltrate and blow up an Israeli factory, how to enter an Israeli camp, how to liberate part of their homeland, rather than trying the odd sortie by rocket from Syria's border. If it came to that, the Syrian army had long-range artillery. But it was the Syrian army that stood facing the Israeli, and had to calculate the results of provocative policies. Gadafi reverted to his familiar theme for action from all fronts simultaneously in a planned and unified battle. When Israel attacked Syria during 1973, Gadafi ignored her pleas for help, insisted that these were skirmishes and not the battle proper, and that nothing decisive was possible until the Arab world committed itself to total confrontation. But Gadafi was also capable of despairing with a not inaccurate account of the impasse:

> The Arab situation is tepid and engulfed in fog and darkness. There is no direction. The Arabs have lost direction. There is no unanimity in support of the Palestinian people. There is no determination to open a *feda'i* war against Israel. There is no determination to conduct a regular war against Israel. There is no force that can be counted on in the arena except Egypt and Syria. The rest, no. Iraq has a force but it is not present. We do not even know who rules Iraq. Jordan has a force but it is finished, for it has reached the inevitable conclusion of any régime that is a lackey of Zionism. The other Arab states have no clear, reliable course.[11]

There were also policy differences between Egypt, Syria, and Libya. The latter two, unlike Egypt, had not accepted the Security Council decision of 22 November 1967. Egypt and Libya had opposite policies on the Pakistan–India–Bangla Desh issue. The Federation between the three had produced little more than a liaison of the superstructures of their governments, and a conscientious exchange of minutiae between their legal and administrative staffs. There were some combined economic projects, especially Egyptian undertakings in Libya; and the Federal Assembly of twenty elected members from each country held sessions in Cairo. It was the very feebleness of the Federation and the policy disorientations of its constituent parts that seemed to convince Libya that something closer and stronger was needed.

In July 1972 on the twentieth anniversary of Egypt's Free Officer coup, Gadafi called for an immediate merger of Egypt and Libya, and the government radio announced that the 'country was impatiently waiting with boundless hope for the reply of President Anwar es-Sadat'. It subsequently emerged that Gadafi had made the original demand for union five months earlier, but that Sadat had asked for time to consider. A week later the Egyptian delegation was closeted in Benghazi with Gadafi and eight of his RCC members, and when they emerged it was to announce that the merger was agreed and would go to referendum in September 1973. The signing of the agreement took place as Israeli commandos invaded southern Lebanon in search-and-destroy attacks on *fedayin* bases. The 'unified political leaderships' of the two states – in fact Gadafi and Sadat – were to supervise the steps towards unity and were to be served by nine committees: on constitutional affairs, political organization, defence, security, foreign affairs, economic organization, juridical and legislative matters, administration and finance, and education and sciences. But all decisions lay with Gadafi and Sadat. A member of Libya's RCC told me that the nine committees were 'just technicians'. At any level below the RCC and doubtfully on that body, there was absolutely no attempt to explore the implications of a unified state or different means towards it. Planners felt and very occasionally said that they were confronted with 'imponderables'. The most prominent civil servants in the country were given no documentation to study the issues in depth. And there was, of course, no serious public debate on the matter; only enthusiastic press and radio homilies to the glories of unity. Jalloud told a student gathering that the unity with Egypt was the one issue that was not open to discussion by them.

It was disclosed that the unified state would comprise twenty-five provinces, ten on Libyan and fifteen on Egyptian territory, with perhaps one straddling the border on combined territory. It was probably through provincial organization and delegation of authority that attempts would be made to allocate money for development projects to suit the starkly different needs of these two diverse countries. But until a few months before the merger deadline, practically nothing more detailed was known. Libya made a public promise that pay and civil service grades for Libyans, though considerably higher than Egyptian rates, would be unaffected by the merger. But in what precise terms these two countries of widely different economic and social structure, and unlike development priorities and needs, would combine, remained a mystery. Such were dismissed as technical details that were not to be allowed to stand in the way of unity.

Gadafi was saying with increasing urgency that if Egypt fell, all North Africa, all the Arab world, was defeated. Orders from Tel Aviv would be carried out in Mauritania. Egypt remained the only force capable of confronting the enemy. If Egypt as the heartland of the Arab cause could not rally, the cause was lost. It was an arguable case. It is certainly true that nothing which affects Egypt can leave Libya untouched; that on her own Libya is of minimal importance and effect; that left to their own devices, Libya's young soldiers and bureaucrats may squander Libya's oil resources on this generation; that it is difficult to see how social forces will arise from within Libyan society to break the sequence of military rule; that closed, insular Libya needs an opening to the wider Arab world and its ideas and influences and social movements, and Egypt is the natural doorway. This is the reasoning used by some radical Libyan unionists. Their conception of unity is different from Gadafi's but based on the hope that he could unleash forces that will enlarge his own restricted calculations. The flaw in this argument that unity with Egypt will rescue Libya from her obsolete past and situate her at last inside a changing Middle East is that Gadafi's influence – and the forces he identifies with and encourages – seek not to promote social and political change but to suffocate it. Resurgent Moslem Brotherhood functions and rising religious xenophobia in Egypt are in part a direct response to Gadafiism.

Inside Egypt the initial reaction to the merger ranged from indifference to downright scepticism. Then Cairo's ministries were taken aback at the speed with which Sadat acquiesced under Gadafi's pressure, and they bent their backs to the paperwork which is the strength of the Egyptian bureaucracy. The last thing Egypt could afford was to refuse a request for unity, above all when it came from such a persistent and wealthy neighbour, and when close friends were so scarce. There is no evidence that the Egyptian government gave the implications of the merger any more serious study than had the Libyans.* But as the months went by, the unity project, like so many of Sadat's gambits, became one more bid by the President to buy time. The Egyptian government was hurtling from one expediency to another: the expulsion of the Russians (before obtaining any *quid pro quo* from either the United States or Israel), and then an invitation to return; promise of a marriage with Libya, and then a courtship of Saudi Arabia and Kuwait and even a rapprochement with Jordan; overtures to win diplomatic support from Western Europe so as to make an impression on the United States; feelers to Washington for the reopening of the Suez Canal and some new diplomatic formula for ending the Middle East imbroglio. Yet simultaneously there was the launching of a nationwide network of 'war' committees to prepare the home front for the battle against Israel. The domestic slogan was 'No voice louder than the battle.' It was ostensibly to stiffen national unity for the battle that Sadat lashed out against the deviationists, the 'irresponsible Left', during student and industrial unrest, while continuing to tilt his régime towards the most conservative sections of the middle class and the new bureaucratic rich. The battle cries were the classic diversionary tactic. The interminable speeches roused the country for the inevitability of the battle that was not joined; and meanwhile a state of national

---

* By 1973 the two countries were considering three alternative unity formulas. The first proposed a unified state achieved fairly rapidly; the second proposed a form of federation; and the third envisaged agreement on a unified foreign policy and then gradual stages towards a combined administration. Discussion on the three formulas was interrupted by the outbreak of the 1973 Middle East War. See *Summary of World Broadcasts*, ME 4352/A/6, 21 July 1973.

emergency was used to obscure and postpone recognition that the system was fraying at the seams.

Until his death, Nasser's tactical skill had managed to balance and control the contesting factions in the Egyptian régime. But the disintegration within Egyptian society was far more profound than simply Sadat's failings or the conflict for office of rival factions might explain. It was a disintegration within Egypt but also throughout much of the Arab world where petit-bourgeois nationalism had proved its disastrous limits. It was widely evident that 'national unity' for the battle against Israel was being used as a form of political blackmail by régimes against masses; that régimes were corrupt and paralysed, while peoples were dispirited and alienated; that despite the conventional distinction between 'revolutionary' and reactionary Arab régimes, no really far-reaching revolution had taken place anywhere, to break creatively with the past and place controls in the hands of sectors thus far denied access to power. Nationalist ideology, even with some provision for socialist aspirations but with these relegated to a subordinate role, had served to mobilize the masses in the assault on old ruling groups. But once nationalists were in power, and confronted with the ineluctable decisions about economics that power involved, nationalism and its nebulous theories of Arab unity had been found wanting. Arab unity under the leadership of the petit-bourgeoisie, squeezed by larger capitalist interests but nervous of what they might lose under socialism, could only be an uneasy unity at the top between vacillating régimes.

This variety of Arab nationalism could not really fight a battle for Palestine, for there was an inherent contradiction between the strategic needs of the *fedayin* and the purposes of Arab régimes. The Arab régimes had only deflected attention from their internal problems by their advocacy of the Palestinian cause. In some circles there was a growing realization that the *fedayin* movements were useless as creatures of the Arab régimes; that prolonged popular struggle was the only way. The Vietnam parallel was quoted even by men like Gadafi. But given the power of Israeli society against the Palestinians, their struggle could not survive or escalate into popular war without a safe rear. Popular war Vietnam-style would require countries directly concerned in supporting the guerrillas to play the role and risk the fate of North Vietnam and Cambodia; and this they had become positively unwilling to do. By now the Palestinian resistance was in a critical condition. Its rout by the Jordanian army in 1970 had been followed by a second annihilation offensive, when fleeing guerrillas forded the river Jordan into Israel and gave themselves up rather than face annihilation at the hands of pursuing Jordanian forces. The Lebanon, the last remaining Arab state where the guerrillas had a measure of freedom to operate, turned on them. In the Left-wing *fedayin* groups and in Fatah's own rank and file, there had for some time been growing disillusionment with the policy of dependence on Arab régimes that had progressively weakened the movement and its freedom of action. There were already signs in 1971 that as the price of Arab assistance in reaching a *modus vivendi* with Fatah at least in Jordan, Yasser Arafat and the Fatah leadership would be called on to help in neutralizing the Left-wing guerrilla groups.

When Fatah finally came out unreservedly for the overthrow of the Hashemite monarchy, it had already lost the means to pursue such a policy. 'In 1965 when Fatah blew up its first water pipe in Israel,' David Hirst wrote, 'it was laying down a challenge not only to Israel, but to Nasser and the whole strategy which he had, through his immense prestige, persuaded most Arabs to accept, namely, that the Arabs must defer the liberation of Palestine until they were really ready, and any freelance operations, dragging them into premature war, were not merely foolish but treacherous.'[12]

Whether the causes emanated from this subservience to Arab régimes, or from internal equivocations and errors, or some mixture of these, the Palestinian resistance had failed to build a mass base of support in the occupied territories. Palestine groups were beginning sharply to criticize the reliance of the movement on refugee populations in refugee camps, the rootless and 'lumpen', without a vanguard guiding force.[13] But by the time this came to be recognized as the most serious weakness, it was late in the day, and the *fedayin* had lost easy access to Israeli territory from the Arab countries along the front line. 'The major error committed by the resistance,' Walid Khalidi, Director of the Institute of Palestine Studies, told Eric Rouleau,[14] 'was to put the cart before the horse and launch hostilities without first establishing the bases indispensable to the success of any guerrilla operations.' Armed struggle had been conceived as a series of forays initiated from outside and not as the armed and therefore final form of a popularly rooted resistance. This failure to elaborate a strategy of popular struggle within the occupied territory was connected with the failure to analyse the structure and development of Israeli society, whose internal unity was maintained through conflict with the external enemy, but within which Israeli Arabs above all, but also strata of Israeli youth, were coming increasingly into conflict with the régime.[15] Eric Rouleau described the central body of the resistance as not so much a coordination centre as an area for the struggles between the contending ideologies of the nationalist and Islamist Right and the Leftists, between contradictory political and tactical concepts and between partisan and personal rivalries. For all the intensity of the contending arguments, the resistance had not been able to formulate a strategy for guerrilla resistance that was autonomous of the Arab régimes and could nonetheless and at the same time take indispensable advantage of their susceptibility on the Palestinian issue. The *fedayin* movements vacillated shakily between one pole of their need and the other; at one time provoking the Jordanian army to a showdown which they lost, and at other times permitting the manipulation of their internal leadership structure by régimes determined to keep a tight rein. The resort to terrorism was an admission of these combined failings and their culmination. Black September was less a structured group than a rallying point for mutually independent terrorist cells which came from the youth of the Palestinian Diaspora desperate at the shortcomings of the resistance. The most clear-thinking of the resistance leaders were alarmed at the danger that terrorism as a tactic, together with the reprisals it must bring, would nurture illusory forms of struggle that would steadily cut off the Palestinian movement from its remaining grass roots.

Gadafi's backing of terrorist groups – he was probably their principal paymaster – was a measure of his enthusiasm for blows, any blows, against Israel. In the nature of his aversion for radical ideology as a politicizing force among the masses, terrorism was a natural choice of means. But it was also a measure of his own despair at the prevarication of the Arab régimes, not least Egypt, about whose policies he was becoming increasingly critical; even though he was pledged to merge Libya and Egypt into a single state at all costs. The culmination of this despair at the feebleness of the battle was his decision to withdraw 600 Libyans sent to fight alongside the *fedayin*; it was not Israel that had stopped them fighting, but Arab régimes, he said.

No wonder that his speeches sounded so frantic. Convinced that he could carry his zeal into Egypt, he pressed for total union, while all around him commentators speculated on the outcome. The two countries are contiguous and, to an extent, complementary. Egypt is poor with too many trained professional people; Libya has too few people and almost no expertise, but more money than she knows what to do with. In theory the combination of Libyan oil money with Egyptian technical ability offered chances of swifter development to both countries: but only if the most painstaking attention was paid to the distinct needs of both. As her own planning was without any conception of the dynamics of development, the danger for Libya of a merger with Egypt was that for every local or manpower problem Libya could not solve, she would import a temporary solution. If Gadafi's intention was to underwrite Egypt's war effort, did he seriously propose to assume the burden of civil and military aid? and if so, what would be the fate of Libya's development plans? Would he not surrender his leverage as an independent entity by having his army of 16,000 absorbed by Egypt's 800,000 men under arms, and his own resources sucked into the Egyptian bureaucracy? Gadafi saw himself influencing Egypt. But would Sadat not turn him into an instrument to cover his flank, as with loud talk about the battle he went in search of mediated solutions? Already, as 1973 opened, Gadafi made a speech which warned that if pan-Arabization of the battle was not realized, then every Arab state would have the right to settle its own problems in the way it found suitable. The implication was that no Arab could blame Sadat for seeking a political settlement, if the other Arab countries had failed to rally to her.

After the downing of the Libyan airliner over Sinai in February 1973 and the Israeli raid on Beirut to kill Palestinian resistance leaders, he launched a blistering attack against Arab states, including Egypt, for thwarting plans he had drawn for retaliation against Israel:

> I personally cannot be held responsible for any pan-Arab failure. Should the Arabs fail again and suffer a calamity, God forbid, I do not want to be among the defeated leaders. This is because I have nothing to do with any defeat ... I cannot endure being one of the Arab Presidents who live and see the Palestinian people stripped of their resistance.

There had never been any doubt of his sincerity; but audacity, even more audacity, was simply not enough.

Meanwhile Libya was also engaged in battles on other fronts. Through Malta and Ireland, it was possible to strike bold blows against imperialism by taking advantage of Britain's declining strength as an imperial power. There was less occasion for confrontation with the United States. Libya's support for Malta gave her time to use the leverage of prolonged negotiations to get more money for the base not from Britain but from NATO, and opportunity to assert her claims for national independence and her search for neutrality. Libya made no secret of the arms she shipped to the Provisionals of Northern Ireland. At the same time Libya was still Britain's largest customer in North Africa and the Middle East. After the withdrawal of the bases, the BAC contract had lapsed into abeyance; with remaining disputes about Britain's debts to Libya arising from base rentals, the undelivered B.A. missile system, and the order for Chieftain tanks. Britain had hoped to salvage the arms deals from the Anglo-Libyan Defence Treaty, but France had edged her way into the space left by Britain's departure as the principal arms supplier.

Since the end of the war in Algeria, De Gaulle's policy had been to modify France's unqualified support for Israel in order to rebuild French relations with the Arab world. The Six Day War provided the occasion to exchange the Israeli market for the potentially far more lucrative Arab one and to take advantage of Arab disenchantment with British and American Middle East policy but uneasiness about turning to the Soviet Union. The Mirage contract generated heated Western responses. United States intelligence sources were quoted as saying that the Mirage jets were destined for Egyptian airfields, and that Nasser had arranged for the Libyan government to do his arms shopping for him. French policy, said Premier Chaban Delmas, was neither pro-Israel nor pro-Arab, but only pro-French; and in any case, French policy was well appreciated by the British government, for France's supplies would prevent Libya from turning to the Soviet Union. Rather Mirages than Migs.

But not everything was bought from France. Soon Libya was once again shopping for arms in Britain, and her arms purchases became as diversified as all her economic arrangements, with the vast preponderance of her trade done with the industrial capitalist world.

Gadafi's pronouncements that he rejects both capitalism and communism stem not from any Maoist-type commitment that the United States and the Soviet Union are equally 'imperialist super-states', but from nationalism and religion. Communism is pernicious because it is godless and abolishes property. Gadafi is as suspicious of China as he is of the Soviet Union. Some ground had been prepared for the exchange of diplomatic representation between Libya and the Peoples' Republic of China, but Peking is still unrepresented in Tripoli because Formosa is still there. The first top-level Libyan delegation visited the Soviet Union in March 1972, two and a half years after the RCC's accession to power. Led by Prime Minister Jalloud, this delegation was reported to have discussed the Palestinian issue, among other questions. Soviet proposals for helping build Libya's industrial sector seem for the most part to have fallen away; in Tripoli it is said this arises from the régime's determination to permit no 'communist' influence whatever in the domestic economy.

Gadafi's – and thus Libya's – relations with the United States

are ambiguous. The young colonel shocked a meeting of
Egyptian intellectuals during a round-table discussion at the
offices of *Al Ahram*[16] by arguing that unlike other great powers,
the United States had not shared in the accumulation from
colonialism. 'All American capital is American,' he told his
astonished audience. 'It is United States steel, copper, United
States rivers . . . that did it (establish a technological society –
R.F.) . . . not the exploitation of the world.' (This was too much
even for editor Heykal who spoke immediately after Gadafi to
say with some feeling: 'America stole a whole continent . . .
Latin America is still colonised until now . . .') Gadafi's version
of the United States role in Libya was that 'America had not
taken money from us . . . she was giving us aid, wheat.' True she
had used Libya for NATO as a base against the Soviet Union.
'This,' said Gadafi, 'was the extent of United States colonialism.'
What of today? 'Now there is oil and the majority of companies
are American . . . but this is a very new road, and the companies
are facing difficult times, an unknown fate . . .'

Gadafi's overriding concern about the United States is that
its foreign policy has not yet 'defined its attitude to our enemy'.
One has the distinct impression that once the United States
changed its policy on the Palestine issue, Gadafi would have little
to quarrel with. He as much as said so in his statement after the
re-election of President Nixon in 1972.

Whenever any US President, whether Richard Nixon, or anyone
else, is able to get rid of the Zionist influence on US policy, that day
will not only be the beginning of the establishment of sound and
healthy relations between this nation and the United States, but will
also be a national day for the United States, to celebrate the restoration
of the right to determine the policy of a major state like the United
States.[17]

If there are stumbling blocks to closer Libyan–US relations, in
Gadafi's opinion Western Europe 'has got rid of the imperialist
trend', and is seeking 'free economic and commercial relations
with countries like Libya.' He told the Lebanese weekly newspaper *Al-Hawadeth*: 'It is out of this understanding that we
directed ourselves towards Western Europe.' Relations with

France have never been better; West Germany is now the largest importer of Libyan oil; Britain's trade with Libya – despite the running battle over the BAC contract monies – is the largest in the Middle East.

As far as the United States' attitude to Libya is concerned, two senior American diplomats are reputed to have helped swing American attitudes in favour of the Gadafi régime.[18] The two were David Newson and Joseph Palmer; the former was American Ambassador in Tripoli, the latter Assistant Secretary of State in Washington; and just before the revolution they swopped jobs. It was Newson who the then British Ambassador to Washington, Mr John Freeman, is said to have called on to discuss the matter of recognition of the new régime. Ambassador Palmer's despatches to Washington prophesied that Gadafi would be a heaven-sent champion of United States interests and the scourge of communism. There is no doubt that Gadafi's interventions in the Sudan and the Yemen are part of an anti-communist and anti-Soviet campaign and exactly what the United States might have ordered. Yet a certain friction ran through Libyan–US relations occasioned by contests within the oil world and over the Palestine issue.

12 The Limits of Nationalism

When in October 1973 Egypt launched the Fourth Arab–Israeli war, it was not Gadafi, his partner in the projected union between Egypt and Libya, but King Feisal of Saudi Arabia who was privy to that attack plan. It proved to be a limited war with limited goals.[1] Until then Sadat's policy of trying to cajole the United States into pressuring Israel into acceptable terms had failed; a military success on the battlefield was calculated to induce Nixon and Kissinger to impose a more stable situation in the Middle East. The offensive launched by Egypt, and joined by Syria, was a conventional military confrontation, fought by a technically proficient army manned by a generation of university-trained and drafted technicians,[2] using textbook tactics. The Egyptian forces knocked out the Israeli positions along the Bar Lev line, but then hesitated, and switched to a defensive strategy when they might have maintained the offensive. The extent to which military or political considerations lay behind this tactic is not yet clear. But even a limited war with limited gains shattered the myth of the invincibility of the Israeli army and its intelligence apparatus. It also broke the myth of the fighting incapacity of Arab armies, and, most important of all, it broke the mood of fatalism and immobilism within the Arab world. But this only temporarily perhaps, for Sadat's post-war tactics proved to be a logical continuation of the search of the Egyptian bourgeoisie and bureaucracy for close and amicable relations with the United States. The re-opening of diplomatic relations between Egypt and the United States was natural enough, as formal recognition that by then Egypt had handed Kissinger her negotiating brief in the dispute with Israel. Simultaneously, inside Egypt the Sadat régime's domestic measures demonstrated that her diplomacy was part of a larger concern by Egypt's rulers to forge a close relationship with imperialist capital. Western and other private capital was sought for the public sector. The most conservative oil-rich states were invited to invest. Some confiscated land was handed back to its former owners. The economy is to be 'liberalized' for private domestic capital, in harness with foreign capital. Libya's oil resources, accordingly, are no longer the most significant source of support on offer.

Perhaps more than anyone else in the Arab world, Gadafi emerged the loser from the 1973 war. Once Sadat and Feisal had been able to combine – and the history of the origins and sequence of this collaboration are as yet untold – Gadafi and Libya were expendable. Saudi Arabia could offer infinitely more pressure with oil resources so much vaster than Libya's; and Saudi Arabia had excellent relations with the United States. The thrust of an Arab drive for the combined use of frontal war and the economic weapon of oil were provided by the Cairo–Riadh axis. Libya was left on the sidelines. When the fighting was over and a ceasefire in operation, Gadafi was heard to be denouncing it as a comic-opera war, and accusing Sadat of a sell-out.[3] (The Palestinians had indeed been edged to the fringes of the event, to be kept there throughout the prolonged negotiations, for the war and its aftermath have less and less to do with the Palestinian issue.) Gadafi refused to attend the Algiers summit in November 1973. He denounced Feisal as 'nothing but an oil merchant'. Relations between Egypt and Libya had rarely been worse. Passport controls were reimposed on Egyptians in Libya, and Egyptians there on official secondment were reported to be returning home.

In this context the Libyan–Tunisian merger proposal of January 1974 looked uncommonly like an act of pique on Gadafi's part: overlooked by Arabs to the east, he would build a union with a country to the west. It was an enterprise even more precipitate and worse prepared than the proposal for union with Egypt had been. And it collapsed even more precipitately, reducing to the level of farce one more attempt to forge Arab unity from on high in presidential proclamation. Arab unity, said Tunisian opposition leader in exile Ahmed Ben Salah, 'must not be used as a whiff of oxygen to save a régime already expiring'.[4] He was referring to the internal state of Tunisia. As for Libya, every abortive unity attempt she tried was serving to discredit her own cause. The month after the Tunisian debacle Gadafi went to Egypt to patch up his differences with Sadat. His speeches were as obsessed with the need for unity as ever before ('If Egypt falls, then the entire Arab nation will collapse'). But by then credibility in Gadafi's capacity for sustained strategy was seriously strained. And, ironically enough, the Arab leader who had pressed hardest for the use of oil as a political weapon had been upstaged by oil-producing régimes that until the war had dragged their feet on every issue from Palestine to oil.

The effect of the war has been to isolate Gadafi and Libya from Middle East political events, to strengthen the Sadat régime with its new-found allies, and also to rigidify the ruling groups in the most conservative Arab states which increasingly in the period after the 1973 war came to dominate events in the Middle East. For the war which initiated the use of oil as a political weapon found not only Algeria and Libya ready to reduce production and place an embargo on shipments to Europe and the United States, but Kuwait, Iran and Saudi Arabia too.

In time – by March 1974 – the embargo imposed by the oil producers to pressure Europe and the United States to alter their policy on Israel was lifted. But by then it was clear that the use of the embargo and production cutbacks during the war were part of a far larger crisis over the control of the world's oil resources, and that oil was tilting the balance of world power.

The world's most advanced capitalist states, led by the United States, had to confront the fact that their economies' survival in the ensuing decade would depend on their oil imports from the Middle East, and this in precisely the period when the oil-producing states were threatening a cutback in production in a concerted policy to husband their oil resources. The embargo, which was in any case applied only partially, was nothing like as important as production levels. The Arab producers have begun to assert their power not only through their insistence on price rises, but also by the assertion of their right to control production rates.

OECD estimates of world oil availability and demand calculate that even without the cutback in production, by 1980 the combined oil needs of the United States, Europe, Britain and Japan will considerably exceed oil production.[5] This period of increased demand coincides with the faltering supply of United States domestic production, so that US demands for a larger share of the world supply will eat deeply into that supply.

Fred Halliday writes:

While the rise in demand within each different imperialist economy will be of roughly the same order, the changes in supply will be asymmetrical. The US will double its demand – from 15 to 25 million barrels – while its domestic supply will falter or even fall round the 12 million mark. Alaskan production, if and when it can be started, will provide around 2 million barrels a day, i.e. only 20 per cent of the increase in demand. This means that US import needs will rise, from under 15 per cent in the early 1970s, to up to 50 per cent by 1980. Europe will continue to import most of its oil, since the North Sea will produce only 2–3 million barrels a day, and Japan too will continue its dependence on imports. The 'energy crisis' is therefore both a general crisis of rising demand but it is distorted by the disproportionate increase in US import needs.[6]

It is the disproportionate demands of the US economy which explain the frenzy with which that government is trying to induce European consumer-governments to allow the State Department to represent their interests in Middle East negotiations; the US anxiety is that European governments will continue in their efforts to conclude a series of bilateral oil deals with individual Middle East producers, and the United States will lose its controlling grip on the allocation and marketing of international oil.

The result of the rise in general oil demand is that producer states can continue to raise their revenues. There have been meteoric rises in the price of oil. In February 1974 a supply of Libyan crude sold for $18·76 a barrel; the more general price at the time was $15·76 but even this was six times the price paid her a few years earlier. (The Gulf price in the same period was in the neighbourhood of $11·65 a barrel.)

Rising oil prices continue to mean rising profits for the oil companies as well as the producer-states. Company profits have in fact never been higher.[7] But there is no denying that the shape of the international oil industry run by giant integrated companies is changing. The monopoly character of the industry, as it had once been controlled by the majors, has been eroded over the years, first by the competitive entry of the independent companies, later by joint ventures, especially forms of partnership between oil states and consumer states; and now, most recently, by producer-state intervention in price-fixing and production targets.

In the Arab oil world the financial reserves of the producers have grown sufficiently large for their movements to affect world money markets and the fate of metropolitan currencies. Instead of investment by advanced capitalist economies in the underdeveloped, though wealthy, oil states, there is the prospect of the ruling classes of these underdeveloped states investing in the economies of the advanced capitalist world: a case of large-scale reverse-direction overseas investment.[8]

Arab oil money can, of course, be re-cycled back into the western economies through large-scale arms purchases and the import of high technology. Hence King Faisal's visit to Washington to call for United States aid to industrialize his country and negotiations between France and Libya. But even with the exchange of oil for western technology, the crisis of Western monopoly capitalism remains, for it is rooted in the declining power of the oil industry and receding western control over the world's energy resources. From being client states of the West the oil states are likely to become more assertive partners, forging in the process ever-closer links between western economies and policy-making and the ruling oligarchies of the richest oil states, and yet at the same time deepening the contradictions between competitive capitalisms, both mature and emergent.

Hinged on the structure of the industry, the exploitation of oil has made Libya inescapably part of the international capitalist system. Though much of the economy is still blatantly pre-capitalist, the dominant mode of production is capitalist, linked to giant multi-nationals resting on American, British, and European monopoly capital and management. Despite its great wealth Libya is dependent in the fullest sense of the word, providing crude oil to the metropolitan centres of the world in exchange for manufactured goods, foodstuffs, even primary materials. Subordinated to international capital in the economy are the remnants of pre- or early-capitalist agrarian production, small-scale trading, an embryonic sector of national capital in commerce and industry, and a growing state sector. The growth of the economy since oil has been phenomenal, but growth has been restricted to this highly capitalized sector and its direct subsidiaries on the one hand; and on the other, to the public sector of the rentier economy's state, which is the direct beneficiary of the Libyan share of oil exploitation. Libya's series of confrontations with the oil companies are attempts to re-negotiate the terms by which the monopolies exploit the country's oil resources. The process is as yet incomplete. It is too soon to tell whether Libya can achieve more than partial control over the exploitation and use of these resources. For the meantime, then, between the multi-nationals and the state, there is thus both collaboration and yet a conflict of interests. On the surface there is blazing hostility and a running quarrel over the pickings; but below this, there is a mutual dependence on oil and the cartel monopoly marketing structure which, by its subsidies – in the shape of oil royalties – to the state, creates a large and constantly expanding public sector.

In an oil economy based on highly sophisticated technology more than in any other post-colonial state, there is thus illustrated not any classic contradiction between the interests of metropolitan bourgeoisies and an indigenous ruling class, but a fundamental source of collaboration. Hamza Alavi[9] has demolished the concept of a 'national' bourgeoisie which is presumed to become increasingly anti-imperialist as it grows bigger, so that its contradictions with imperialism sharpen. This, he argues, is derived from an analysis of colonial and not post-colonial experience. In the post-colonial state, 'the mutual relationship of the native bourgeoisie and the metropolitan bourgeoisie is no

longer antagonistic; it is collaborative'.[10] In large part this is
embedded in the need for access to technology to sustain and
develop the economic operations of the new state. Collaboration
implies separate interests and a hierarchy of interests which in-
volves a degree of conflict in their relationship and a tension
underlying it. Convergence of interest does not dissolve into
an identity of interests. There is nonetheless an element of
mutual dependence even in the context of oil economies in
which producer-states command such excessive resources.

It is the nature of the post-colonial state which is crucial to an
understanding of the role of Libya's army régime. The coup
d'état is a recurring phenomenon in post-colonial societies on all
the continents of the Third World which are neither part of
the advanced capitalist world nor socialist. The coup d'état
brings to power a military–bureaucratic oligarchy which runs the
country through its power over the state machine. The state
apparatus in the post-colonial state is inherited from the withdrawing – or ejected – colonial power; and in the nature of its
pre-independence function, to institutionalize the subordinate
relationship of the colonial population and society, it is over-
developed. Yet it is, after independence, not the instrument of
any single indigenous ruling class.[11]

In Libya under the monarchy, the functions of the domestic
state were controlled by a traditional oligarchy, linked with
incipient elements of a new bourgeoisie, under the direct tutelage
of metropolitan power. The seizure of power was not so much a
revolution made by the petite-bourgeoisie as one that has made
way for its speedier formation. Under the Revolutionary Command Council, political power rests in a small army group that
rules through its control of the state machine on behalf of a range
of domestic social class interests, which are not identical but are
mediated through the all-powerful and relatively autonomous
state. By comparison with post-colonial states in which there are
competing interests between indigenous bourgeoisie, landed
classes, peasantry, proletariat, and petite-bourgeoisie, Libya's
social formation is relatively simple; and the state's role as
mediator between the interests of conflicting groups, relatively
uncomplicated. There is no policy against the development of an

indigenous bourgeoisie; but the growth of this class has been and will continue to be limited by the state's own economic ventures and its control over the country's economic resources. There is no policy against the acquisition of private land; but there is no powerful entrenched landed class. There is a working class; but it is tiny, and its organization and class action are government controlled. There is a great body of rural and urban poor, illiterate, sick, and under-employed; but one patronized by an oil-rich state which dispenses oil royalties as sheltered employment and welfare disbursements. There is a large and growing petite-bourgeoisie, which is mostly urban, ranging from small businessmen and shopkeepers to professionals, intellectuals, and students, and a huge spreading stratum of public officials. In new states the advent of the petite-bourgeoisie is directly related to the increased numbers of officials in the state machine and the public sector. In an oil state, where massive resources are channelled directly to the state, the representatives of this bureaucracy manage the use of a handome national surplus and its allocation. Under an army régime like Libya's it is not the petit-bourgeoisie which rules directly – and a national bourgeoisie is virtually non-existent – but a military–bureaucratic faction which directly commands the power of the state. The army acts as a ruling class in charge of a statist economy.

In successive Arab countries (Egypt, Iraq, Syria, Sudan, and Libya) the petite-bourgeoisie's closeness to power has run through young army officer movements. The army becomes not just the leading force of the petite-bourgeoisie revolution but one elevated above it and in control of it. The military in power is strongly self-confident; hostile towards autonomous political organization, mass movements, even civilian life as a whole. It mediates the interests of the petite-bourgeoisie, as its armed, organized, and most efficient representatives. Though it is not a class by virtue of its ownership of capital and means of production, it exercises the power of decisions over resources and the use of state capital. Most of these régimes have practised extensive nationalization measures and have built large public sectors of the economy. Nationalization has generally arisen out of the struggle for independence in the economic as well as the political sense; in the absence of a dynamic and independent national bourgeoisie, this was one way of trying to give the economy a self-sufficient base. But when control was made no more accessible after the revolution to those strata of the population denied it before, economic power as much as political proceeded to accrue in the hands of a state which claimed to mediate the interests of all classes but which in fact was relatively autonomous of them all.

By contrast with the trained bureaucracy, the members of Libya's Revolutionary Command Council, the Free Officers and the ranks of the army are not generally recruited direct from the petite-bourgeoisie. They spring rather from the rural depressed in the interior and the under-employed or less established strata in the towns. But once in power the army, and its subordinate partner the bureaucracy, imposes on army, state, and populace the essential ideology of the petite-bourgeoisie. This is in part because the development of the state apparatus and its allocation of formidable resources is accompanied by a massive rise in consumption, but also because the army-led revolution, in which the masses play no organized autonomous role, consciously adopts the ideology common to the petite-bourgeoisie of the Arab world.

Writing on this ideology, Michel Kamel[12] shows how in most Arab countries the petite-bourgeoisie forms a broad social base, comprising small landowners, craftsmen, small traders, government employees, officers and rank-and-file in the army, students and intellectuals, and those engaged in small-scale production in town and countryside. The Arab revolutions, notably after 1952 in Egypt, enlarged this class still more, as a result of agrarian reform laws which favoured the middle-sized peasantry, the rewards to this class from the nationalization of foreign capital, the extension of public services and education, and the expansion of the army. If, Kamel writes, ideology is conceived as an integral set of philosophical, ethical, juridical, and political concepts, the working class and the capitalist order are seen to have their distinct ideology and characteristic ideological method. But the petite-bourgeoisie, because of the intermediate position it occupies, because of the duality of its character and its transitory nature, has a complex outlook constituted of scattered and heterogeneous ideas. It cannot adopt the ideological approach of either of the two poles of struggle, since one of them leads to the abolition of property, while the other leads to the concentration of capital and its power and thus threatens the petite-bourgeoisie with the fate of the propertyless. The petite-bourgeoisie thus projects a 'third' ideology and searches for a 'third' way, not identified with either major class, and seemingly above class. This is Gadafi's Third Theory: the Libyan Socialist Union charter's 'non-exploiting capitalism' a formula that did not originate in Libya, and which expresses at the same time hostility towards big capitalism and a defensiveness towards capitalists property relations. Capitalism is capitalism only if it grows beyond a certain size and beyond the control of the petite- and middle-bourgeoisie.

Because the petite-bourgeoisie is not a homogeneous class but one that vacillates between the needs of small traders and farmers and petty officials, often close to the masses; and the interests of those higher up the social and employment pyramid like larger landowners and businessmen, professionals, technicians, and the higher ranks of the administration, the ideology of the petit-bourgeoisie is essentially wavering and pragmatic. It has constant shifts of emphasis, reflecting the shifting state of interests within this large, amorphous class. But it does seek consistently not to assert class interests within the society but to reconcile them. The 'non-exploiting bourgeoisie' is called upon to struggle for socialism like everyone else. The stress is on the need for an equilibrium between exploiters and exploited. The reconciliation of shifting interests is done under the aegis of the state and through state-initiated and state-run politics. Yet even the Arab Socialist Union is organized not as an alliance of class interests, united for the same objectives, but as a collection of individuals who have the right to express themselves as individuals but not as representatives of any class. Gadafi is insistent that the Libyan Arab Socialist Union will not permit any manifestations of class struggle. Such is to be controlled by the state.

This leads to another characteristic of this ideology: a distrust of the masses and their autonomous action. The Baathist theoretician Michel Aflaq claimed that his movement represented 'the entire nation which is still in slumber, ignorant of its reality, unaware of its identity, forgetting its needs. We have preceded it, thereby represent it.' This is precisely Gadafi's view of his own group's role in his country, and throughout the Arab world for that matter. This tutelage of the nation finds expression in the working methods and style of politics once these are allowed. Political instruments are created from the top; any already in existence are dissolved. Popular organization is not for the exercise of popular power or initiative but as an instrument for mobilization by the state and for gathering intelligence. The populist demagogy is passionate, but it disguises the manipulation of the people by the carefully fashioned instruments of the state. At times struggle against vested interests is encouraged, even initiated, as in the Libyan cultural revolution against bureaucracy; but it is controlled and liable to be frozen when it reaches a critical mobilizing phase. The theory of the nation as a whole united for socialism means that exploitation is not an expression of class struggle but a deviation from the nation's morality. If the non-exploiting bourgeoisie exploits after all, this is corruption, not class action, and as such is dealt with by the juridical or semi-juridical powers of the state rather than by the mobilization of counter-class action.

The Arab nation, Gadafi has said, dispenses with struggles for Right or Left on its territory. This is not to say that the state mediates as a neutral or that all ideologies are equal. The rejection of any conception of the class structure of society and sources of conflict has led in turn to a rejection of the independent role of dispossessed classes, whether workers or semi-peasants on the land or in the modern sector. In Libya especially, where class formation is significantly less developed than in most other parts of the Middle East and the Maghreb, the pressures of an indigenous large bourgeoisie are relatively absent: but so, too, are those of a proletariat and genuine peasantry. The petit-bourgeoisie is correspondingly more assertive than ever. Libya is perhaps the expression *par excellence* of the army-run state dominated by petite-bourgeoisie ideology and unchallenged by the organized expression of any diverging interest.

The search for a third way between capitalism and socialism and the rejection of the ideologies of these systems also leads to a search for more 'authentic' roots. Islamic socialism is the inevitable result, for several reasons. In the first place, it expresses a genuine rejection of the impositions of the imperialist West. In the second place, the religious doctrine already exercises a profound influence on vast masses of the people, especially in the rural areas. And thirdly, the Islamic ethos preaches the equality of all believers regardless of wealth or occupation. Islam as an ideology and a set of rules for the organization of social life inhibits the emergence of a class view. Islam also provides a language in which ritual and symbolic interactions either deliberately ignore the societal economic structure or minimize its significance. Emphasis is laid instead on the value of belonging to a community; and the community is that of all believers. Libya has been untouched by any reform movement within Islam and the influence of men like Mohamed Abdu who opened the way to a secular rather than religious nationalism. In Libya Islam plays an important part in projecting the ideal of a strong and unified state from which all internal dissension has been eradicated.

Though Gadafi's Libya abominates the organized right as much as the organized Left, and the Moslem Brotherhood equally with Marxism, his own ideological compound of nationalism, religion, and social reform serves to clear the way for the Brotherhood's message, rather like John the Baptist did for Christ. The pull of religious brotherhood is invariably stronger in the countries which have been moved less by social revolution and class organization. Libya is an ideal breeding ground for the belief of the Moslem Brothers, and a source of inspiration to their counterparts in Egypt, regrouping visibly under Sadat's policy of conciliating the right, and stirred by the political assertion of Islam by the reactionary states of the Arab world.

Not that there are serious sources of opposition within Libya. There is dissent perhaps, but not organized opposition;

and even dissent is heavily repressed. The danger is not of any civilian challenge to the army régime, but of an army finding no way to build civil institutions, to delegate authority and to evoke real popular participation, and instead, entrenching itself and its bureaucratic methods of control. Such may well subject Libya to an endless coup syndrome.

In the absence of any dominant ownership-class to which the state can be subordinated – and in the special situation of the post-colonial state – the military is likely to continue to fill this lacuna.

There may well be inner army conflicts, even army power up-heavals. Army coups made by one faction of the officer corps tend to provoke others. Gadafi's own influence rests on the fact that he was virtually the sole architect of the 1969 coup plan. He is most vulnerable to currents of discontent among his fellow Revolutionary Command Council members, and among the inner group of Free Officers, who acknowledge his leadership, but regard the revolution as their property as well as his, and must increasingly resent Gadafi's imperious, and even punitive, control of them.

But whichever way Libya's internal politics shift, the political and economic mould in which she is cast, as an oil *rentier* state with any army-run corporate political system, has set too hard for short-term political changes to alter that shape significantly.

Like their military counterparts in several other Third World countries, the Libyan military régime has ambitious plans to develop the economy, and more means than most. But the development approach is characteristic of this style of statist, technocratic planning. The state is actively to intervene in production, and to dominate it. Planning and execution are to be the responsibility of technicians and experts. The masses of people are to be beneficiaries of an authoritarian paternalism; there is to be no participation or mobilization from below.

The economy will be wealthier than ever but also more dependent on its sole generator of growth, oil. The attempts to diversify the economy will result in the development of an industrial and possibly an agricultural sphere (though this is of more doubtful endurance) of high technology and capital intensity, but these sectors will be less integrated than ever with the rest of the Libyan economy and the country's productive forces, and more like a transplanted vertical sector of foreign capitalist production.

Now that the world balance of economic power is tilting so dramatically, how much long-term advantage will Libya seize? With incomplete and yet unprecedented control over the production and allocation of the world's supply of energy, the oil states will have undreamt-of resources, even by the standards of oil-rich states. Some countries like Algeria and Iraq have already begun to develop a supportive economic infrastructure and a more balanced economy. Others like Saudi Arabia and Libya have virtually non-existent industry and agriculture, and are liable to intensify the *rentier*-state characteristics of their economies, with oil production and its industrial benefits operating as an enclave and in considerable isolation from the rest of the economy and social system. The ruling classes of the oil shaikhdoms will integrate their régimes more securely within the international capitalist system, even if their financial power will enable them to function more independently than hitherto. But it should be possible in Libya to recognize the crisis as an opening for the exploited populations of the world, not in the interests of élite minority ruling groups exclusively, but an opening for the masses of people; to use the power tilted in the direction of their countries to find the means to forge a concerted strategy of social transformation. This kind of change can, however, not be bureaucratically improvised from above without the mobilization of the masses of the people, and without their assertion of their need for social control of the productive forces and political systems of their countries. It is also not a change which can be asserted by military régimes bounded by the ideology and the aspirations of petite-bourgeois nationalism. So Libya may well miss her chance to re-make herself, and to take advantage of the power which her assertive policies in the sphere of oil have helped to achieve.

References

Chapter 1 A Perverse Revolution

1. Jacques Berque, *French North Africa: The Maghreb Between Two World Wars*, Faber & Faber, 1967, p. 104.
2. These were among the answers to several score questions handled by Gadafi at a marathon six-hour-long press conference in Tripoli in April 1973.
3. Berque, op. cit., p. 72.
4. ibid.
5. Jacques Berque, *The Arabs*, Faber & Faber, 1964, p. 239.
6. Hisham B. Sharabi, *Nationalism and Revolution in the Arab World*, van Nostrand, 1965, pp. 12–16.
7. Berque, *The Arabs*, p. 191.

Chapter 2 Hostage to History and Geography

1. Charles Daniels, *The Garamantes of Southern Libya*, Oleander Press, Harrow, Middlesex, 1970, p. 20.
2. ibid., p. 23.
3. John Wright, *Libya*, Ernest Benn, 1969, p. 55.
4. ibid., p. 70.
5. See the references to the work of J. Poncet in Talal Asad, 'The Bedouin as a Military Force' in C. Nelson, T. Asad, and D. Cole (eds.), *The Desert and the Sown*, University of California Press, forthcoming.
6. B. G. Martin, 'Kanem, Bornu and the Fezzan: Notes on the Political History of a Trade Route', *Journal of African History*, X, I, 1969, pp. 15–27.
7. Samir Amin, 'Underdevelopment and Dependence in Black Africa – Their Historical Origin and Contemporary Forms' United Nations African Institute for Economic Development and Planning, IDEP Reproduction 277.
8. Notes on Ghadames, Laing to Horton, 26 October 1825, quoted in A. Adu Boahen, *Britain, the Sahara and the Western Sudan, 1788–1861*, Oxford University Press, 1964.

9. Majid Khadduri, *Modern Libya: A Study in Political Development*, Johns Hopkins, 1963, p. 9.

10. E. E. Evans-Pritchard, *The Sanusi of Cyrenaica*, Oxford University Press, 1949, p. 98.

11. Nicola A. Ziadeh, *Sanusiyah: A Study of a Revivalist Movement in Islam*, Leiden, 1958, p. 46.

12. E. E. Evans-Pritchard, op. cit., p. 1.

13. ibid., p. 4.

14. ibid., pp. 1–2.

15. H. A. R. Gibb, *Mohammedanism*, Oxford University Press, 1949, p. 13.

16. Ziadeh, op. cit., pp. 6–7.

17. Evans-Pritchard, op. cit., p. 16.

18. Public Record Office, WO, 18 January 1903, 'Notes on the History of the Senusi'. Note by Colonel Count Gleichan, Dir. Intelligence, Egyptian Army.

19. Evans-Pritchard, op. cit., p. 14.

20. Samir Amin, op. cit. See Ahmad el Kodsy, 'Nationalism and Class Struggles in the Arab World', *Monthly Review*, 22, 3, July–August 1970, pp. 3–18, for a description relating to the Arab world in general – Egypt excepted – as trading societies which derived their surplus not from the peasantry in their own regions but from the intermediary commercial function of long-distance trade. Ibn Khaldun, he points out, first analysed the Maghreb societies in this way.

21. Rosalba Davico, *La Guerilla Lybienne (1911–1912): Imperialisme et résistance anti-coloniale en Afrique du Nord aux années 20*, unpublished.

22. ibid.

23. Evans-Pritchard, op. cit., p. 98.

24. ibid., pp. 88, 26, 99.

25. Davico, op. cit.

26. By the sixties the Berber population of Libya was calculated at about 4 per cent.

27. Lars Eldblom, *Structure foncière, organisation et structure sociale: Une étude comparative sur la vie socio-économique dans les trois oasis Libyennes de Ghat, Marzouk et particulièrement Ghadames*, Lund, 1968, cited by Davico, op. cit.

28. See Evans-Pritchard, op. cit., p. 51, and E. L. Peters, 'The Tied and the Free: An Account of Patron-Client Relationships among the Bedouin of Cyrenaica', in *Contributions to Mediterranean Sociology*, J. Peristiany (ed.), Mouton, 1968.

References

29. Peters, op. cit., p. 175.
30. Evans-Pritchard, op. cit., p. 51.
31. Peters, op. cit., p. 185n.
32. Evans-Pritchard, op. cit., pp. 44–5.

Chapter 3 Resistance but Conquest

1. Ambrosini, cited by Evans-Pritchard, op. cit., p. 107. See also W. C. Askew, *Europe and Italy's Acquisition of Libya 1911–12*, Duke University, Durham, North Carolina, 1942.
2. Davico, op. cit., p. 5.
3. ibid.
4. The Davico paper has details of those who took part in the Azzizia meeting and of the tribes and leaders that comprised the two camps.
5. Public Record Office, WO 106/1532, 3 November 1913.
6. Public Record Office, WO 106/1532, Intelligence Department, War Office, Cairo, 11 October 1913.
7. ibid.
8. Public Record Office, WO 106/1553.
9. Evans-Pritchard, op cit., p. 150.
10. Public Record Office, WO 32/5260(674), contains alarming reports from the British Military Mission in Berlin on 'Turkish Nationalist Intrigue': reports of a conversation with a Turkish participant at this Congress who was reported to have brought a message from Lenin that 'the whole of Asia is at the present passing through critical times and it is the duty of all Nationalists of whatever country to cooperate with the Russian government in order to destroy the British empire'.
11. Evans-Pritchard, op. cit., p. 155.
12. ibid., p. 167.
13. ibid., p. 156.
14. The following account of the guerrilla war of the Cyrenaican Bedouin is drawn from the pages of Evans-Pritchard's book (mostly from pp. 159–73) since none has surpassed it and no detailed Libyan history of the war is yet in existence. Libyans have commented that British writers tend to weight their accounts by a deeper interest and affinity with the interior rather than the coastal populations, and one more predisposed to Cyrenaica than Tripolitania.
15. ibid., pp. 188–9.
16. Wright, op. cit., has a skilful summary of this period in Libyan history.

17. Evans-Pritchard, op. cit., p. 225.
18. ibid., p. 207.
19. K. S. McLachlan, 'Agricultural Land Use and Crop Patterns 1911–1960', in J. A. Allan, K. S. McLachlan, and Edith T. Penrose (eds.), *Libya: Agriculture and Economic Development*, Frank Cass, 1973, p. 48.
20. ibid., p. 51.
21. Wright, op. cit., p. 169.
22. ibid., p. 170.
23. ibid., p. 170.
24. ibid., pp. 180–81.
25. ibid., p. 182.
26. Freya Stark, *The Coast of Incense*, John Murray, 1953, p. 162.
27. Public Record Office, WO 32/10159, Report by the Chief Political Officer on the 'Work of the Political Branch 9HQ MEF and the Occupied Enemy Territory Administration of Eritrea, Cyrenaica and Tripolitania between 1 July and December 1942.'
28. Public Record Office, FO 371/134, 20 April 1944. This file was opened in 1972.
29. Public Record Office, WO 32/10159.
30. Public Record Office, FO 371/134.
31. ibid.
32. Public Record Office, WO 32/10159, Chief Political Officer, 17 August 1942.
33. Public Record Office, FO 371/134.
34. Khadduri, op. cit., pp. 31–3.

Chapter 4 Independence through Cold-War Diplomacy

1. Michael Brett, 'The U.N. and Libya; a review of Libyan Independence and the United Nations' in *Journal of African History*, Vol. I, 1972, pp. 168–70.
2. David Horowitz, *From Yalta to Teheran*, Penguin Books, 1967. See especially Chapter 5.
3. C. Grove Haines, 'The Problem of the Italian Colonies', *Middle East Journal*, October 1947, Vol. 1., No. 4, pp. 417–31.
4. Adrian Pelt, *Libyan Independence and the United Nations: A Case of Planned Decolonisation*, Yale University Press, 1970, p. 61. Much of the account in this chapter on Libya's accession to independence through the agency of the United Nations is based upon material in this record.
5. Henry Serrano Villard, *Libya: The New Arab Kingdom of North Africa*, Cornell University Press, 1956, p. 24.

References

6. Parliamentary Debates, Fifth Series, Vol. 377, cols. 77–8, 8 January 1942.
7. *The Times*, 2 June 1949.
8. G. H. Becker, 'The Disposition of the Italian Colonies, 1941–1951', Thèse 87, University of Geneva.
9. Public Record Office files on Libya between 1951 and 1956 are still confidential print.
10. Villard, op. cit., pp. 33–4.
11. United Nations Resolution 289(iv) of 21 November 1949.
12. Official Records, General Assembly, Fourth Session 1949, First Committee, 278th meeting, 30 September 1949, p. 20.
13. The choice of the United Nations Commissioner in Libya was the decision of Secretary-General Trygvie Lie and of Andrew Cordier, the United States' man at the hub of UN affairs who orchestrated, among other policies, the United Nations operation in the Congo when the Lumumba government was overthrown.
14. Pelt, op. cit., p. 140.
15. ibid., p. 128.
16. ibid., p. 155.
17. ibid., p. 167.
18. ibid., p. 168.
19. ibid., p. 169.
20. ibid., p. 835.
21. This information was supplied to the writer by the interpreter present at the key meeting between King Idris and Adrian Pelt.
22. United Nations, Official Records of the General Assembly, Fifth Session 1950, Vol. 1, pp. 411–12.
23. Pelt, op. cit., p. 826.
24. ibid., p. 641.

Chapter 5 Palace Power

1. Evans-Pritchard, op. cit., p. 105.
2. Villard, op. cit., p. 44.
3. Khadduri, op. cit., especially pp. 171–9.
4. Sharabi, op. cit., pp. 48–50.
5. One such family was the Muntassers of Tripoli, one or more of whose various branches was generally represented in government, whether inside in the Cabinet or abroad as ambassadors. Others included the Salem Qadi family of Misurata, the merchant family of the Ben Zikris of Tripoli, the Baqir family which married a daughter to the Crown Prince, the Kubar family originally from

Gharian, and the Ben Sha'ban family of the Berber community of Zawia.

6. Khadduri, op. cit. See for instances pp. 240–43.

7. Four governments, one federal and three provincial, had ruled in their several capitals, each administering a cumbersome and extravagant administrative machine. In addition to the fifteen federal ministries the provinces had an average of eight each, and Tripolitania and Cyrenaica had each employed more civil servants than the federal government (Wright, op. cit., p. 260).

8. A road was needed to connect the Fezzan interior with the Mediterranean coast. The lowest tender, for £1,900,000, was won by Sayyid Abd-Allah Abid, but two years later he submitted claims for a further £4,000,000. The government tried to stifle the criticism that ensued by elevating one of its most vocal critics to a re-shuffled Cabinet, and then by urging the King to dissolve a troublesome Parliament; the King declined. See Khadduri, op. cit., pp. 301–3.

Chapter 6 A Base for Imperialism

1. Khadduri, op. cit., p. 226.

2. Villard, op. cit., p. 141.

3. ibid., p. 142.

4. Wright, op. cit., p. 234.

5. *Christian Science Monitor*, 20 October 1963.

6. Parliamentary Debates, 13 June 1961.

7. According to *The Times* (14 September 1969), CYDEF (The Cyrenaica Defence Force) led by General Bushar had 300 Vigilant anti-tank guided missiles, 100 of which had warheads. The Tripolitania Defence Force (TRIDEF) had 400. The British Aircraft Corporation had been supplying CYDEF and TRIDEF with ground-to-air defence weapons.

8. Stockholm International Peace Research Institute, *Arms Trade with the Third World*, Paul Elek, 1971, p. 589.

9. Roger Owen, *Libya: A Brief Political and Economic Survey*, Chatham House, 1961, p. 13.

10. *Sunday Ghibli*, 29 March 1964. The King's broadcast said he had yielded to the intense desire of the people that he remain their monarch. 'Dear Brothers,' he added, 'put it down to old age; the ways of an old man are imperfect.'

11. *Daily Telegraph*, 16 August 1964.

12. United States Security Agreements and Commitments Abroad, Part 9. Hearings before Sub-Committee on US Security Agree-

ments and Commitments Abroad of the Committee on Foreign Relations, US Senate 91st Congress.

13. *U.S. News and World Report*, 21 August 1967.

14. *Christian Science Monitor*, 19 June 1967.

15. John S. Badeau, *The American Approach to the Arab World*, Council on Foreign Relations 1968, p. 9. This writer adds 'When the clamour for the closure of Wheelus started the United States had to ask itself: "does it then have such importance that the United States should consider going the whole way to protect it?" At the time no satisfactory answer could be obtained, partly because no current estimates were made available, partly because of differing estimates in the military and diplomatic communities' (p. 118).

16. John Stanley and Maurice Pearton, *The International Trade in Arms*, Chatto and Windus, 1972, p. 190.

17. *Financial Times*, 22 April 1969.

18. George Thayer, *The War Business*, 1970, p. 264.

19. *Flight International*, 20 September 1967.

20. 'Arms and the Super Salesman', *Sunday Times*, 2 June 1968.

Chapter 7 The Intervention of the Army

1. The 'official history' of the background, planning, and execution of the Libyan revolution appeared in Libyan newspapers in serialized instalments in September 1969 and at intervals during the next two years. There were also articles in Tripoli's *al-Yawm* of 5 September 1969; Gadafi's interview with Middle East News Agency, 10 September 1969; Gadafi's interview with Egyptian television reported in Libyan newspapers of 15 October 1969; and his interview with the Sudanese *al-Ayyam* reported in Tripoli's *al-Ra'id* of 26 September 1969 and 6 December 1969.

2. In September 1970, on the first anniversary of the coup, Gadafi and some of the other members of the Revolutionary Command Council reminisced about the coup and its background on Libyan television. The statements here quoted are taken from a translated transcript.

3. Interview with writer in Tripoli, June 1971.

4. This came out in cross-examination during the court martial of the Musa Ahmed and Adam Hawwaz group.

5. The twelve members of the Revolutionary Command Council were as follows:

Colonel Mu'ammar Gadafi
Major Abdul Salaam Jalloud

Major Beshir Saghir Hawady
Captain Mukhtar Abdullah Gerwy
Captain Abdul Moniem Taher al-Huny
Captain Mustapha Kharuby
Captain Kheweildy Hamidy
Captain Mohamad Nejm
Captain Ali Awad Hamza
Captain Abu Bakr Yunis Jaber
Captain Omar Abdullah Meheishy
Lieutenant Mohamed Abu Bakr Mgarief (killed in a motor accident in August 1972).

6. After the coup Libyan military cadets were switched to the Egyptian Military Academy. They did one year's training there, and then a second in Benghazi.

7. Articles written during his student days can be found in back copies of the *Fezzan* newspaper. From Fezzan he went to Misurata where he met Meheishy. After graduating from the Military Academy in 1965 he went on a six-months signals course to Britain to an army school for education at Bovington Hythe in Beaconsfield. When he returned to Libya he enrolled in the arts faculty at Benghazi university to do a history degree. He did not complete the degree course, but during it he wrote an essay criticizing Rommel's desert tactics. Despite his disavowal of all ideological politics, both Arab nationalist movement and Baathist groups claim they had his allegiance for a time at least. Abu Bakr Yunis admitted he had joined the Baath Party briefly. In his younger days Meheishy had the reputation of being interested in Marxism.

8. Huny came from Zanzour, west of Tripoli, of a 'citizen' milieu not typical of the interior; Gerwy was born in Tripoli's Old City; Nejm in Benghazi; Kharuby at Zawia; Awad Hamza at Gamenas in Cyrenaica of a father who was a school janitor; and Mgarief was born at Marble Arch in Cyrenaica.

9. It was this group which Nasser addressed during his first visit to Libya and to whom he advised policy: not to antagonize the United States; not to rush ahead with oil nationalization; to shop for arms in France. These three tactics were part of his 'balanced politics' for the Arab camp.

10. Lieutenant Rifi became Governor of the Fezzan.

11. For a comparison between Arab and African military régimes see Amos Perlmutter, 'The Dynamics of Evolution and Cleavage in Arab and African Military Régimes'; mimeographed.

12. On the counter-coup plot and trial see Gadafi's radio and telephone interview recorded by the Libyan News Agency, 11 December 1969; and the Libyan Press Review reports of 1, 8, 10, and 21 August and 20 October 1970.

13. To give two examples only: Air force captain Meftah Sharef had been one of the two Libyan pilots who before the coup had flown their aircraft into Algeria and had been sentenced to five years' imprisonment under the monarchy. In prison he met Suleiman Maghrabi; it was at his suggestion that Maghrabi had been made the new régime's first Prime Minister. Major Abdul Matloub was one of the middle-ranking 'Baghdad group' of officers who had been in contact with Gadafi before the coup.

14. Libyan Press Review, 25 July 1970. The details of the plot disclosed by Gadafi suggest that at least part of it was the operation described in Patrick Seale and Maureen McConville, *The Hilton Assignment*, Temple Smith, 1973. Omar Shalhi's scheme to hire foreign mercenaries to free Colonel Shalhi and other prominent figures of the old régime from prison in Tripoli proved abortive even before it got moving.

Chapter 8 Religion as Politics

1. *Middle East Journal*, Spring 1970, Vol. 24, No. 2, from a set of translations of proclamations, statements, addresses, and interviews.

2. Writer's interview with several signatories to the petition.

3. A fortnight after his Cabinet appointment the Minister of Education and National Guidance resigned; he had been discovered to have Tunisian nationality.

4. Constitutional Proclamation, 11 December 1969, gazetted 25 December 1969; Article 18 said:

The Revolutionary Command Council is the highest authority in the Libyan Arab Republic. It exercises the functions of supreme sovereignty and legislation and draws up the general policy of the state on behalf of the people. In such capacity it may take all measures deemed necessary for the protection of the revolution as well as the régime stemming from it. Such measures take the form of constitutional proclamations, law orders or resolutions. Measures adopted by the Revolutionary Command Council may not be challenged before any body.

Article 19 empowered the RCC to appoint a Council of Ministers and to dismiss it from office. The Council of Ministers was to study and prepare all drafts of laws consistent with the policy drawn up by the Revolutionary Command Council and submit them for consideration and promulgation thereby.

5. The RCC comprised nine captains and two lieutenants, apart from Gadafi who promoted himself to Colonel after the coup. Of the pre-coup complement of about 600 officers, 170 were retained; those removed included 40 colonels, 75 lieutenant-colonels, and 150 majors. The four-month period of RCC anonymity was thought to be due to the need to entrench its control before it revealed the junior rank of its members.

6. In the fourth Cabinet, appointed towards the end of 1971 there were three RCC members only, holding the premiership and the portfolios of Defence and the Interior; likewise there were three RCC members in the fifth cabinet of July 1972.

7. *Figaro*, 30 September 1969.

8. The Italian community comprised about 30,000 persons. For details of the expropriation measures see RCC Decision on Usurped Land, 21 July 1970, and Decision on Agrarian Reform and Land Reclamation Corporation, 15 July 1970.

9. Law No. 3 on Illicit Profits, 19 January 1970.

10. The People's Court was presided over by a member of the RCC and comprised four other members representing the armed forces, the Islamic university, the Supreme Court, and the police force.

11. For details of the sentences passed on the defendants see Libyan News Agency report, 16 November 1970. Four former prime ministers were among those found guilty and sentenced; one of them *in absentia*.

12. Tripoli rally, 16 October 1969.

13. Interview with *al-Balagh*, 30 November 1969.

14. I. M. Arif and M. O. Ansell, *The Libyan Revolution: A Source Book of Legal and Historical Documents*, Vol. 1; 30 September 1969–30 August 1970, Oleander Press, Harrow, Middlesex, 1970.

15. Libyan Press Review, 23 November 1970. A government-initiated women's organization was set up instead.

16. Law 58 of 1970, Official Gazette, 1 May 1970.

17. See the ten reasons set out in the RCC Statement Setting up the Popular Organization, June 1971.

18. Article 18 of the Libyan ASU Charter.

19. ibid., Article 11.

20. The extracts of the debate are taken from Summary of World Broadcasts, ME/3954, 4 April 1972.

21. Law 71 of 1972 and Explanatory Note.

22. It was during this period that the international press carried

reports of an internal crisis in the régime, and of an attempted coup, which proved totally unfounded.

23. Press conference, RCC headquarters, April 1972.

24. *Le Monde*, 8 June 1970.

25. RCC Decree, 11 October 1972.

26. There are several textual versions of the Third Theory, see seminar address by Gadafi to the Arab Socialist Union, Cairo, 9 February 1973, published by the Libyan Ministry of Information and Culture.

27. Speech at Zwara, 15 April 1973, published by the Ministry of Information and Culture.

Chapter 9 The Economic Environment

1. According to the 1964 census the population was 1·56 million compared with 1·09 million ten years earlier. The 1970 population estimate was 1·94 million. A new census was due during 1973. Two thirds of the population was in Tripolitania, mostly in the northern fringes and in Cyrenaica, where the density was about 50 per square mile; elsewhere population density was below 1 per square mile. Tripoli City and environs had a population of 380,000 and Benghazi 280,000. The population of Sebha, capital of the Fezzan, was below 50,000.

2. B. Higgins, *The Economic and Social Development of Libya*, prepared for the government of Libya, United Nations Technical Assistance Programme ST/TTA/K/Libya/3, 1953, p. 164.

3. J. A. Allan, 'Agricultural Development in Libya since Independence', paper presented to African Studies Association of the United Kingdom, Symposium on Islamic Northern Africa, 1971.

4. There was also the Libyan Finance Corporation (LFC), and the Libyan–American Technical Assistance Service (LATAS), which changed later to the Libyan–American Joint Services (LAJS).

5. Ali Ahmad Attiga, 'The Economic Impact of Oil on Libyan Agriculture' in *Libya: Agriculture and Economic Development*, J. A. Allan, K. S. McLachlan, and Edith T. Penrose (eds.), Frank Cass, 1973, pp. 9–18.

6. Libyan Arab Republic, *General Economic Background Information*, Tripoli, 30 May 1971.

7. H. Mahdavy, 'The Patterns and Problems of Economic Development in Rentier States: The Case of Iran', in M. A. Cook, *Studies in the Economic History of the Middle East from the Rise of Islam to the Present Day*, Oxford, 1970, pp. 428–67.

8. Robert Mabro, 'La Libye, un État Rentier?' in *Projet* 39, November 1969, pp. 1,090–1,101.

9. RCC Decree, 27 October 1970.

10. Summary of World Broadcasts, ME/3816/A/12, 19 October 1971.

11. Thus for instance, a French consortium of six companies, together with a government survey department, won a several-million-pound project to investigate soil and water resources along the coastline together with two desert areas. It was, by all accounts, a dubious research proposition thrown together in a hurry, with the French team under pressure from its government to telescope the period for investigation and evaluation. Political expediency gave no time to modify aspects of the scheme recognized at initial planning sessions as faulty. The work was already in progress when the original French contract was whittled down. The desert areas were handed over to a Polish team. The reason was to be sought in ruffled Franco-Libyan relations at the time and a decision to make a gesture in the direction of the socialist bloc.

12. Calculating from the 1960 Census of Agriculture, Hilal found that by the sixties one in four landlords in western Libya owned 37 per cent of all private land, with holdings of between twenty and 100 hectares; and a third of the landed peasantry had less than five hectares each.

   The system of land tenure varied from west to east and by region and district. Thus in the eastern region the percentage of tribally owned land under the monarchy was twice as high as in the west, and even this was considered an underestimation since the 1960 census had failed to include tribal grazing land.

   Overall agricultural statistics produced in 1963 showed that whereas the average farm size in the whole country was twenty-eight hectares, in some coastal areas in the Tripoli region farms were smaller than two hectares and a third of agricultural holdings occupied only 3 per cent of arable land. Source: Ministry of Planning and Development. Department of Economic and Social Affairs, Agricultural Planning Section: Dr Susan Lalevic and Eng Milena Lalevic, *Libyan Agriculture in the Light of Statistical Data*.

13. Jamil M. Hilal, *Family, Marriage and Social Change in some Libyan Villages*, M.Litt. Thesis (No. 68 of 1969), Durham University.

14. By 1940 Italian ownership, private and government, had acquired approximately a quarter of the cultivated area. Italian colonizing efforts more than doubled the farmland area under use but it was for use by Italian settlers.

In 1956 an agreement between the Libyan and Italian governments resulted in the former settlement farms in the east being returned to the Libyan government; the same happened to farms vacated by Italian owners in the west.

15. NASA, the National Agriculture Settlement Authority.

16. Policy statement, 18 December 1972, at a meeting with the public sector companies in Tripoli.

17. There are certain drawbacks to these statistics. The criterion of 'large' units has differed from one year to the next, which makes comparative conclusions difficult. If there are only three enterprises of a type, no statistics are published. Above all, since most enterprises in Libya are small the selective material on 'large' enterprises is not indicative of the condition of small-scale production in the country.

18. R. Mabro, 'Labour Supplies and Labour Stability: A Case Study of the Oil Industry in Libya', *Bulletin, Oxford University Institute of Economics and Statistics*, Vol. 32, 4 November 1970, and Employment and Wage Rates, in Allan, McLachlan, Penrose (eds), op. cit.

19. In 1971 there were 20 per cent increases for unskilled workers, 16 per cent for skilled and semi-skilled, and 10 per cent for clerks, technicians, and professionals. In May 1972 government-employed craftsmen won increases.

20. Hilal, op. cit.

21. M. Cheshkov, 'Élite and Class in the Developing Countries', *Social Sciences Today* 4, USSR Academy of Sciences, 1970, pp. 142–56.

22. Economist Intelligence Unit, *Quarterly Economic Review* 1, 1972, p. 4.

23. This calculation was based upon the 1969 extraction rate, which has since been reduced.

Chapter 10 The Oil State Beyond the State

1. In 1943 when the British military occupation had just installed itself, the State Department directed a query to the Foreign Office on behalf of American oil companies: its information was that a British oil company would shortly attempt to get a concession embracing the whole of Libya: could the British government confirm that American companies would be given the opportunity to share in oil exploration and marketing? Public Record Office, FO 371/976. The reply was reassuring, after several inter-departmental amendments: 'The State Department may be

assured that American oil interests will receive *equality of*' (this was deleted and substituted by '*equitable*') '*treatment* on a basis of reciprocity in Libya as elsewhere'. Public Record Office, FO 371/976, 25 March 1943.

2. During 1958 when the Italian oil tycoon Enrico Mattei tried to get a concession for ENI in the Fezzan near the Algerian border, dealings with the Libyans had reached an advanced stage, but then the Americans stepped in and the concession went instead to Phillips. *The Times*, 22 November 1957.

3. Abdul Amir Q. Kubbah, *Libya: Its Oil Industry and Economic System*, 1964. See pp. 64–72 on the 1955 Petroleum Law.

4. OPEC Statistical Bulletin, 1968.

5. Bank of Libya Twelfth annual report, p. 81.

6. The Majors or Seven Sisters of the oil industry used to be counted as ESSO, Shell, BP, Gulf, Texaco, Standard, and Mobil. Another two are now included among the giants: Indiana Standard, which operates in twenty-five foreign countries, and CFP.

7. Apart from ESSO and Oasis the principal companies operating in Libya by 1965 were Mobil-Gelsenberg; BP (49 per cent owned by the British government), 50 per cent of the Libyan operations of which was owned by Bunker Hunt; Amoseas, which is California Standard and Texaco (Caltex); Shell; CFP, which is 35 per cent owned by the French state; and Texas Gulf Libya, with a share held by Sinclair Oil.

8. *Petroleum Intelligence Weekly*, 31 May 1965.

9. See 'Middle East Oil and the energy Crisis', *MERIP Reports* (Middle East Research and Information Project), 20 and 21, for an account of the organization of the international oil industry in a changing Middle East. For a brief description of changes in oil price fixing by 1974, see 'West Awaits New Oil Prices', by Peter Hillmore, *Guardian*, 15 March 1974, p. 21.

10. See Wanda M. Jaclobski, 'Libya's Oil Pricing and Tax Dilemma', *Petroleum Intelligence Weekly*, 19 April 1965, pp. 6–9.

11. In September 1962 there had been an announcement of new concessions opened for bidding, but it was abruptly withdrawn.

12. *Petroleum Intelligence Weekly*, 13 September 1965.

13. *Petroleum Intelligence Weekly*, 1 November 1965.

14. ibid., 29 November 1965.

15. ibid., 28 February 1966.

16. ibid.

17. *Oil and Gas Journal*, 5 December 1966.

18. *Petroleum Intelligence Weekly*, 14 March 1966.

References

19. *Wall Street Journal*, 8 February 1972, pp. 1 and 14, report by Stanley Penn.
20. *Los Angeles Times*, 12 October 1969.
21. *Petroleum Intelligence Weekly*, 9 January 1967.
22. *Financial Times*, 15 August 1969.
23. Oasis internal memorandum, September–October 1969.
24. *Financial Times*, 29 September 1970.
25. For the technical arguments against over-production and gas flaring and the case against Occidental, see the *Financial Times*, 4 June 1970.
26. For a full account of the progress of the negotiations see 'Tripoli's 33 Day Dramatics', *Arab Oil Review*, March–April 1972.
27. From 1971 to 1972 there was a 20 per cent reduction in production. Cutbacks were ordered during critical rounds of negotiation with the companies but as part of a longer-term conservation policy; in April 1971 the government began to implement an amendment to the Petroleum Law to prohibit the burning of hydrocarbon resources and excessive flaring of gas. In the latter period drilling has begun to slow down. (Only sixty-five wells were drilled in the first three quarters of 1971 compared with 206 in the same period of 1970.) There were small finds by ESSO and Aquitaine but no major discoveries. Part of the decline in activity is explained by the age of concessions; recognizing this, some foreign-owned companies relinquished a number of concessions. The government turned over 118,000 square kilometres to the state oil company LINOCO. A large part of this area is in western Libya where the development of minor discoveries is not economic due to the need to build a larger pipeline and a new ocean terminal. The oil companies insist that the rise in price and tax rate are the reasons for the drilling and exploration decline; though this is not expected to fall any further since under the Tripoli agreement each major operating group is committed to maintaining a minimum exploration activity.
28. These figures are compiled from oil company, Libyan Oil Ministry, OPEC, and Bank of Libya reports.
29. Odeh Aburdene, 'An analysis of the impact of the economies of Iraq, Iran, Kuwait, Libya and Saudi Arabia upon the Balance of Payments of the US for the years 1963–8', Ph.D thesis, Fletcher School of Law and Diplomacy at Tufts University, Medford, Massachusetts.
30. The Organization of American States produced figures showing that oil companies in Latin America were re-investing only about

5 per cent of their profits during the 1960s, whereas the total for manufacturing was 58·4 per cent from 1960–64 and 52·3 per cent from 1965–7. See M. Tanzer, *The Political Economy of International Oil and the Underdeveloped Countries*, Temple Smith, 1970.

31. IMF Report for 1972.
32. *Financial Times*, 7 July 1971.
33. *Oil and Gas Journal*, 10 May 1971, p. 46.
34. *United Business Services*, 30 August 1971, cited in Adelman, see below.
35. M. A. Adelman, *The World Petroleum Market*, 1973, Chapter VIII, note 32, for the calculation.
36. M. A. Adelman, 'The Oil Industry as an International Tax Collecting Agency', Tokyo, 26 April 1972, under the auspices of the Institute of Energy Economics.
37. *New York Times*, 11 February 1971, p. 4, cited in Adelman, ibid.
38. Sir David Barran to the Fuel Luncheon Club, London, 16 February 1971.
39. 'Is the Oil Shortage Real? Oil Companies as OPEC Tax-Collectors', *Foreign Policy*, No. 9, Winter 1972–3, pp. 79–80.
40. The principal importers of Libya's oil are Italy (20 per cent in 1972); West Germany (25 per cent); Britain (14 per cent); and France (14 per cent).
41. France had originally entered Libya's oil industry by persuading her of the virtues of joint ventures. Under the monarchy The National Libyan Petroleum Corporation–LIPETCO–entered into partnership with Société Nationale de Pétroles Aquitaine, a subsidiary of the French state-owned oil corporation. At the time, in 1968, this was a major French inroad into an Anglo–American reserve.
42. Algerian assistance to Libya's oil industry was extremely important not least for the experience Libya gained from her more aggressive oil policy and her pioneering search for markets. In turn, back in February 1971, when Algeria's Sonatrach was locked in battle with France, Libya had loaned Algeria $100 million to tide her over the crisis.
43. *Economist*, 30 July 1971, p. 51.
44. M. A. Adelman, 'Is the Oil Shortage Real?', *Foreign Policy*, No. 9, Winter 1972–3, pp. 69–107.

Chapter 11 The Search for Arab Unity

1. Maxime Rodinson, *Israel and the Arabs*, Penguin Books, 1968, p. 86.
2. Fawwaz Trabulsi, 'The Palestine Problem: Zionism and Im-

perialism in the Middle East', *New Left Review*, September–October 1969, pp. 53–89. See especially pp. 79–80.

3. Rodinson, op. cit., pp. 25–6.

4. Libyan Arab Republic, Ministry of Education and National Guidance, 17 April 1971.

5. The intervention prompted Sadat's boast that the new Federation had 'teeth'.

6. The Chad news agency announced that Libya had indicated her willingness to hand over all Frolinat members on her territory. The Chad security forces were to draw up the list but Chad had agreed that the name of the Frolinat leader Dr Abba Siddick would not be on it. *Summary of World Broadcasts*, ME/4180/B/1, 29 December 1972, Fort Lamy Radio, 26 December 1972.

7. *Le Monde*, 25 February 1971.

8. *Summary of World Broadcasts*, ME/4114/A/1, 10 October 1972.

9. ibid., ME/3851/A/8, 29 November 1971.

10. Edouard Saab, *Le Monde*, 18 November 1970; see also the *Guardian*, 8 June 1970.

11. 9 March 1973.

12. The *Guardian*, 11 April 1972.

13. Samir Franjieh, 'How Revolutionary is the Palestinian Resistance?', *Journal of Palestine Studies*, Vol. 1, No. 2, Winter 1972.

14. *Le Monde*, 11 and 12 January 1973.

15. See Haim Hanegbi, Moshe Machover, and Akiva Orr, 'The Class Nature of Israel', *New Left Review*, No. 65, January–February 1971.

16. *Al Ahram*, 7 April 1972.

17. *Summary of World Broadcasts*, ME/4142/A/5, 11 November 1972.

18. Seale and McConville, op. cit., p. 179.

Chapter 12 The Limits of Nationalism

1. See *MERIP Reports*, 'The October War', No. 22, published by the Middle East Research and Information Project, Cambridge, Mass., for an account of the politics of the October 1973 war.

2. According to *MERIP Reports*, 22, ibid., under General Shazli some 50,000 students had been integrated in the Egyptian army's electronic arms section.

3. Gadafi told Eric Rouleau of *Le Monde* on 23 October 1973: 'This war is not my war. Sadat and Assad took their decision and worked out their plan without my consent, without consulting me, without even informing me. And yet our three countries are members

of a federation whose constitution clearly states that war or peace could only be decided by a unanimous vote by the three presidents. We also disagree about the manner of conducting the campaign. I had once submitted to them a strategic plan, but their general staffs decided otherwise. I still think that my plan is better. Even if Egypt and Syria were to defeat Israel, I cannot lend my name to a comic-opera war ... I'm in profound disagreement with Presidents Sadat and Assad even on the aims of their war. For me, the essential thing is not to take back from Israel the territories she conquered in 1967, but to free the Palestinians, all the Palestinians, from the Zionist yoke.'

4. Ahmed Ben Salah, 'Le Peuple Tunisien en a Assez', *Afrique-Asie*, 48, 21 January 1974. See also *Afrique-Asie*, 49, 4 February 1974, pp. 10–13.

5. It has been calculated that by 1980 the combined oil needs of the United States, Europe, Britain, and Japan will total 58 million barrels of oil a day. Between them these countries have in the last 13 years taken 61 per cent of the world's oil supply. It is calculated that total world demand by 1980 will be 93 million barrels a day, but world oil supply by present predictions of production levels will be 10 million barrels less.

6. Fred Halliday, 'The Saudi Oil Kingdom,' *New Left Review*, 80, July–August 1973.

7. Exxon, for instance, announced a 12 per cent increase in dividends in 1973. The oil companies justify their rising profits with the argument that they are needed to capitalize the search for new sources of energy. According to *MERIP*, 20, op. cit., by 1970 the largest American petroleum companies had interests in at least one other phase in other raw energy resources. The results of this concentration of energy resources in the hands of relatively few companies had enabled these companies to manipulate even higher prices and profits in the United States. Thus the 1973 and 1974 American energy crises were 'nothing more or less than a well-coordinated attempt by the oil companies and the energy companies to extort higher prices for energy to maintain the profit margins that once depended on the total control of low-cost crude in the Middle East and elsewhere.'

8. *New Left Review* 80, p. 1.

9. Hamza Alavi, 'The Post-Colonial State', *New Left Review*, 74, July–August 1972. See also Hamza Alavi, 'Bangla Desh and the Crisis of Pakistan', *Socialist Register*, 1971, pp. 289–317.

References

10. Alavi writes:

   The classical Marxist theory postulates a fundamental contradiction between the metropolitan bourgeoisies and the indigenous or 'national'
bourgeoisies of the post-colonial societies. It concludes that the 'bourgeois-
democratic' revolution in the colonies, of which independence is only the
first phase and which continues in the post-colonial situation, necessarily has
an 'anti-imperialist' character. It is true, of course, that the native bourgeoisie
plays an anti-imperialist role and contributes to the national independence
movement against the colonial power, but only up to the point of independence. In the post-colonial situation there is a double reorientation of alignments, both of the indigenous bourgeoisie and of the erstwhile 'comprador'
class of merchants, building contractors and the like. The latter, unable to
compete on equal terms with giant overseas concerns, demand restrictions
on the activities of foreign businesses, particularly in the fields in which they
aspire to operate. They acquire a new 'anti-imperialist' posture. On the other
hand, as the erstwhile 'national' bourgeoisie grows in size and aspires to
extend its interests and move from industries which involve relatively un-
sophisticated technology, such as textiles, to those which involve the use of
highly sophisticated technology such as petro-chemicals and fertilisers, etc.
they find that they do not have access to the requisite advanced industrial
technologies. Their small resources and scale of operation keep the possibility of developing their own technology, independently, out of their reach.
For access to the requisite advanced industrial technology they have to turn
for collaboration, therefore, to the bourgeoisies of the developed metropolitan
countries or to socialist states. This they do despite the fact that the terms
on which the collaboration is offered are such that it hamstrings their own
independent future development. As it grows in size and extends its interests
the so-called 'national' bourgeoisie becomes increasingly dependent on the
neo-colonialist metropolitan bourgeoisies. (*New Left Review*, 74, pp. 74–5.)

11. Alavi, ibid., pp. 72–3.
12. Michel Kamel, 'Political and Ideological Role of the Petit-
    Bourgeoisie in the Arab World'; mimeographed, n.d.

Bibliography

The footnote references to the chapters will give the best indications of the sources on which I have drawn. For those wishing to study Libya in more detail, the following is a brief list of books, articles, and reports that I found most useful; the list makes no pretensions at being complete, though some of the publications mentioned, especially the general works, have lists of references.

A bibliography that goes up to the sixties is R. W. HILL, *A Bibliography of Libya*, Durham University 1959.

General works

ROGER OWEN, *Libya: A Brief Political and Economic Survey*, Chatham House Memoranda, Royal Institute of International Affairs, London, May 1961. This is a brief (46-page) summary of material that takes the account up to 1961.

A more up-to-date general summary is the entry on Libya in *The Middle East and North Africa*, Europa Publications, 1970, pp. 471–96.

JOHN WRIGHT, *Libya*, Ernest Benn, 1969, is a useful general history and one that is especially good on the Italian conquest and occupation, and has extensive references to Italian material.

The *Area Handbook for Libya*, Stanford Research Institute, December 1969, printed by the US Government Printing Office, Washington DC, is one of a series of handbooks prepared under the auspices of Foreign Area Studies of the American University, and designed 'to be useful to military and other personnel who need a convenient compilation of basic facts about the social, economic, political and military institutions and practices of various countries'. The contents of the handbook are said to represent the work of the authors (who are unnamed) and not to represent the official view of the United States government. This is a comprehensive and compact summary, whatever the political and strategic uses to which it, and its like, have been put.

Bibliography

People and History

The standard works on the Sanusi are:

E. L. PETERS, 'The Tied and the Free: An Account of Patron–Client Relationships among the Bedouin of Cyrenaica' in J. Peristiany, *Contributions to Mediterranean Sociology*, Mouton, 1966; 'Aspects of the Family among the Bedouin of Cyrenaica' in M. F. NIMKOFF (ed.), *Comparative Family Systems*, Boston, Houghton Mifflin, 1965; and 'Some Structural Aspects of the Feud among the Camel-Herding Bedouin of Cyrenaica', in *Africa*, July 1967.

E. E. EVANS-PRITCHARD, *The Sanusi of Cyrenaica*, Oxford University Press, 1949.

NICOLA A. ZIADEH, *Sanusiyah: A Study of a Revivalist Movement in Islam*, E. J. Brill, Leiden, 1958.

On other ethnic groups, apart from material in the general works cited, there is LOUIS DUPREE, 'The non-Arab Ethnic Groups of Libya', *Middle East Journal*, Vol. XII, no. 1, Winter 1958, pp. 33–44. For an account of the early Garamantes see CHARLES DANIELS, *The Garamantes of Southern Libya*, Oleander Press, Harrow, Middlesex, 1970.

On history up to and including the Italian period, John Wright's book includes a number of references. MISS TULLY *Letters Written During Ten Years' Residence at the Court of Tripoli*, Arthur Barker, London, 1957, republished from the original edition of 1816, is a lively account of the Court of the Tripoli Regency in the late eighteenth century by the sister of the British consul of the day.

The full history of the guerrilla resistance against the Italian occupation must await the completion of the work by Rosalba Davico, whose paper on 'La Guérilla Lybienne (1911–1932): impérialisme et résistance anti-coloniale en Afrique du Nord aux années 20' is as yet unpublished, though it was delivered at the Colloque internationale d'études historiques et sociologiques, Cinquantenaire de la République du Rif, Paris, 18–21 January 1973.

The existing histories of the war are written from the viewpoint of the colonizer.

Transition to Independence

On Libya's *Transition to Independence*, the most painstaking and voluminous account is written by the international civil servant who supervised the transition. This is ADRIAN PELT, *Libyan Independence and the United Nations: A Case of Planned Decolonisation*, published for the Carnegie Endowment for International Peace, Yale University Press, 1970, 1,016 pages. This account is supported by considerable

United Nations documentation and repays close reading of, as well as in between, the lines.

G. H. BECKER, *The Disposition of the Italian Colonies 1911–1951*, thesis of the University of Geneva, is useful for the reasoning behind the Anglo-American decision in favour of Libyan independence.

On constitutional development see:

MAJID KHADDURI, *Modern Libya: A Study in Political Development*, Johns Hopkins Press, 1965 and ISMAIL RAGHIB KHALIDI, *Constitutional Developments in Libya*, Khayat's College Book Cooperative, 1956.

Politics

The politics of the régime must be traced from official speeches and versions of documents that issue from time to time from the Revolutionary Command Council and the ministries. Laws appear in the official Gazette. The Ministry of Information and Culture produces the speeches of Colonel Gadafi in several languages not long after they have been delivered. The same Ministry produces an annual publication on *The Achievements of the Revolution*.

MEREDITH O. ANSELL and IBRAHAIM MASSAUD AL-ARIF (eds.), *The Libyan Revolution: a source book of legal and historical documents*, Vol. 1, 1 September 1969–30 Aug. 1970, (Oleander Press, Harrow, Middlesex), carries a list of the contents of the Official Gazette of Libya for that period, selected translations from official and semi-official documents, and the Proceedings of the Libyan Intellectual Seminar of May 1970.

Economics

Libya: Documents on Economic Development 1960–1971, Inter Documentation Company AG, Poststrasse 14, Zug, Switzerland, is a collection of published and unpublished documents, available on microfiche, assembled during the project jointly conducted by London University, School of Oriental and African Studies, and the University of Libya. The documents are mainly concerned with agricultural development as this was the area most closely researched. There is also material on the national economy and trade, on labour and manpower, and on construction and housing developments.

Other material on agriculture includes the Libyan–London Universities Joint Research Project, J. A. ALLAN, K. S. MCLACHLAN, and EDITH T. PENROSE (eds.), *Libya: Agriculture and Economic Development*, Frank Cass, 1973; J. A. ALLAN, 'Land Use and Cropping Patterns: Present Position and Recent Changes'; 'Some Recent

Developments in Libyan Agriculture', *Middle East Economic Papers 1969*, American University of Beirut; and an earlier report is S. LALEVIC, MILAD A. SCHMEYLA, and MILENA LALEVIC, 'Agriculture in Libya and a Plan for its Development'; Ministry of Planning and Development, Tripoli.

On manpower see the following:

Kingdom of Libya, Ministry of Planning and Development, the chapter on Manpower Development of the Second Five Year Plan, July 1969; mimeographed.

R. MABRO, 'Labour Supplies and Labour Stability: A Case Study of the Oil Industry in Libya', Bulletin Oxford University Institute of Economics and Statistics, Vol. 32, No. 4, November 1970.

ILO Integrated Manpower Planning and Organisation Project, 'Population and Labour Force Projections for Libya, 1965–1985', Tripoli, August 1970; draft mimeograph.

UNDP/ILO Integrated Manpower Planning and Organisation Project. Libya 'Report on Survey of Wages Problems in Libya', May 1971; mimeographed.

'Report of the Manpower Situation', Ministry of Planning, Tripoli, 1972; mimeographed.

For material on the economy in general see:

Central Bank of Libya, Annual Reports.

Libyan Arab Republic, Survey of National Economy Covering 1968 and certain Main Indicators for 1969, mimeographed.

Libyan Arab Republic, General Economic Background Information, UNDP, Tripoli, 30 May 1971; mimeographed.

Libya Statistical Abstract, 1968, 1969.

National Accounts 1962–71.

Libyan Arab Republic, Ministry of Planning, Census and Statistical Department: Report of the Annual Survey of Large Manufacturing Establishments 1969, 1970; Report of the Annual Survey of Petroleum Mining Industry, 1969, 1970, and Supplements;

Quarterly Bulletin of Statistics;

Report of the Annual Survey of Large Construction Units, 1969, 1970; External Trade Statistics;

Monthly Statistics of Production and Employment in Selected Large Manufacturing Establishments.

For an approach to the rentier state see:

H. MAHDAVY, 'The Patterns and Problems of Economic Development in Rentier States: The Case of Iran', in M. A. COOK (ed.), *Studies in The Economic History of the Middle East from the Rise of Islam to the Present Day*, Oxford University Press, 1970.

ROBERT MABRO, 'La Libye, Un État Rentier?' *Projet* 39, November 1969, pp. 1,090–1,101.

Oil

The standard, though by now very out-dated, work on Libya's oil industry is ABDUL AMIR Q. KUBBAH, *Libya: Its Oil Industry and Economic System*, Arab Petro-Economic Research Centre, Baghdad, 1964. The best way to follow recent developments is in issues of the *Petroleum Intelligence Weekly*, the *World Petroleum Magazine*, and the *Oil and Gas Journal*. *Arab Oil Review* is published in Tripoli in Arabic and English.

There is by now a large literature on oil in general, which I do not cite here. Much of it explains the technicalities of the industry and is written by specialists not greatly interested in the politics behind oil and therefore disinclined to probe behind the official line of the industry. Sources I found which do try to question some of the assumptions of the industry are cited in the footnotes to the chapter, notably work by Aburdene and Adelman, and MERIP publications. See also LOUIS TURNER, *Multi-nationals and the Developing World: Conflict or Co-operation?* Allen Lane the Penguin Press, 1974.

Newspapers and Periodicals

For general coverage of current events, newspapers and periodicals remain indispensable, especially *Le Monde*. *Arab Report and Record* produces résumés of political, economic, and social developments month by month. *La Documentation Française*, 29–31 Quai Voltaire, Paris 7, has a documentation service on the Maghreb which includes Libya.

The most useful Libyan news sources in English are the *Libyan Press Review*, published by Septimius Advertising and Public Relations Agency, Tripoli, and the daily news bulletins issued by the Ministry of Information, which record official statements, events, and sometimes translated items from the Arabic press. The BBC's *Summary of World Broadcasts*, Middle East series, is indispensable for versions, often verbatim, of official speeches.

Index

More about Penguins and Pelicans

Penguinews, which appears every month, contains details of all the new books issued by Penguins as they are published. From time to time it is supplemented by *Penguins in Print*, which is a complete list of all titles available. (There are some five thousand of these.)

A specimen copy of *Penguinews* will be sent to you free on request. For a year's issues (including the complete lists) please send 50p if you live in the British Isles, or 75p if you live elsewhere. Just write to Dept EP, Penguin Books Ltd, Harmondsworth, Middlesex, enclosing a cheque or postal order, and your name will be added to the mailing list.

In the U.S.A.: For a complete list of books available from Penguin in the United States write to Dept CS, Penguin Books Inc., 7110 Ambassador Road, Baltimore, Maryland 21207.

In Canada: For a complete list of books available from Penguin in Canada write to Penguin Books Canada Ltd, 41 Steelcase Road West, Markham, Ontario.